THE PASSAGE OF ARMS

An archaeological analysis of
prehistoric hoards and
votive deposits

RICHARD BRADLEY

OXBOW BOOKS

Oxford and Oakville

Published by Oxbow Books
Park End Place, Oxford OX1 1HN

Second edition 1998

First edition published by
Cambridge University Press 1990

© Richard Bradley 1990, 1998

ISBN 1 900188 58 9

The CIP record is available from the British Library

Printed in Great Britain
at the Alden Press, Oxford

For George Eogan

The detective need only know the rules and play the game, and he has the criminal trapped, has won a victory for justice. This fiction infuriates me. Reality can only be partially attacked by logic. Granted, we police officers are forced to proceed logically, scientifically, but the factors that spoil things for us are so common that all too frequently only pure professional luck and chance decide the issue ... But in your novels chance plays no part at all, and if something looks like chance it's represented as some kind of destiny or divine dispensation. You writers have always sacrificed truth for the sake of your dramatic rules ... Our rules are based on probabilities, on statistics, not causality; they apply only in general and not in particular ... But you fellows in the writing game don't worry about that ... Instead you set up a world that you can manage. Drop the perfection if you want to get anywhere ... Otherwise you'll be left behind, fooling with useless stylistic exercises. But now I must come to the point.

Friedrich Dürrenmatt, The Pledge

Contents

Plates

Figures

Figures

Preface

This is a book about artefacts, written by someone with a limited appetite for artefact studies. That is a paradox that this preface must explain.

The source materials for this book, as for most studies of European archaeology, are catalogues of artefacts, for these provide the chronologies within which we work. Many have been imaginative and original, but their cumulative effect can be depressing. There is no denying the extraordinary energy and organisation that have gone into their making, but at times it seems as if little has come out again. Do they really tell us all there is to know about this material, or have these projects become an end in themselves, innocent of both questions and answers, like the five volumes of Beachcomber's *List of Huntingdonshire Cabmen*?

It is one thing to organise the component parts of the archaeological record, and quite another to explain how it came into being. In the case of the finest artefacts – so often those on which our framework depends – it is relatively easy to classify them, but much more difficult to show why they should have survived in such numbers. And in failing to ask that question loudly enough, it seems to me that we have lost our way. If we are to investigate this material to good effect, we must also account for its deposition. That is the problem addressed in the following chapters.

I was first attracted by this subject on a visit to Danish museums in 1980. The high quality of their displays brought home very graphically the role played by the deliberate destruction of prehistoric artefacts, among them some of the most elaborate ever made. This set me wondering about the true character of some of the hoards and river finds of the British Bronze Age, which had generally been studied as a source of chronological information. The same was true of metalwork deposits over large areas of North-West Europe; so much so that catalogues of hoards or of individual artefact types were widely available but made virtually no contribution to our understanding of prehistoric society.

Soon those superficial similarities came to seem less important than the more theoretical problems posed by the consumption of valuables in non-market societies, and yet here was a body of material perfectly suited to this kind of analysis. Despite the position that it occupied in our libraries and museum collections, it remained largely unstudied at a time when 'social archaeology' was emerging as a distinctive discipline. Intentional deposits of artefacts also posed problems for those working in another new field of research: the formation of the archaeological record. Surely, here there was scope for a more ambitious project.

I took support from the work of a number of friends and colleagues who shared similar attitudes to the problem, even when they pursued quite different lines of enquiry. Our discussions came to persuade me that the division of the prehistoric sequence among period specialists had done much to obscure the most striking patterns exhibited by this material. Others were lost because archaeologists were working on too limited a geographical scale. This book seeks to redress the balance.

Between 1982 and 1988 I attempted to define my views in a series of articles. During that time I not only found it necessary to revise some of my first thoughts on this subject: I also became convinced that the issues could only be tackled by a more lengthy treatment. This is the result. Let me emphasise that it is *not* a synthesis of all that can be said about hoards and votive deposits. It is a personal essay about some of the ways in which they can be studied, and some of the reasons why this should be done. One of my friends who was kind enough to look at the typescript said that it was really 'a conversation about archaeology' – and that is what I intended. The book is conceived within strict geographical and chronological limits. It is concerned mainly with evidence from North and North-West Europe, seen almost entirely through the medium of published sources, and it is restricted to the pre-Roman period. It would take another author and another book to deal with the evidence from the first millennium AD.

Preface

A number of friends have spared the time to go through the typescript, and more often than not I have taken their advice. I must thank John Barrett, Bob Chapman, Mark Edmonds, Martin Henry, Marisa Ruíz-Gálvez, Steve Shennan and Sander Van der Leeuw for doing all they could to save me from the error of my ways. Their efforts were greatly abetted by Melanie Hall and Frances Raymond, who tried to make sense of my English and worked out what I should have said. Tess Durden and Riki Bowden removed more errors from the manuscript, and Katherine ensured that I kept some sense of proportion while all this was going on. Jim Smith prepared the index. Adam Hadley's contribution speaks for itself, for he produced lucid illustrations from the most unprepossessing originals.

When I began this research, it was difficult to persuade people that there was a problem to investigate; still less that votive deposition was one of the most important transactions in prehistoric society. When I completed the manuscript I realised how far our attitudes had changed, for on the front page of a national newspaper was an account of Francis Pryor's work at Fengate Power Station, where a massive timber causeway seems to have formed the focus for a whole series of intentional offerings, from weapons to human remains. No longer were these regarded as chance finds – the basic point had already been accepted. But if that means that some of this book will seem familiar, it also guarantees a critical audience.

Someone who will not be surprised by developments of this kind is George Eogan. He was one of the first scholars publishing in English to recognise that deliberate deposition really is a problem, and he has taken the trouble to consider the problem on a European scale. He is a master of the artefact record, in a way that the writer is not, and he brings to his archaeology a curiosity and enthusiasm that we would do well to emulate. This book is for him.

Acknowledgments

I am grateful to the following individuals and institutions for providing the plates: the Trustees of the British Museum, London (Plates 3, 4, 5, 6, 10 and 11); Musée Denon, Chalon-sur-Saône (Plate 14); Nationalmuseet, Copenhagen (Plates 7, 8, 9 and 12); Barry Cunliffe (Plate 13); Ulf Erik Hagberg (Plate 1); and Francis Pryor (Plates 2 and 15). I must also thank Louis Bonnamour, Stuart Needham and Poul Otto Nielsen for their help in selecting the illustrations.

The epigraphs used in the book are included by kind permission of the following: Gillon Aitken for the extract from *Finding the Centre* by V. S. Naipaul; Jonathan Cape and the Estate of Pablo Neruda for the extract from *Extravagaria* translated by Alastair Reid; Diogenes Verlag Ag Zurich, Jonathan Cape, Alfred A. Knopf Inc. and Pan Books Ltd for the extract from *The Pledge* by Friedrich Dürrenmatt (*The Pledge* was first published as *Das Versprechen* in 1958 © 1985 by Diogenes Verlag Ag Zurich. First published in Great Britain 1959 by Jonathan Cape in English translation © Alfred A. Knopf, Inc. 1959 © Pan Books Ltd, 1985); Faber and Faber Ltd for the extract from *The Silver Bough* by Neil Gunn; Routledge and Princeton University Press for the quotation from the English translation of *Monsieur Teste* by Paul Valéry. The extract from 'Flowering Death' is from *Selected Poems* by John Ashbery. Copyright © John Ashbery, 1985. All rights reserved. Reprinted by permission of Viking Penguin, a division of Penguin Books USA, Inc.

Rereading *The passage of arms*

Introduction

I wrote *The passage of arms* almost ten years ago and have been working on other projects since that time. The appearance of a paperback edition introduces the book to a wider audience, but it also provides an opportunity for the author to look at it again.

There are several ways of reissuing a study of this kind. One is to treat it as a historical document whose status is already assured. The writer may introduce the work by describing the intellectual climate in which it was composed, but the book itself cannot be changed. The same applies to collections of essays, which all too often have the same subtext: this work was ahead of its time, it was unjustly criticised when it first appeared, but, despite this temporary setback, it retains its relevance today. A fashionable alternative is to invoke 'the death of the author', in that way disowning all responsibility for the weakness of the argument or the ways in which it might have been misunderstood (Hodder 1987).

I do not favour either of these approaches. *The passage of arms* was the result of a period of research during the 1980s, but it concluded a project which I did not intend to take any further. As a result, I can read it now with a certain detachment. There seems little justification in presenting it as a sacred text which stands apart from the intellectual fashions of the day. Still less would I be justified in arguing that it was ahead of its time, anticipating the course of archaeology over the following years. It seems more helpful to look at this book as I would a study by someone else.

The passage of arms

Over the last few weeks I have examined a number of Ph D theses. This has created the right attitude of mind in which to reread *The passage of arms*. In each case my procedure has been the same: I have been critical but, I hope, not unduly negative. I have noted the arguments that seem unsatisfactory, I have identified a few errors of fact and I have listed some vital references that should also be consulted. In a more positive spirit, I have also identified those ideas that deserve further development in the future. This is my report.

These notes are intended to guide the reader to other ways of thinking about this material. They are not an attempt to have the last word on a subject where there is so much left to say. The book was written to provoke debate and to stimulate fresh research. I cannot judge how far it has succeeded in these objectives, but I do know that by issuing it in a cheaper edition Oxbow Books are making it more accessible to the people for whom it was intended. Eight years after its first publication, I hope that it has some life in it still.

Major revisions

Anyone examining a doctoral thesis will distinguish between two kinds of revision to the text. 'Major revisions' are those that are fundamental to the argument, and they must be undertaken before the text can be considered further. 'Minor amendments' are of less substance, but they have to be completed before the candidate is passed.

Three *major revisions* are needed to *The passage of arms*.

1. The first is to the argument in Chapter Two, which traces the changing significance of axes in hoards and votive deposits from the beginning of the Neolithic period to the end of the Early Bronze Age. In this case the text comes close to my present position, but, perversely, it never acknowledges the implications of the argument.

It was probably true to say that axes were deposited in a structured manner around and beyond the agricultural frontier. There is some evidence of this in Britain, Ireland and Brittany, but the clearest indications come from Scandinavia. In *The passage of arms* I suggested that these artefacts were symbols of a new relationship between people and the natural environment and that they were of most significance in those areas where agriculture had been adopted by the indigenous population. Unfortunately, this argument overlooked the possibility that the deposition of such material could already have been practised during the Mesolithic period. Moreover, the emphasis on votive deposits containing axe heads meant that other kinds of offering were largely ignored.

This approach was unsatisfactory, for it failed to follow the argument to its logical conclusion. The Neolithic period has been characterised by three quite independent elements: domesticated plants and animals, monuments, and a new material culture characterised mainly by pottery and ground stone axes. To a large extent these originated in the heartland of Neolithic Europe, and by the time that they were adopted by hunter gatherers beyond the agricultural frontier their significance was transformed. Thus Ertebolle pottery may have played a role in Mesolithic society, and the same could have been true of the earliest domesticates (Jennbert 1984): at first they were employed according to local social conventions. Yet when we discuss the deposits of axes in watery locations, these are supposed to have originated spontaneously, as a kind of 'side-effect' of agriculture. In fact it is now quite clear that imported axe heads, and occasional Ertebolle pots, were being placed in bogs before the subsistence economy had changed (Karsten 1994). That is hardly surprising since recent research in Scandinavia has shown that votive deposits were an important feature of the indigenous Mesolithic. In Norway, for example, there is a regular association between features of the natural topography and deposits of Mesolithic axes (Klungseth Lødøen 1996), and, in Sweden, human and animal bones were being deposited in water some time before the adoption of agriculture in the same area (Larsson, Meikeljohn and Newall 1981). That should not occasion any surprise as the native population of northern Scandinavia – the Saami – were making rather similar votive offerings as late as the eighteenth century AD (Zachrisson 1984). In the light of this evidence, it may be more helpful to suggest that offerings of organic material and artefacts were first made by hunter gatherers and that these practices were *transformed* during the Neolithic period, when they were undertaken on an increasingly large scale. During the Mesolithic period they may well have played a part in mediating between the human and natural worlds. With the changing social relationships associated with farming such transactions merely assumed a greater importance. I have discussed this material in more detail in a recent study (Bradley 1998, chapter 3).

2. The second weakness of *The passage of arms* concerns the rather rigid distinction that is made in Chapter One between 'ritual' and 'non-ritual hoards'. In my account of the Bronze Age material in Chapter Three it reappears as the difference between 'votive' finds and 'utilitarian' deposits. This scheme was criticised in Timothy Champion's review of the book (Champion 1990) and has been questioned by other writers since (for example, Vandkilde 1996).

It is ironic that my first attempt to characterise the metal hoards of the Bronze Age questioned this division, contending that all these deposits should be interpreted in the same way (Bradley 1982). That tradition of thinking is particularly common in Scandinavia, but by the time I wrote *The passage of arms* and several of the articles leading up to it I had changed my mind. That was because I had become convinced by the arguments associating some of these groups of metalwork with the activities of smiths. Certain collections included groups of raw material or metalworking residues, whilst others appeared to consist of newly made artefacts. A common feature of these 'utilitarian' collections was the presence of scrap. In the book I sought to distinguish these assemblages from the finds made in graves or rivers where, it seemed, material had been deposited in places from which it was unlikely to be recovered. Although I commented on certain ambiguities in recognising 'non-ritual hoards', I did not appreciate the problems inherent in this distinction. Appeals to the contexts in which material was found say nothing about the character or role of ritual activity; they merely argue against a practical interpretation for these collections on the grounds that they would have been difficult to recover. As Dickens (1996) has pointed out, specialised artefacts might have been hidden on dry land when they were not in use, and in any case they may have remained undisturbed because they were protected by social sanctions.

At the same time, the fact that certain collections of metalwork may have been created by smiths is not necessarily an argument for a practical role in the distribution of bronze artefacts. That presupposes what may be an anachronistic interpretation of the role of metal production in prehistoric society, one which was too strongly influenced by the late work of Gordon Childe (1958). Despite the criticism of his ideas found on pages 26–7, a weakness of *The passage of arms* is that it takes little account of the production of metalwork and places so much emphasis on the final deposition of a number of specialised artefacts. It does not consider the possibility that metalworking was itself a highly specialised process, involving a number of arcane, even dangerous procedures. It may well have been accompanied by what we would identify as ritual. That would certainly be consistent with what is known about metal production in the ethnographic record (Herbert 1984, Hosler 1994, Reid and MacLean 1995, Budd and Taylor 1995) and might help to explain why this process so often took place in isolation on, or even beyond, the boundaries of the domestic sphere.

Instead of referring to 'utilitarian' hoards, I propose that some of these deposits should be referred to by the neutral term 'metalworking' deposits. This emphasises the particular significance of the *transformation* of the material, and does not make any assumptions about the reasons why some of it was buried. In writing *The passage of arms* I was troubled by the arguments that linked this group of deposits to the activities of smiths – the contents of these hoards were clearly very different from those found in other collections – but I may have been quite wrong to regard the production of bronze artefacts as a straightforward process, akin to industrial activity in the modern world. On a less theoretical level, a new approach to this evidence may explain why it was never retrieved – it was as much an offering as the swords found in rivers and lakes. That is important, as metal analysis suggests that the collection and recycling of scrap metal went on over a much longer period than the hoards that were supposed to provide the principal evidence for that process.

3. As I said earlier, I would have been wiser to maintain the interpretation of metalworking hoards that I put forward in 1982 than to follow the more cautious line that I published eight years later. That change of position was particularly unfortunate as it prevented me from following another line of enquiry that I outlined in Chapter One of *The passage of arms*. My third major revision concerns the proposition that prehistoric artefacts had a distinctive life history that extended from their production, through their period of use to their final deposition.

I referred all too briefly to the approaches summarised in Appadurai's edited book *The social life of things*, and though I quoted from Kopytoff's chapter on the 'cultural biography' of artefacts, I did not follow that model systematically (Appadurai ed. 1986). In retrospect I might have been well advised to trace the careers of a series of artefacts from their creation to their final deposition, charting the moments in that process when their significance changed. Although I did draw certain analogies between gift exchange and the provision of offerings, I did not appreciate how much of their social significance may have been fixed *when they were first made by the smith*. Nor did I appreciate how important it was to establish the relationship between those smiths and their patrons. At the time I felt that there was too little material to discuss, but, with the benefit of hindsight, it is clear that there were a number of obvious links between special-ised or high status settlements and the production of metal artefacts – the evidence from the Late Bronze Age ringwork at Springfield Lyons provides a typical instance in Britain (Buckley and Hedges 1987, 11–12) – whilst in the Rhineland Hansen (1991) has observed that ingots were buried in the graves of a limited section of society. In the same way, recent work in Ireland suggests a recurrent relationship between the hill forts of the same period and votive deposits in nearby bogs and lakes (Grogan et al. 1996). At times it seems as if the history of particular artefacts was preordained, from the moment that they were made to the time when they were removed from circulation. This approach is particularly tempting in the light of recent studies which consider the use damage acquired by specific artefacts in the course of their history (Taylor 1993, 58–78; Bridgford 1997). It seems particularly ironic that I should have found this 'biographical' approach so difficult to apply to Bronze Age archaeology since it was to form the core of my next research project: an exploration of the Neolithic 'axe trade' conducted jointly with Mark Edmonds. This work took exactly the opposite course to *The passage of arms,* for the main body of this study was a detailed analysis of a series of production sites (Bradley and Edmonds 1993). It may provide a stimulus for research on later periods.

In Chapter One of *The passage of arms* I also quoted Meillassoux's interpretation of the North American potlatch, emphasising his idea that one reason for destroying particular artefacts was to protect their special significance and to prevent them from being used as general purpose valuables. This provides a convincing interpretation of the deposition of King Arthur's sword Excalibur, which is described in the opening section of the book, but it is an approach which is especially powerful when it is combined with a study of the cultural biography of artefacts. Instead of taking this line, I emphasised the social prestige that might accrue through conspicuous gifts to the gods. That interpretation was influenced by another interpretation of the potlatch. Those two readings of the evidence are not necessarily incompatible with one another, for it remains important to come to terms with the increasing quantity of material deposited in watery locations during the Later Bronze Age. The rate of deposition may have increased, and it is surely more than a coincidence that these changes came at a time when grave goods were less frequently deposited with the dead. I may have been right to argue that a long established tradition of votive deposition was gradually transformed, but I would have been wiser to offer a more broadly based interpretation of that practice. By studying the life history of different artefacts we are less reliant on piecemeal comparisons with the ethnographic record.

Minor amendments

In a doctoral thesis *the minor amendments* consist of corrections to the text, but in this case I shall also take the opportunity of bringing the story up to date by referring to a few important papers that have been published since 1990.

Corrections

The main corrections concern two important questions of chronology, although these do not have radical implications for the argument contained in the text. Both relate to Chapter Two of *The passage of arms*. The first is on pages 48–57 which discuss the sequence of monuments in Neolithic Brittany in relation to depictions of axe heads and finds of these artefacts themselves. In this section I argue that objects of the kind that had been depicted on menhirs in the open air were increasingly concealed beneath enormous mounds. Symbols which had possessed a public character became the private possessions of a few individuals in death. This interpretation was based on the widely held view that the *grands tumulus* of the Carnac region were later in date than the small passage graves found beside them. More recent work at Le Petit Mont, Arzon, has shown that this was not the case, for there that sequence is reversed (Lecornec 1994). Not only were the passage graves on that site a secondary development, they incorporated broken fragments of the carved stones associated with the first monument to be built there.

That simplifies the field evidence from southern Brittany, but it does not do much to undermine the argument in *The passage of arms*. It still seems as if some of the carved menhirs were meant to resemble enormous axe heads and these features may have been associated with artefacts of exactly this kind, at the foot of the upright stones and beneath the heart of the mounds. Other axe heads are associated with passage graves where they might be associated with the interior of the monument. At Gavrinis it still seems likely that the famous carvings of axe heads were associated with abstract imagery that referred to states of altered consciousness (Lewis-Williams and Dowson 1993). The main difference between these interpretations and those advanced in 1990 is that there is less evidence that axe heads changed their contexts over time.

The second correction concerns the Late Neolithic sequence in Britain. In *The passage of arms* I followed the widely held view that during this period two major artefact traditions were in use simultaneously, even though their contents were very different from one another. One of these traditions was associated with

Peterborough Ware and was sometimes found in association with individual burials. The other was Grooved Ware, which was more often associated with ceremonial monuments. The latter tradition included a notable proportion of axes from highland quarries. I suggested that the same duality might be recognised in the Early Bronze Age when weapons and personal ornaments are a particular feature of the burial record, whereas copper and bronze axes are often recorded from bogs and rivers.

That view needs some revision for it no longer seems likely that the currency of Peterborough Ware and Grooved Ware was the same. More probably, they were used in succession before Grooved Ware was replaced by Beaker pottery (Gibson and Kinnes 1997). That makes it more difficult to postulate a direct connection between the Neolithic single burials and those associated with metalwork. The relationship between axes and watery locations may have remained the same between the two periods, although most of the first deposits of metal axes are found in Ireland where Grooved Ware has only recently been identified; on the other hand, stone axes have long been known from watery locations in that country. The situation is confusing, but it seems as if the neat duality between finds of Early Bronze Age tools and weapons was less firmly rooted in earlier developments than originally appeared.

Additional information

There are also points where it is possible to supplement the argument in *The passage of arms* by referring to the results of more recent work. I should stress that this is only mentioned where it bears on the themes of the different chapters. This is not the occasion to review all the literature of the last eight years.

Chapter One of the book introduces most of the main debates in the archaeology of hoards and votive deposits, but it could be useful for the reader to refer to a more recent discussion of these themes. In this chapter I complained that period specialists seemed to be unaware of the literature discussing other bodies of material: virtually the same debates are repeated between proponents of a 'practical' explanation for discoveries of fine metalwork and those who interpret the same material as votive offerings. Since *The passage of arms* was written, this dialogue has extended to the interpretation of the gold work from Snettisham (Fitzpatrick 1992).

Chapter Two raises rather different issues. The discussion of Neolithic deposits in Southern Scandinavia rests on a much more secure basis with the publication of Sarup, where an entire causewayed enclosure has been excavated (Andersen 1997). In the same way, the production and exchange of Early Bronze Age artefacts are much easier to discuss in relation to two important projects which have been published since 1990. The first is O'Brien's field investigation of the copper mines of south-west Ireland. His report also offers a comprehensive review of work on other sites dating from this period in Britain and Continental Europe (O'Brien 1994). The second is Shennan's monograph *Bronze Age copper producers of the Eastern Alps* which reports on his excavations at the Klingiberg in Austria and considers the social and economic setting of artefact production in Central Europe (Shennan 1995). It provides a wealth of detail which is absent from the account of this area on pages 86–93 of *The passage of arms*.

One further point concerns the contents of Chapter Two. Pages 80–85 ask the question why early metalwork should have been so important, concluding that it was adopted in some areas less for its functional properties than for its exotic character. That may still be correct, but at some point the situation did change. It is easy to suppose that stone axes were just as efficient as those made of copper and bronze, but, somewhat unexpectedly, this is not borne out by recent experiments conducted in the United States (Mathieu and Meyer 1997). It may be that in my attempt to demystify Early Bronze Age technology I gave too little weight to functional considerations

The contents of Chapter Three can be supplemented in other ways. At the time of writing I was aware of the recent discovery of metalwork and timber structures at Fengate Power Station / Flag Fen, but it was too soon to build them into my account. That can now be remedied. The full extent of this work has now been published (Pryor ed. 1992). This must be among the few places where votive deposits have been excavated on a large scale. Pryor and his colleagues provide a graphic account of this evidence, although I am not convinced by the 'functional' explanation for the siting of this complex suggested in the final section of this report.

Another important project in Eastern England has been the radiocarbon dating of human remains from the East Anglian Fens. On one level this provides another instance of the deposition of human bones in watery locations discussed on pages 107–9 of *The passage of arms*, but the results of this work have a still greater impact for they show that this practice was already under way during the Early Bronze Age (Healy and Housley 1992). It follows that the placing of human remains in water is not a new development of the Later Bronze Age. Rather, it seems to have built upon an already existing tradition of deposition which had run in parallel with the richly furnished barrow burials of the third and second millennia BC. The new evidence reinforces the association between the dead and water deposits suggested in Chapter Three, but raises the possibility that only the later of these may have been associated with the provision of large quantities of weaponry. Until the Middle Bronze Age most finds of daggers were from graves on dry land.

Two other publications concern the process of metal production. In Chapter Three I used the finds from Petters Sports Field, Egham to illustrate the complexity of much of this evidence. My discussion was based on preliminary reports of this material, but a definitive account of these finds has now appeared (Needham 1990). It does not differ greatly from my brief summary of the metalwork deposits on this site, but Needham's discussion provides a critical review of the problems of recycling which should be read alongside my account of this phenomenon.

The second new development concerns the tentative suggestion in *The passage of arms* that certain artefact types may have played a dual role in Bronze Age society, as tools and ornaments and as standard units of metal. I had originally made this suggestion in a festschrift for Mats Malmer where I compared some of the interpretations of hoarding in the Late Bronze Age and Viking economies (Bradley 1988). Now Malmer has put this idea to the test, showing very clearly that certain kinds of Bronze Age metalwork in Scandinavia did conform to a standard system of weights (Malmer 1992).

A final question raised by Chapter Three concerns the principal patterns of deposition in Later Bronze Age Europe. Here there are a number of new developments to report. First, it has become quite clear that *The passage of arms* considered too small an area, so that a number of traditions which involved the deposition of weapons or other artefacts in water were overlooked. For example, this applies to finds from Italy (Bianco Peroni 1979) and to the contents of the extraordinary sacred wells constructed during this period in Sardinia (Lilliu 1988, 521–44). Of similar importance has been the recognition of a further tradition of river metalwork in the Iberian Peninsula. This has been studied in considerable detail in recent years, and one of the major developments has been Ruiz-Gálvez's re-interpretation of the contents of the River Huelva 'shipwreck' as a votive deposit (Ruiz-Gálvez 1995).

Another important publication is Hansen's study of Urnfield metal deposition in the Rhine – Main region of Germany, which appeared a year after *The passage of arms* (Hansen 1991). This book identifies many of the same relationships as Chapter Three and also suggests that the contexts in which an object was deposited might change with the distance that it had travelled from its source. His work also illustrates a pattern mentioned only in passing in Chapter Three. The evidence of clay moulds certainly suggests that particular forms of artefact were produced which never entered the archaeological record. Hansen illustrates an interesting variant of this pattern: as well as different regional traditions of deposition, there may be local traditions that dictated that specific types of object *should not be deposited at all*. On a European scale a good example is provided by one type of winged axe whose distribution extends from Central Europe to the Atlantic, with a conspicuous gap in the pattern of find spots in east and central France (Fig. o).

Chapter Four of *The passage of arms* was an extremely selective account of some material dating from the Iron Age. It can be amplified on two levels. First, there are good general accounts dealing with a more extensive body of votive deposits, extending well outside the geographical area considered in the book. Thus the contributors to a volume edited by Haffner in 1995 discuss the broader character of 'Celtic' offering places, whilst Randsborg

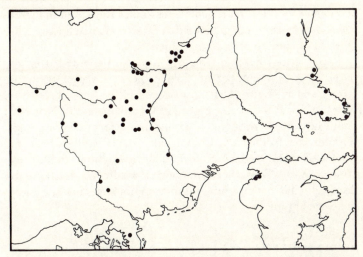

Fig. o A regional tradition of 'non-deposition'? The distribution of one form of winged axe according to Hansen (1991). The find spots extend from Central Europe to the Atlantic coastline, but none occur in other parts of France where metalwork of the same date is frequently discovered. Hansen suggests that it may not have been appropriate to deposit such objects in this area.

(1995) provides an interesting discussion of those located around the Roman frontier and their interpretation in relation to Classical literary sources.

Other new publications concern the particular questions discussed in the text. One important theme of Chapter Four is the increasing emphasis on natural fertility during this period. This is a central point in Brück's account of the treatment of the dead in the Late Bronze Age / Early Iron Age and is reinforced by the studies of intentional deposition of artefacts and animal bones at settlement sites published by Hill (Brück 1995; Hill 1995). This work emphasises the symbolic role of the corn storage pit as a receptacle for structured deposits. Hill also emphasises the importance of settlement boundaries, and their significance is reinforced by Hingley (1993) in an important review of finds of currency bars. At the same time, our understanding of wetland deposits is expanded by Coles's recent account of wooden figure sculptures (Coles 1990). When I wrote *The passage or arms* I complained that these remained undated; her work has begun to remedy the situation.

Research on the Late Iron Age has also benefited from the publication of a number of field projects. Excavation at the temple site at Thetford has now been published in full (Gregory 1992). Work at the vitally important sanctuary sites of Northern Gaul has been brought together in a recent monograph (Goudineau, Faudet and Coulon eds. 1994), and so have the results of recent work on *Viereckschanzen*. (Bittel, Schiek and Müller 1990). These accounts add a wealth of detail to the discussion in Chapter Four, but they do not appear to contradict the basic argument.

Future prospects

So far I have paid most attention to those areas where the ideas expressed in *The passage of arms* require amendment or where the text could be expanded in the light of new information. I would like to end this discussion by drawing attention to other points which still present problems and to comment on my basic approach to the evidence.

In the final chapter of *The passage of arms* I considered some of the other ways in which the book might have been written. In particular, I discussed the possibilities of interpreting votive deposits according to the literature of the Classical and Early Medieval worlds, extrapolating from that evidence to the character of earlier practices. This is exactly what Randsborg has now done in his account of the great weapon deposit from Hjortspring, which carries the ambitious subtitle *Warfare and sacrifice in early Europe* (Randsborg 1995). This is a most attractive discussion and is certainly to be recommended as an alternative account to *The passage of arms* which is mentioned only once in its pages. My problem is that Randsborg has not taken enough account of the sheer variability of the evidence. Thus he uses the character and frequency of the artefacts in this well excavated deposit to provide a compelling reconstruction of warfare in the Scandinavian Iron Age, but then he applies the same interpretation to Bronze Age weapon hoards. This is less convincing. In the same way, he moves between literary and archaeological sources covering enormous tracts of time and space as if he were discussing a unitary phenomenon. That has never been established in the first place.

The alternative approach is to stress the many different ways in which particular practices were adapted and manipulated in the past and to place less emphasis on the only period in that history to be illuminated by literary evidence. The archaeological record does not stand alone, but it is sufficiently robust to show that ritual deposition was extremely varied. It is by identifying the various transformations in that particular practice that *pre*history can be written. In doing so, it is perfectly permissible to draw on written sources and on the ethnographic record, but these are part of the creative process, and do not supply any ready-made conclusions. Randsborg's book is one source of inspiration for new work, but others can include studies of purely archaeological material, like Treherne's recent account of the warrior ethos in late prehistoric Europe (Treherne 1995).

There is another danger in treating hoards and votive deposits as a unitary phenomenon, for there are many empirical patterns that are still very difficult to explain. Among those identified in *The passage of arms* are: the complementary distributions of artefacts in hoards and river deposits, discussed on pages 114–29; the chronological relationship between votive deposits and hoards containing scrap metal considered on pages 150–3; or even the apparent 'downgrading' of the axe head as a symbol. As the distinction between 'ritual' and 'utilitarian' deposits becomes difficult to sustain, these patterns are harder to interpret than they were when the book was written.

Other points have not been discussed in enough depth since 1990. There is a need for a more searching account of the adoption of metals in outlying areas of Europe. Were the new types of artefacts really used and deposited according to the conventions already laid down in the Neolithic? And were they categorised in different ways in areas remote from the sources? The discussion on pages 85–90 lays the foundations for a much more ambitious study.

In the same way, the adoption of iron still raises many problems, but these are too rarely identified in studies of ritual activity. On page 153–4, I made the provocative suggestion that perhaps iron could not be treated as a substitute for bronze 'because these two raw materials had different *meanings* for those who used them'. No one was provoked and this hypothesis remains to be explored.

That also applies to the idea that the changing character of Late Iron Age votive deposits reflects a process of standardisation: weapons were replaced by copies in miniature and coins began to be used. I argued that ritual practice had changed and that what had originally been a form of conspicuous consumption came much closer to the Roman conception of sacrifice as payment for services rendered. Here, more than anywhere else, we might recognise the impact of a market economy, but the idea has apparently been passed over in silence. Would it be useful to look at it again?

Coda

In Eric Ambler's novel *Passage of arms*, published in 1959, a Western tourist is caught up in the arms trade. He becomes involved in the shipping of stolen weapons from Malaya to Indonesia. The book exposes his naivety faced with social and political relationships that are beyond his immediate experience. The adventure almost ends in disaster, but he learns from the perils of confronting an unfamiliar culture. I did not discover this book until my own had been published, and yet it seems as if they have more than their titles in common. Attempts to come to terms with another culture present their problems, and these are multiplied when that culture is long extinct. Any dialogue between them will involve misunderstandings. In this essay I have tried to learn from my experience.

I have emphasised what I regard as unfinished business. The 'archaeological analysis of prehistoric hoards and votive deposits' has only just begun. In offering some pointers to future work I am well aware that this will be the last edition of *The passage of arms*. We need a new generation of projects to take the story further. And then it will be time for another book entirely.

References

Ambler, E. 1959. *Passage of arms.* London: Heinemann

Andersen, N. 1997. *The Sarup enclosures, vol.* 1. Aarhus: Jutland Arch. Soc.

Appadurai, A. ed. 1986. *The social life of things.* Cambridge: University Press

Bianco Peroni, V. 1979. Bronzene Gewässer- und Höhenfunde aus Italien. *Jahresbericht des Instituts für Vorgeschichte der Universität Frankfurt A. M. 1978–79*, 321–35

Bittel, K., Schiek, S. and Müller, D. 1990. *Die keltischen Viereckschanzen.* Stuttgart: Theiss

Budd, P. and Taylor, T. 1995. The faerie smith meets the bronze industry: magic versus science in the interpretation of prehistoric metal-making. *World Archaeology* 27, 133–43

Bradley, R. 1982. The destruction of wealth in later prehistory. *Man* 17, 108–22

Bradley, R. 1988. A comparative study of hoarding in the Late Bronze Age and Viking economies. In Burrenhult, G., Carlsson, A. Hyenstrand, A. and Sjøvold (eds.), *Theoretical approaches to artefacts, settlements and society; studies in honour of Mats P. Malmer*, 379–87. Oxford: BAR (S366)

Bradley, R. 1998. *The significance of monuments.* London: Routledge

Bradley, R. and Edmonds, M. 1993. *Interpreting the axe trade. Production and exchange in Neolithic Britain.* Cambridge: University Press

Bridgford, S. 1997. Mightier than the pen? An edgewise look at Irish Bronze Age swords. In J. Carman (ed.), *Material harm: archaeological studies of war and violence*, 95–115. Glasgow: Cruithne Press

Brück, J. 1995. A place for the dead: the role of human remains in Late Bronze Age Britain. *Proceedings of the Prehistoric Society* 61, 245–77

Buckley, D. and Hedges, J. 1987. *The Bronze Age and Saxon settlements at Springfield Lyons, Essex.* Chelmsford: Essex County Council

Champion, T. 1990. Review of R. Bradley, 'The passage of arms'. *Antiquaries Journal* 70, 479–81

Childe, V. G. 1958. *The prehistory of European society.* Harmondsworth: Penguin

Coles, B. 1990. Anthropomorphic wooden figures from Britain and Ireland. *Proceedings of the Prehistoric Society* 56, 315–33

Dickens, J. 1996. A remote analogy? from central Australian tjurunga to Irish Early Bronze Age axes. *Antiquity* 70, 161–7

Fitzpatrick, A. 1992. The Snettisham, Norfolk, hoards of Iron Age torques: sacred or profane? *Antiquity* 66, 395–8

Gibson, A. and Kinnes, I. 1997. On the urns of a dilemma: radiocarbon dates and the Peterborough problem. *Oxford Journal of Archaeology* 16, 65–72

Goudineau, C., Faudet, I. and Coulon, C. (eds.) 1994. *Les sanctuaires de tradition indigène en Gaule Romaine.* Paris: Errance

Gregory, A. 1992. *Excavations in Thetford, 1980–1982: Fisons Way.* East Anglian Archaeology 53

Grogan, E., Condit, T., O'Carroll, F., O'Sullivan, A. and Daly, A. 1996. Tracing the late prehistoric landscape in North Munster. *Discovery Programme Reports* 4, 26–46. Dublin: Royal Irish Academy

Haffner, A. (ed.) 1995. *Heiligtümer und Opferkulte der Kelten.* Stuttgart: Theiss

Hansen, S. 1991. *Studien zu den Metalldeponierungen während der Urnenfelderzeit im Rhein-Main-Gebiet.* Bonn: Habelt

The passage of arms

Healy, F. and Housley, R. 1992. Nancy was not alone: skeletons of the Early Bronze Age from the Norfolk peat fen. *Antiquity* 66, 948–55

Herbert, E. 1984. *Red gold of Africa*. Madison: University of Wisconsin Press

Hill, J. D. 1995. *Ritual and rubbish in the Iron Age of Wessex*. Oxford: BAR

Hingley, R. 1993. Iron Age 'currency bars': the archaeological and social context. *Archaeological Journal* 147, 91–117

Hodder, I. 1987. Reading Bell reading 'Reading the past'. *Archaeological Review from Cambridge* 6.1, 87–91

Hosler, D. 1994. *The sounds and colours of power: the sacred metallurgy of ancient West Mexico*. Cambridge, Massachusetts: MIT Press

Jennbert, K. 1984. *Den productiva gåvan*. Lund: Acta Archaeologica Lundensia

Karsten, P. 1994. *Att kasta yxan in siön*. Lund: Acta Archaeologica Lundensia

Klungseth Lødøen, T. 1996. Concepts of landscape in Mesolithic Western Norway. Paper to the conference *From Jomon to Star Carr,* University of Durham 1996. Publication forthcoming

Larsson, L., Meikeljohn, C. and Newall, R. 1981. Human skeletal material from the Mesolithic site of Ageröd, Scania, *Fornvännen* 76, 161–7

Lecornec, J. 1994. *Le Petit Mont, Arzon-Morbihan*. Rennes: Documents Archéologiques de l'Ouest

Lewis-Williams, D. and Dowson, T. 1993. On vision and power in the Neolithic: evidence from the decorated monuments. *Current Anthropology* 34, 55–65

Lilliu, G. 1988. *La Civilita dei Sardi*, third edition. Turin: Nuova ERI

Malmer, M. 1992. Weight systems in the Scandinavian Bronze Age. *Antiquity* 66, 377–88

Mathieu, J. and Meyer, D. 1997. Comparing axe heads of stone, bronze and steel: studies in experimental archaeology. *Journal of Field Archaeology* 24, 333–51

Needham, S. 1990. *The Petters Late Bronze Age metalwork: an analytical study of Thames Valley metalworking in its settlement context*. London: British Museum

O'Brien, W. 1994. *Mount Gabriel. Bronze Age mining in Ireland*. Galway: Galway University Press

Pryor, F. ed. 1992. Current research at Flag Fen. *Antiquity* 66, 439–531

Reid, A. and MacLean, R. 1995. Symbolism and social contexts of iron production in Karagwe. *World Archaeology* 27, 144–61

Randsborg, K. 1995. *Hjortspring. Warfare and sacrifice in early Europe*. Aarhus: Aarhus University Press

Ruiz-Gálvez, M. 1995. *Ritos de paso y puntos de paso. La Ria de Huelva en el mundo del Bronce Final Europeo*: Madrid: Servico de publicaciones Universidad Complutense

Shennan, S. 1995. *Bronze Age copper producers of the Eastern Alps*. Bonn: Habelt

Taylor, R. 1993. *Hoards of the Bronze Age in Southern Britain*. Oxford: British Archaeological Reports (British Series 228)

Treherne, P. 1995. The warrior and his beauty: the masculine body and self-identification in Bronze Age Europe. *Journal of European Archaeology* 3.1, 105–44

Vandkilde, H. 1996. *From stone to bronze: the metalwork of the late Neolithic and earliest Bronze Age in Denmark*. Aarhus: Jutland Archaeological Society

Zachrisson, I. 1984. *De samiska metalldepåerna år 1000–1350*. Umeå: University of Umeå, Department of Archaeology

Chapter 1

A mirage, but permanent

> How many facts we have fallen through
> And still the old façade glimmers there,
> A mirage, but permanent. We must first trick the idea
> Into being, then dismantle it.
> John Ashbery, 'Flowering Death'

As his hand went in once more, he could hear the trampling surge of blood in his ears, for he knew now that he had found a hoard of gold, that he was not only discovering treasure trove but creating archaeological history in his own land. Hoards of bronze had been found, but never a hoard of gold. His hand brought forth a penannular gold bracelet – with a second bracelet dangling from it, swinging, swinging towards the opening and just about to slip through when he made a grab at it and caught it, but the lunula slipped from the fingers of his other hand and for a moment he was entangled and confused.

Neil Gunn, The Silver Bough

Introduction

Stories of lost or hidden treasure exert a fascination that has always coloured our ideas about the past. Such accounts have a very long history and some can be found in the earliest European literature.

In *Le Morte D'Arthur*, for instance, the king receives his sword from the Lady of the Lake (Fig. 1) and on his death it is to the water that it must return. Thomas Mallory describes the scene:

'My time hieth fast,' said the king. 'Therefore,' said Arthur unto Sir Bedevere, 'Take thou Excalibur, my good sword, and go with it to yonder water side, and when thou comest there I charge thee throw my sword in that water, and come again and tell me what thou seest'. (*Morte D'Arthur*, Book xxi, Chapter 5)

The knight is reluctant to follow this instruction:

By the way he beheld that noble sword, that the pommel and the haft

Fig. 1 King Arthur receives Excalibur from the Lady of the Lake: an engraving after the Victorian painter Daniel Maclise, illustrating Tennyson's *Morte D'Arthur*.

was all of precious stones; and then he said to himself, 'If I throw this rich sword in the water, thereof shall never come good, but harm and loss.' And then Sir Bedevere hid Excalibur under a tree.

When he returns, Arthur knows that the knight has disobeyed him. Again Sir Bedevere is dispatched, and again he hides the sword. Only on the third occasion are the orders carried out:

Then Sir Bedevere departed, and went to the sword, and lightly took it up, and went to the water side; and there he bound the girdle about the hilts, and then he threw the sword as far into the water as he might; and there came an arm and an hand above the water and met it, and caught it, and so shook it thrice and brandished, and then vanished away the hand with the sword in the water.

Not until this task has been performed can the king depart. He is carried away in 'a little barge with many fair ladies in it... Among them all was a queen, and all they had black hoods, and all they wept and shrieked when they saw King Arthur'. The king is taken over the water to his death.

An equally powerful myth is recorded in the *Nibelungenlied*, the major epic of the Germanic world, which itself incorporates an older Norse tradition (Vestergaard 1987). Here we find the same association between treasure and water. In this case the story concerns the treasure of the Nibelung dynasty:

It was as much as a dozen wagons fully loaded could carry away from the mountain in four days and nights, coming and going thrice a day! It was entirely of gems and gold, and even if one had paid all the people in the world with it, it would not have lost a mark in value! (*Nibelungenlied*, Chapter 19)

The treasure was brought from Nibelungland as dowry for the princess Kriemhild, but it fell into the hands of Hagen, who 'took the entire treasure and sank it in the Rhine at Locheim, imagining he would make use of it some day: but this was not destined to happen'. That treasure is the 'Rhine gold' of Wagner's famous opera.

Both those examples call to mind some of the most enigmatic parts of the archaeological record, and also some of the ways in which they have been understood. *Le Morte D'Arthur* recalls the numerous discoveries of swords and other weapons in watery locations across North and North-West Europe (Torbrügge 1971). The *Nibelungenlied* also recalls the extraordinai y wealth of artefacts recovered from major rivers, including the Rhine itself. At the same time, the two accounts evoke some of the interpretations that have been placed on these strange deposits. *Le Morte D'Arthur* suggests a connection between the rites of passage and the deposition of weapons. Even the king's departure in the barge creates a link between water and death. Sir Bedevere's behaviour is revealing in another way. It seems that Excalibur had to be consigned to the waters so that its special powers would be extinguished with Arthur's death. The knight, however, was influenced by its fine appearance and the presence of precious stones. If the sword had remained in circulation, it could have brought him wealth and power, and so at first he hid it.

Kriemhild's treasure was intended as dowry, and would have played a part in the cycle of gift exchange so characteristic of heroic society. There was no intention of taking it out of circulation permanently, yet the story makes the same connection between portable wealth and water, in this case a major river. Hagen's motivation is obvious. He did not intend to destroy this material, still less to offer it to the gods: it was *hidden* in the river, and he intended to retrieve it. By the end of the *Nibelungenlied*, however, everyone who knew the hiding place of that treasure had been killed, and it remained there for the archaeologist to find it.

It is paradoxical that these acts should play such a central role in European literature, whilst water finds enjoy a marginal status in archaeological writing. Michael Schiffer's comprehensive review of the formation of the archaeological record devotes only two of its 350 pages to votive deposits (1987, 79–80). By contrast, the present book suggests that such collections are of fundamental importance to our perception of early society.

The classification of deposits

It is understandable that certain archaeological problems should be echoed in the literature of the Middle Ages, when we consider that intentional deposits of fine artefacts can be traced over an enormous time span and a vast geographical area. They have been studied most intensively in North and North-West Europe, but they have counterparts in other continents and, to some extent, in the ethnographic record. Valuables would have been hidden during every period of history, whilst the specific association between fine artefacts and watery locations seems to develop in the Neolithic period and continues virtually uninterrupted into the first millennium AD. It is the later stages of this sequence which are echoed in these two sources. Such deposits change from one period and one cultural setting to another, but throughout this lengthy sequence we find that same contrast between votive deposition and concealment. In the following pages we review the different schemes by which these finds have been classified, ranging from the empirical to the more theoretical. Later sections extend the discussion to consider the wider significance of votive offerings in non-market societies.

Find context

The empirical evidence has been classified in many ways, although few of the schemes available at present make any attempt to explain the formation of these deposits. Indeed, the terms in which such finds have been considered have hardly changed in a hundred years. The fundamental distinction is between the deposition of artefacts which *could* have been recovered and those which would have been difficult or impossible to retrieve. In general that distinction corresponds to the contrast between finds which were deposited on dry land and those which were placed in water. Like most simple schemes, it has many exceptions. Not all dry-land finds would have been easy to locate. For every example whose position might have been marked, by a stone or a recognisable feature of the landscape (see Stein 1976, Karte 12 A–D), there were others that were buried too deeply. Some finds which seem to have come from dry land may have been deposited when conditions were very different, for example the weaponry found in former river channels or lakes (e.g. Needham 1979, 111–13 and 127–8). Not all the artefacts from peat bogs need have been deposited when these were watery locations. Some of the Bronze Age metalwork found in the English Fenland may have been placed there when conditions were much dryer (see Pryor 1980a, 488–90); in such cases the change to a watery environment came only later. In either case the *Nibelungenlied* sounds a warning against too confident an interpretation, for it is clear that Hagen sank the treasure in the Rhine with the express intention of recovering it later. The story may be a rationalisation of an archaic practice, but it cautions us against any easy solution.

Single finds and multiple finds

A still simpler distinction has been offered between single and multiple finds (Kubach 1985). Although these terms are self-explanatory, their implications are not so easy to grasp. Single finds may come from either land or water, and until recently they had attracted little attention. It has been all too easy to dismiss these discoveries as chance losses, although their fine condition often makes this seem unlikely (Jensen 1972; Kubach 1985). Multiple finds raise more problems, since it is usually presumed that they were deposited together at the same time. On dry-land sites this is a convention which underpins a long series of chronological studies (Déchelette 1924), but where material is supposed to have been stored for later recovery it is possible that certain items were added and that others were removed from the original collection. In some cases what are described as single finds may be the residue of such accumulations. Finds from wet locations raise different problems again. A number of the bog hoards retain evidence of their original arrangement (e.g. Hagberg 1988; Pl. 1), and for this reason they do seem to possess a certain integrity, but when artefacts were placed in water they generally lost any detailed context. Virtually all the river metalwork in Europe has been recovered by dredging, and even where the locations of these finds have been recorded accurately, there is no reason to suppose that items which were discovered together were originally deposited at the same time. Indeed, the deposition of valuables in wet places may have occurred for as much as two millennia. The only prospect of securing adequate information would be by excavation in bogs (Pl. 2) or even underwater (e.g. Rychner 1987, 15–18), and this might not be enough to identify a process of intermittent deposition.

Plate 1 Part of the Bronze Age shield hoard from Fröslunda, Sweden, at the time of excavation. Fourteen of these artefacts were deposited in shallow water on the same occasion. Photography courtesy of Ulf Erik Hagberg.

Tools, weapons and ornaments

Another factual distinction is between collections of these three types of material. In the Bronze Age there is some reason to suppose that objects in each of the different categories could have been made and distributed separately, if only because their production imposed very different technical demands (Rowlands 1976). It is true that the finer weapons are often found separately

Plate 2 A Bronze Age sword under excavation close to a timber upright at Fengate Power Station. Photograph courtesy of Francis Pryor.

from other groups, and the same is the case for certain types of personal ornament (Pl. 3). Reference to the burial record suggests that sometimes such distinctions were based on gender (Sørensen 1987). Others may reflect fundamental differences of status, but there is a danger of adopting too schematic an approach to this material. Simpler weapon types are more closely associated with finds of tools (Ehrenberg 1977, 17–19), whilst other items traditionally described as tools, such as the Early Bronze Age axes in Ireland, can carry elaborate decoration (Harbison 1969). In any event the three groups are not mutually exclusive. We need a fourth category to accommodate a series of distinctive hoards in which the separation breaks down. The sig-

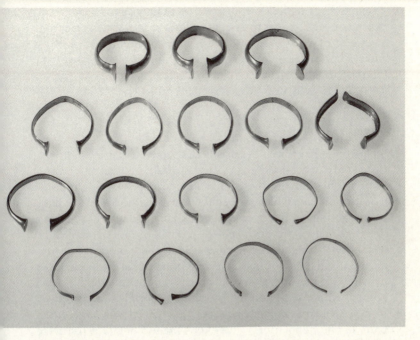

Plate 3 Two hoards of gold ornaments from Bexley, Kent. Photograph: British Museum.

nificance of this interesting group of 'mixed' hoards will be considered later (p. 121).

'Wet' finds and dry-land finds

The simple distinction between 'wet' finds and dry-land finds lends itself to subdivision, although the process can be taken too far. The 'wet' finds may be divided between river finds, finds from lakes, discoveries from springs and finds from bogs (Hundt 1955; Zimmerman 1970). There seems little reason to suppose that these distinctions are important, and, generally speaking, they reflect the natural features of the different areas being studied. The finds from dry land have a rather more complicated structure and can sometimes be studied in greater detail. Here the most important distinctions are between finds of elaborate artefacts from settlements, discoveries of grave goods, and those deposits which appear to exist in isolation. The latter come from a variety of locations, and some were apparently marked by stones (Levy 1982). Other distinctive groups are associated with hilltops, mountain passes (Bianco Peroni 1979; Mayer 1979), caves and rock fissures (Maier 1977; Warmenbol 1988a).

'Ritual hoards'

So far these have been essentially descriptive schemes, although close study of these different contexts has helped us to interpret some of the finds: in these terms secular deposits should occur in locations from which they could be recovered, but votive finds would be impossible to retrieve. In Denmark, where a number of metal hoards are documented in detail, a more complicated method of distinguishing between 'ritual' and 'non-ritual' groups has been suggested on the basis of ethnographic evidence. Janet Levy (1982) has offered several criteria for identifying these two groups. *Ritual* deposits might occur in special locations away from settlements, and may have been associated with only certain parts of the population. These finds might contain a restricted range of items, including specific categories of sacrificial animals or food, and particular kinds of personal valuables. Associations with food appear to be especially widespread, and such locations may see the ritual slaughter of animals, the consumption of ritual meals and the provision of ritual libations.

This scheme has its problems, for not only is it difficult to apply some of these criteria to the archaeological record: the fact that the list is compiled by cross-cultural generalisation is also open to criticism. It combines a series of practices which have been divorced from their local contexts and brought together to create an ideal 'primitive' world. The ethnographic present becomes a direct analogue for the prehistoric past, but at the expense of draining those activities of their original meanings (see Rowlands and Gledhill 1977, 146–7).

In this particular case Levy has a second source of information in the writings of the Roman historian Tacitus, although she can only use his account to any effect by assuming that society in Bronze Age Denmark, the subject of her detailed study, had similar beliefs to those described in the *Germania* almost a millennium later. By combining these two approaches she suggests much more specific criteria for recognising what she terms 'ritual hoards'. The special locations selected for such deposits should include wet places, such as bogs, springs or wells; other suitable places could be burial mounds, shrines or groves. She suggests that collections of material buried at a great depth also belong in this category. Among the objects that she believes may dominate these groups are ornaments, weapons and those artefacts 'with apparent cosmological referents', such as figurines or musical instruments. The contents of ritual hoards might be set out in a formal arrangement and would sometimes be associated with the remains of food, in most cases animal bones.

Levy's study is confined to the Danish Bronze Age, but ritual deposits have a much longer history in Scandinavia. Such 'offerings' have been studied in the field by Stjernquist (1970) through a campaign of excavation at spring deposits in southern Sweden. These provide considerable support for Levy's work, but, as we shall see, they witnessed a long history of intentional deposits, extending from the Neolithic period into the first millennium AD. During the latter period excavation provides further material for comparison, and some of the great deposits of war booty in Northern Europe have been investigated by this means (Ilkjaer and Lønstrup 1983). Although they fall outside the period considered in this book, they have much in common with Levy's description of ritual hoards.

Non-ritual hoards

These finds have also been the subject of detailed study, extending over more than a century. Levy distinguishes these from Bronze Age ritual hoards according to the following criteria. They may be found in dry ground and would be buried less deeply than the other deposits. Their position could be marked by a stone, and they might include small personal valuables and a high proportion of tools. Food remains should not be found in these deposits. Some of the metalwork could have been damaged or broken before it was deposited and might include raw material or metalworking residues. For the most part these criteria are not derived from comparison with the ethnographic record. Rather, they comprise a residual category of deposits which do not conform to her group of ritual hoards.

In fact very similar criteria have governed the interpretation of utilitarian hoards since the nineteenth century. In this case such groups have been characterised according to their likely owners and the industrial processes which might have taken place when they were deposited. Again this discussion has concentrated on the Bronze Age, and in particular on its later phases.

The major categories that are thought to identify the owners of these deposits are 'personal hoards' and 'craftsmen's hoards' (Hodges 1957). This classification does not take account of the contexts in which the material was discovered and is based exclusively on the types of artefact in these collections. Thus small groups of intact tools, weapons or ornaments may be regarded as personal property which had been concealed or stored to await later recovery. This interpretation has been particularly popular where ornaments and weapons are the simpler types which are also discovered on settlement sites. The craftsmen's hoards are defined according to rather similar procedures and comprise a range of intact tools, including those used for woodworking or leatherworking. Again these artefacts can be found singly in contemporary settlements.

We can contrast these groups with two categories of 'industrial' hoards, both of which are defined according to a specific reconstruction of how the bronze industry was organised. 'Merchants' hoards' are thought to consist of freshly made pieces that were stored together to await distribution to the customer. Sometimes these objects were still unsharpened, and in certain cases they came from the same mould. 'Founders' hoards', on the other hand, are more closely connected with the accumulation and recycling of scrap metal and some may be the remains of workshops (Pl. 4; Evans 1881, 458–9; De Mortillet 1894, 338). Although they do contain complete objects, many of the artefacts are extremely fragmentary and seem to have been broken up as scrap metal. The objects in these collections can reveal signs of use-wear and may show evidence of heating. In specific hoards they are accompanied by metalworking residues, including casting jets, ingots, slag and even moulds.

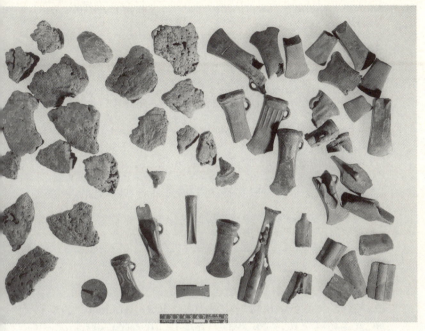

Plate 4 A Late Bronze Age scrap hoard from Addington Park, Greater London. Photograph: British Museum.

The locations in which utilitarian hoards are found have rarely been studied in much detail, but already it is clear that in some areas they occur very close to contemporary settlements. Moreover artefacts of very similar character, including metallurgical debris, can be found within the occupation sites themselves.

The main characteristics of these groups are summarised in Table 1. This analysis has the advantage that it is flexible. All too often studies of such deposits have been concerned with content rather than context. This is a tradition that can be traced at least as far back as the work of Sir John Evans (1881). It has remained important because of the way in which prehistoric chronology has been compiled, by studying groups of associated material. Since so little is known about the circumstance in which this material was deposited, it is perhaps a moot point whether such chronologies can be entirely reliable, but in the present account they are followed for want of anything better.

Table 1. *Criteria for identifying 'ritual' and 'non-ritual' hoards (after Levy 1982)*

'Ritual' hoards
Locations (specialised): Bogs; springs; wells; groves; burial mounds; deep pits.
Range of items (restricted): High proportion of weapons; high proportion of ornaments; ceremonial objects; animal bones or other food remains.
Condition of artefacts: Mainly whole objects; formal arrangement.

'Non-ritual' hoards
Locations (unspecialised): Dry land; with marker stone.
Range of items (less stereotyped assemblage): High proportion of tools; simpler personal ornaments; simpler forms of weapon; multiples of one type.
Condition of artefacts: Often damaged and/or broken; metalworking residues; freshly made objects

Levy's analysis combines the study of hoard contents with an investigation of their context. This is a more recent development in European archaeology and requires greater research, but its value is shown by the quotation from *Le Morte D'Arthur*, for King Arthur chose both *the object to be deposited and the place where this was to happen*. The close interrelationship between the composition of such deposits and their setting in the cultural landscape is a major theme of this discussion.

Approaches to the evidence

Given so much variety, it might seem strange to assert that hoards and votive deposits have not received their due from archaeologists, but this is undeniable. In many areas only certain segments of a longer history of deposition have been studied in any detail. As we shall see, the scope of current research also depends on deep-rooted regional traditions in the interpretation of this material. This has meant that in Northern Europe a range of deposits extending from the Neolithic to the Viking period has been analysed in some depth, whereas in Central and Western

Europe too much attention has been paid to Bronze Age finds, with the result that few of the schemes described so far could be applied to deposits of other periods. There is the additional problem that specialists in different periods take the term 'hoard' to mean different things.

Traditions of interpretation

Not only is research impeded by the approach taken to the Bronze Age material: essentially similar finds from different areas of Europe are studied according to quite different traditions of research (cf. Eogan 1983, 4). This can be expressed in terms of three schools of thought. In Central Europe there has been a tendency to investigate the circumstances that led to the *deposition* of hoards, and this has involved an attempt to write political history. In Northern Europe, on the other hand, there has been a much greater willingness to envisage a long-running tradition of votive offerings, extending from the Neolithic period into the first millennium AD, and correspondingly less enthusiasm for connecting the deposition of bronze hoards with the organisation of the metal industry. In Western Europe these priorities are reversed, and until quite recently most of the deposits considered in this book were interpreted in utilitarian terms.

To some extent these contrasts can be explained by non-archaeological considerations. They appear to have been influenced by the more recent history of those areas. At its simplest it appears that the interpretation of this material in Central Europe has been coloured by the region's long history of invasion from outside, a history in which political authority and territorial boundaries could change from one generation to the next (Sklenàr 1983). It is no accident that so many countries in Central Europe emerged as independent states only recently; even then this sometimes happened through the confederation of traditionally opposed ethnic groups. An interpretation that emphasises the effects of hostile incursions into these territories could draw on a long history of invasion.

By contrast the Scandinavian experience would have been coloured by both literary and artistic sources that emphasised the role of fine objects and the close association between this world and the supernatural. The links between prehistory and the early historical period were strengthened further because this area remained outside the Roman frontier. The earliest literary sources come from a society in which the supernatural was still part of everyday affairs, and some of these texts belong to a period when the tradition of votive deposits was only just at an end. At the same time, the landscape of Scandinavia contains a most distinctive rock art, in which elaborate objects, apparently of Bronze Age date, seem to have been used in mysterious ceremonies (Fig. 2; Malmer 1981, chs. 7 and 12). In some cases it has even seemed profitable to combine the information from sources that are separated by more than a thousand years, and to interpret some of these scenes with the aid of the oldest literary traditions (Gelling and Davidson 1969). In Northern Europe archaeology has played an important role in defining national identities, and antiquities have been recorded systematically for many years (Kristiansen 1981). In a society in which the literary and artistic evidence would have been familiar, there was little reluctance to favour a votive interpretation for the deposits of prehistoric material.

Western Europe, on the other hand, experienced a major break in its archaeological sequence with the expansion of the Roman Empire, and here there was less continuity between the prehistoric material and the evidence from the Migration period. Indeed, that break was so abrupt that the periods on either side of the Roman occupation are often studied by different people, using quite different methods (Driscoll 1988). Although there were literary references to the deposition of fine objects, archaeologists, particularly in Britain and France, tended to take a pragmatic approach to the archaeological record. Deposits that might have appeared enigmatic were explained in common-sense terms, and until recently any interpretation that relied too heavily on ideas of 'ritual' activity was regarded with suspicion. Thus explanations were often circumstantial and anecdotal. Most attention was paid to the 'utilitarian' hoards, which were possibly related to Bronze Age metalworking. Here prehistorians felt that they were on safer ground, and at times the metal industry was interpreted as if it were directly comparable to an industry in the contemporary world, with its 'merchants', 'traders' and 'middle-

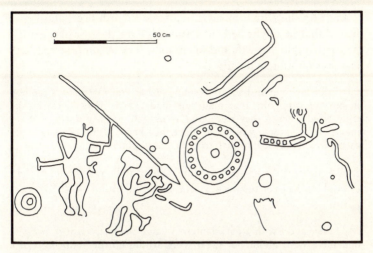

Fig. 2 An example of the prominent role played by metalwork in Scandinavian rock art. The illustration shows part of a larger design in Kville parish in Bohuslän, western Sweden. (After Nordbladh and Rosvall 1981)

men'. This interpretation was particularly acceptable during the nineteenth century, itself a period of rapid economic growth. It may be no accident that its most influential advocate, Sir John Evans, was a successful business man (Evans 1955, 115–17).

This is not to suggest that the interpretations put forward in these three areas were completely mutually exclusive, or that they were mistaken and naive. Archaeologists were not the dupes of their own preconceptions. There is no doubt that each of these interpretations can shed light on certain of the specific deposits. The problem is that the deposits themselves did not show as much variation as the theories developed to account for them.

Historical interpretations

There are some advantages in relating the formation of hoards to the historical situation at the time, for this has the signal merit of accounting for both the deposition and the non-recovery of so much archaeological material. The best-known example comes from the diary of Samuel Pepys.

The passage of arms

In 1667 the Dutch burnt part of the English fleet, and Pepys feared that he might be held responsible for the disaster. Anticipating trouble, his wife hid his money. The account in his diary is worth quoting in detail:

[She] did give me so bad an account of her and my father's method in burying our gold, that made me mad ... My father and she did it on Sunday when they were gone to church, in open daylight in the midst of the garden, where for aught they knew, many eyes might see them; which put me into such trouble ... (19 June)

It was not until October of that year that Pepys was confident enough to recover his money, and again he found cause for complaint:

My father and I with a dark lantern ... into the guarden with my wife and there went about our great work to dig up my gold. But Lord, what a tosse I was for some time in, that they could not justly tell me where it was ... ; but by and by, poking with a spit, we found it, and then begun with a spudd to lift up the ground; but good God, to see how sillily they did it, not half a foot under ground and in sight of the world from a hundred places if anybody by accident were near-hand ...

Having located his hoard, he had another problem:

I was out of my wits almost, and the more from that upon my lifting up the earth with the spud, I did discern that I scattered the pieces of gold round about the ground among the grass and loose earth; and taking up the iron headpieces wherein they were put, I perceive the earth was got among the gold and wet, so that the bags were all rotten ... At last [I] was forced to take up the headpieces, dirt and all, and as many of the scattered pieces as I could with the dirt discern by the candlelight ... and then all people going to bed, W. Hewer and I did all alone, with several pales of water and basins, at last wash the dirt off of the pieces and parted the pieces and the dirt, and then begun to tell; and by a note which I had of the value of the whole (in my pocket) do find there was short above a hundred pieces, which did make me mad. (10 October)

Another campaign of excavation took them through to two o'clock in the morning. After a sleepless night Pepys resumed work, using a more sophisticated method:

And then rose and called W. Hewer, and he and I, with pails and a

sive, did lock ourselfs into the garden and there gather all the earth
about the place into pails, and then sive these pails in one of the summer-
houses (just as they do for dyamonds in other parts of the world); and
there to our great content ... we did make the last night's forty-five
up to seventy; so that we are come to about twenty or thirty of what
I think the true number should be, and perhaps within less; so that
I am pretty well satisfied that my loss is not great and do bless God
that it is well; and do leave my father to make a second examination
of the dirt. (11 October)

Several features of this account are revealing. The hoard was
buried when its owner feared for his safety. It consisted of high-
value coinage (gold) and was buried at no great depth below
the surface. It had been placed in containers for easy recovery,
but these had deteriorated during the four months that they had
been in the ground. The hoard was buried just outside Pepys'
house, but its position had not been marked, and despite every
effort part of the hoard was never recovered. Pepys' account
is graphic, but, without it, would we be able to interpret a deposit
of this kind?

In this case the problem is not too serious – we know too
much about the seventeenth century for votive offerings to be
a serious option. On the other hand, it would only be possible
to offer a detailed explanation for its burial if a number of other
hoards had been buried at the same time. This certainly happened
during the English Civil War (Fig. 3; Kent 1974, 190–2), but
our ability to make such connections depends entirely on the
precision with which such finds can be dated. Here we encounter
a serious problem. Unless coins carry the date of issue, it is very
difficult to recognise 'hoarding horizons' of this kind, and the
same applies even more powerfully to deposits of other types
of artefacts, which can rarely be dated within much less than
a century.

In fact this kind of interpretation easily falls into a circular
argument. A series of rather similar deposits are believed to represent valuables that were hidden but never recovered, probably
at a time of crisis. Sometimes we can suggest a plausible historical
context for such deposits, but this can all too easily be treated
as evidence of date. When further finds come to light, their chronology seems assured, and the 'historical' interpretation of the
material is strengthened. A specific example of this process is

The passage of arms

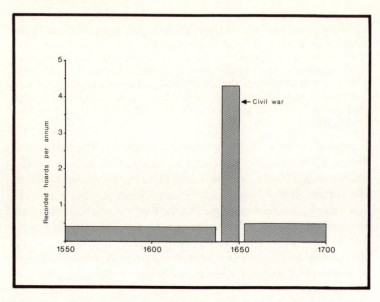

Fig. 3 The mean number of coin hoards per annum recorded from the English Civil War, compared with their frequency in earlier and later periods. (Data from Kent 1974)

provided by Late Iron Age coinage. It has been tempting to identify a peak of coin hoards in the Channel Islands with the disruption occasioned by the Gallic Wars, and for a time this seemed to provide a fixed chronological point on which other studies could build. That equation has since been questioned (Fitzpatrick and Megaw 1987, 439–41), but not before the same chronology had been extended to the development of pre-Roman coinage in Britain, with all its implications for the development of contemporary society.

In Pepys' case most of the coins were recovered, but by definition the archaeological record is composed of deposits that were abandoned or lost. Perhaps it is here that the 'political' interpretation of such finds has more to offer. Material may have been hidden or stored in the ground during many or most periods of prehistory, but only when circumstances prevented its recovery would it have stayed in the archaeological record. Peaks in the frequency of such deposits tell us most about the conditions under which these collections were lost. We have less idea of why they were hidden in the first place.

This question has been raised in a useful discussion of British Bronze Age hoards (Burgess and Coombs 1979). In this case it is quite clear that multiple deposits have a discontinuous history on dry land, whereas water finds are a regular feature of the archaeological sequence. The majority of the dry-land finds belong to the later stages of both the Middle and Late Bronze Ages. It would be quite inappropriate to regard these as periods of crisis or conflict just because so many hoards remained in the ground, but it is extremely striking that groups of material should have been deposited in both these contexts at times when there is evidence for the building of fortifications (Bradley 1984, ch. 5; Darvill 1987, ch. 5). Perhaps these really were periods of political instability. This argument can be amplified if we turn to other contemporary artefacts. Ian Hodder (1979) has made the interesting suggestion that it is under exactly those circumstances that material culture may be employed to emphasise ethnic distinctions. In fact the two periods that seem to show the greatest deposition of hoards also see the development of much sharper boundaries between ceramic style zones (Bradley and Hodder 1979). In the Late Bronze Age there is even a tendency for defended or defensible sites to be concentrated within those territories (Fig. 4).

If this view is correct, it has very serious consequences for traditional studies of chronology. It might mean that individual types – even entire schools of metal production – might be absent from the hoards on which the basic sequence of bronze industries depends. This is not such an extreme argument. Unlike stone, metalwork can be recycled, and in principle there is no reason why it should ever have entered the archaeological record – it needed to be lost, discarded or offered if it were to do so. There is another type of evidence that indicates the kinds of metal artefacts in circulation. This is provided by the increasing number of clay and stone moulds that have been recognised during recent years. It has always been problematical that some of the moulds for specific types of artefact are found outside the distribution of the finished products (e.g. Needham 1981, 37–40): now we

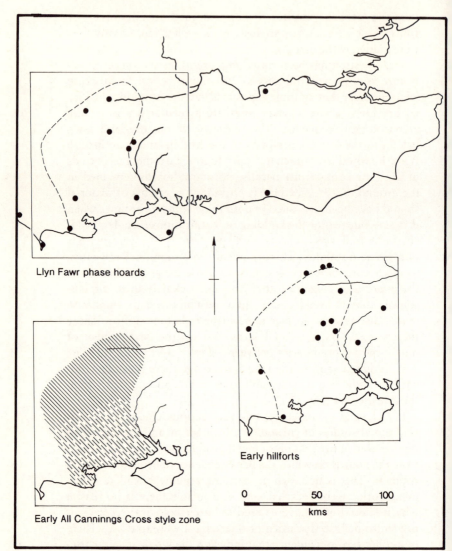

Llyn Fawr phase hoards

Early hillforts

Early All Canninngs Cross style zone

0   50   100
kms

Fig. 4 The distribution of the latest bronze hoards in southern England, compared with the extent of the early All Cannings Cross ceramic style zone and the distribution of the first hillforts in the region. Density of shading indicates density of findspots of pottery. (Hoard distribution after Thomas 1989; pottery style zone and hillfort distribution based on Cunliffe 1984b, the latter with additions)

have the more serious problem that clay mould fragments exist for types of object that never seem to have entered the archaeological record (Needham 1980, 209). The implications of this observation are rather startling. We may be conducting our research on the basis of a very biased sample of the metalwork in circulation. For this reason it is extremely important to investigate the circumstances under which supposedly utilitarian hoards would have been deposited and never recovered. Unless we produce satisfactory answers to that question, we can never be sure that this approach is the right one.

Practical interpretations

If the strength of those arguments is that they force us to consider why so many deposits were left in the ground, the value of this tradition is its scepticism of overblown interpretations. Its weakness is its relentless empiricism.

This tradition is at its best when it engages in meticulous analysis of the composition and condition of individual groups of material, and at its worse in its dismissal of some of the more arresting parts of the archaeological record. Discussion of the 'wet' finds exemplifies this latter tendency. For many years there was a real reluctance to accept that these were a valid category of evidence, and archaeologists preferred to seek essentially anecdotal explanations for these finds. Within this tradition, the major progress came in the German-speaking world, perhaps because German scholars commanded a wider range of European archaeological literature than their colleagues in Britain and France. Their endeavours first brought the sheer scale of this problem into focus. Torbrügge's study of European river finds remains the fundamental review of this material (1971). Within a decade most Anglophone archaeologists had been won over, but in France there is still some scepticism (Mohen 1977, 199; Gaucher 1981, 31).

The main arguments in favour of a distinct class of river deposit – not necessarily of metalwork – are the quantity, fine condition and restricted range of the objects that have been recovered, especially compared with the more fragmentary finds from settlement excavations (Needham and Burgess 1980). In the broadest sense they seem to be offerings. Such discoveries are by no means confined to the metal-using period – nor to prehistory in general – but were often dominated by what has been characterised as 'male' equipment (Fitzpatrick 1984). These artefacts (Pl. 5) seem to have most in common with the contents of rich graves, and in some regional sequences river finds alternate with the provision of fine artefacts in burials. In other cases the two forms of deposit have mutually exclusive distributions, again suggesting that 'wet' finds have a distinctive identity of their own (Torbrügge 1971). A number of authorities have argued against this position by stressing the sheer variety of mundane activities that could have accounted for deposits of this nature, and not all of the suggestions can be rebutted. They stress the accidental loss of artefacts from boats or at river crossings. They raise the possibility that some of the groups of weaponry result from battles at fords, or even from naval engagements. Other objects, they argue, may have been eroded into the rivers from settlements or burials on their banks or could even have been swept into the waters by flash floods. Some of these ideas probably can be rejected – settlement excavations very rarely produce whole objects of the same quality as those in the rivers (Needham and Burgess 1980); the spearheads retain traces of their shafts and would have floated long enough to have been recovered (Hooper and O'Connor 1976) – but the main objection to such piecemeal solutions is the sheer number of artefacts being discussed. A more worrying tendency is for the same case histories to be repeated in the archaeology of one period after another. For example the Iron Age metalwork from La Tène has been discussed as if other water deposits of weaponry were unknown (De Navarro 1972, 17–19). In the same way, no sooner had the integrity of Bronze Age finds from the Thames won general acceptance than a corpus of Neolithic axes from the same river was published, arguing that this material resulted from chance losses and the erosion of nearby settlements (Adkins and Jackson 1978).

The strength of this tradition is its meticulous attention to detail. The contents of some of the dry-land hoards have been analysed with great subtlety, and it is easy to appreciate how closely some of these were related to the process of metalworking. Archaeometallurgists have paid careful attention to the finds of

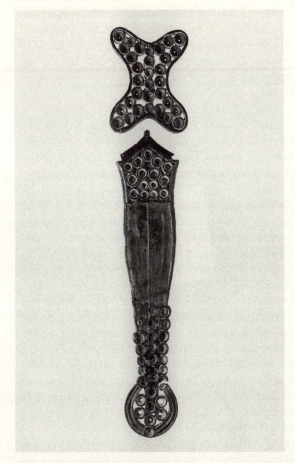

Plate 5 An example of river weaponry: an Iron Age dagger and its sheath from the River Thames at Cookham. Photograph: British Museum.

industrial debris in these hoards, and the slag, ingots and occasional moulds have all been documented (e.g. Northover 1982). The same applies to the traces of manufacture and use on the objects themselves. Indeed, there have even been attempts to identify objects made in the same moulds, through a process akin to the die-linking used by numismatists (Flanagan 1978).

A particular feature of this approach has been the application of metal analysis, which has not only confirmed the traditional idea that bronze scrap was being recycled, but has also provided indications of more basic 'metal circulation zones', linking the sources of the natural ores to the wider regions over which they were distributed (Northover 1982; Needham, Leese, Hook and Hughes 1989).

Whilst this work has often indicated how closely hoarding could be allied to the production and distribution of metalwork, certain ambiguities still remain. Objects could be broken for more than one reason, and we should not assume that *all* these fragments are to be linked with the circulation of scrap metal. Similar broken pieces can be found in burials, and the half-melted fragments of bronze that look so much like industrial by-products also resemble some of the metalwork that is found with contemporary cremations (e.g. Herrmann 1966). In addition, heat-altered artefacts can be found in rivers (e.g. Pryor 1980b, 13–14). For these reasons it would be wrong to suppose that every collection of damaged pieces was associated with the activities of smiths. A set quantity of bronze might have been as acceptable as the offerings of whole artefacts that characterise Levy's 'ritual' hoards. Some ambiguity is inescapable, and only where casting jets, slag, ingots or moulds can be identified in these deposits is their interpretation at all clearcut. Even so, the evidence of widespread recycling provided by metal analysis is impressive and generally convincing. It seems that it became of growing importance during the Bronze Age sequence.

Some archaeologists have attempted to go beyond the simple identification of metallurgical debris in dry-land hoards and have put forward quite specific interpretations of how these deposits were related to the production and distribution of bronzes. The widespread dissemination of particular styles of bronzework attracted attention from an early stage, together with the extensive distribution of hoard finds, few of which seemed to be associated with settlements. The most influential interpretation was that of Gordon Childe (1958), if only because it formed part of a more general attempt to account for the distinctive character of European society. He suggested that bronzesmiths led a mobile existence outside the tribal framework of the time:

The life of the smiths and pedlars who manufactured and distributed these wares was doubtless hard and perilous. They were rewarded neither with great riches nor with a high rank in society ... European metal-workers were free. They were not tied to any one patron or even to a single tribal society. They were producing for an intertribal, if not an international, market ... Their very itinerary and far-flung commercial contacts [would] fertilise native genius ... Whoever had the perseverance to earn initiation into the appropriate mysteries of techniques ... could escape the necessity of growing his own food and shake off the bonds of allegiance to an overlord or the more rigid fetters of tribal custom. (1958, 169)

This endorsement of free enterprise is unexpected from a life-long Marxist and has been criticised (Trigger 1980, 161–2). It is not demanded by the empirical evidence. The hoards themselves can be interpreted in other ways, and are just as likely to result from a system of part-time specialisation taking place *within* the social fabric. The production of the most complex artefacts was perhaps the work of skilled bronzesmiths attached to an élite (Rowlands 1976). This may account for the existence of separate hoards containing tools, weapons or ornaments, and for the increasing evidence of metalworking found on the richest settlement. Moreover a survey of the ethnographic literature suggests that the type of industrial organisation postulated by Childe would be unprecedented (Rowlands 1971).

At a less detailed level the conventional interpretation of these Bronze Age finds is echoed in the archaeology of other periods. In the case of Viking silver hoards this is not because the models have been borrowed from the prehistorian (Hårdh 1976; Graham-Campbell 1982). Rather, both were periods in which large areas of Europe became dependent on a supply of exotic metalwork. It was necessary to use this sparingly and to make complicated arrangements for recycling worn and broken objects, particularly when there could be fluctuations in the rate at which fresh metalwork became available. We shall return to this point in Chapter 3.

Within the prehistoric period this approach to Bronze Age studies has had a powerful influence. It has coloured our interpretation of dry-land deposits of Iron Age metalwork (e.g. Clarke 1954) and groups of Neolithic stone axes have sometimes been seen as the stock carried by prehistoric traders (e.g. Healy 1984,

125). As mentioned earlier, even the terminology used in such discussions has a period flavour and seems to be rooted in the entrepreneurial capitalism of the last century.

Votive interpretations

We have seen how scholars working in the North European tradition tend to interpret their evidence in terms of votive deposition. To some extent this approach has been influenced by their access to literary and artistic sources, but there are specifically archaeological issues to consider here. Finds from this area of Europe are better preserved than most, and their discovery has been documented systematically over a longer period. For this reason we have more details of the major deposits than are available in other parts of Europe.

This information is often revealing and its existence obviously influenced Janet Levy's study. The discovery of food remains is of particular significance here. As she has pointed out, these do accompany a number of finds of metalwork, especially those from watery locations, but it is necessary to add that similar finds are also recorded in isolation during both the Neolithic and Iron Age periods. In southern Sweden it can even be shown that the prehistoric animal bones excavated from a number of springs have a different species composition from the finds on contemporary settlements (Stjernquist 1970); the same is true of the faunal remains from Iron Age weapon deposits in Scandinavia (Todd 1987, ch. 6). In addition, there are discoveries of isolated pottery vessels which seem to have contained food offerings (Becker 1947 and 1971). These could hardly have been stored for later recovery. A purely mundane interpretation is still less likely where ploughs were deposited in watery locations (Glob 1945). Those discoveries belong to the Iron Age, but much earlier finds of Neolithic disc wheels may have had a similar character (Van der Waals 1964).

Even more striking are those deposits which consist of groups of human bones or even preserved corpses. These have a lengthy history, beginning in the Neolithic period (Bennike, Ebbesen and Bender Jørgensen 1986), but with a major group of bog bodies dating from the Iron Age (Fischer 1979; Tauber 1979). It is perfectly possible that some of these finds result from accidents or from casual burial, but in other cases that interpretation is impossible. The bones represent incomplete bodies and may even show evidence of butchery. Some individuals had met a violent death before their corpses were placed in pools and weighted down. These deposits are not confined to Scandinavia, although this region has seen the most detailed analysis of the evidence (Dieck 1965).

In all these cases there is circumstantial evidence of formal deposition. Some of these finds actually occur together with portable artefacts, or in close proximity to such discoveries. It is not surprising that the idea of ritual hoarding should have become so firmly established. Some of the artefacts from Northern Europe also provide support for this interpretation. So far much of our discussion of metalwork has concerned deposits of tools, weapons or personal ornaments. Scandinavia, however, includes a fourth category of contemporary material, which has been described as 'ceremonial equipment' (Levy 1982, 82–3). Comparable finds are less common in other regions. They include such extraordinary objects as the Trundholm sun chariot, the Gundestrup cauldron or the huge bronze horns known as lures (Pl. 6). Again the lures are commonly discovered in watery locations. Their specialised role is emphasised by their depiction in rock art, and since they are virtually absent in any other context, there seems every reason to accept them as intentional deposits.

For the most part these interpretations do carry conviction, but again there is the danger that a single reading of the evidence will involve some loss of detail. The Scandinavian literature is at its weakest when it deals with the collections of broken pieces and metallurgical debris that play such a dominant role in the archaeology of other areas. As we have seen, Levy does distinguish these finds from the ritual hoards of the Danish Bronze Age, but others treat all the hoards together. In some studies this may arise from a purely semantic confusion, and the problem may have been created by the over-extension of this one term 'hoard'. In other cases, however, it seems as if scholars are attempting to manage without a category of utilitarian hoard (e.g. Larsson 1986). This may yet prove to be an acceptable position, but it does need to be justified.

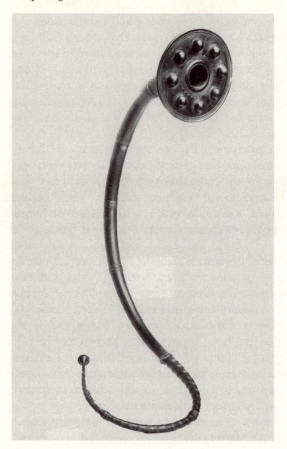

Plate 6 A bronze lure from Tellerup, Funen. Photograph:
Nationalmuseet, Copenhagen.

Archaeological source criticism

Common to all three approaches is a concern with archaeological
source criticism. This term describes the study of how our information has been acquired and the biases which it exhibits (Kristiansen 1974). This is of obvious importance to the present
enquiry. Some rivers have been dredged more intensively than
others, and different periods have seen the reclamation of wet-

lands. If various types of deposit were buried at different depths, it is vital to understand the agencies that have brought them to light, for only in that way can we decide what weight to place on the available sample. Is the rate of discovery still increasing, in which case our evidence may be unrepresentative, or has it already passed a peak? Were certain types of artefact favoured by collectors at the expense of others? And how far has our knowledge of chance finds been influenced by the purchasing policies of public and private institutions? Are the larger items over-represented among the river finds? And to what extent has state legislation affected the reporting of discoveries?

These questions are not the only ones that could be asked, but all relate directly to any assessment of how well particular material may be suited to sustained analysis. In this respect there does seem to be unanimity. The rates of discovery of different types of artefact have been documented in many areas (Fig. 5; Kristiansen ed. 1985). The depths at which discoveries occurred are analysed increasingly often. The different agencies responsible for chance discoveries have been identified, and in one case archaeologists monitored a period of dredging in order to obtain a more representative sample of the artefacts from a major river (Blanchet and Lambot 1977; Blanchet, Cornejo, Lambot and Laurent 1978). Some hoards and offering places have been carefully excavated (Verron 1983), and the positions of others have been investigated using metal detectors (Östergren 1985), aerial photography (Lawson 1980, 281) and even phosphate survey (Callmer 1980). Such research has considerable potential, and its publication may yet bring the different schools of interpretation closer together. At that level the decisive influence will come from the artefacts themselves. But at another level there are already signs of a still more significant change of attitude.

Material culture studies

The traditional approach to hoards is to treat them as a series of closed associations, essential for the construction of artefact chronologies. This is one of the mainstays of the typological method, and it is a basic tenet of this research that 'types' exist as fixed entities. This may not have been the case in prehistory,

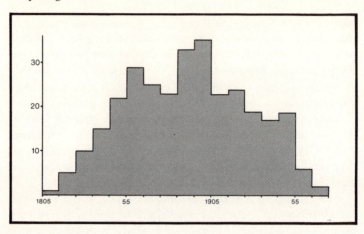

Fig. 5 The dates of discovery of Neolithic and Early Bronze Age metal hoards in Zealand, Denmark. (After Kristiansen 1985)

when the meaning and value of particular objects could have been less stable. The discussions summarised in the previous section have been pursued with a rather limited conception of the part that material culture must have played in past society. Recently, that position has come in for criticism, and there have been attempts to reinstate material culture studies at the heart of prehistoric research. As Appadurai has said, 'commodities, and things in general ... constitute the first principles and the last resort of archaeologists' (1986, 5). This section highlights those elements of the discussion which could be relevant here.

The first area to come under scrutiny is the study of production and exchange. Here there are several strands to the argument. The analysis of production systems has been criticised because it stresses economics rather than culture as the basis of social relations (Miller 1987, 46–9). This is a tradition which goes back to Marx, but because most literature privileges production above consumption it may betray an ethnocentric view of the world, in which Western assumptions are imposed quite inappropriately on other societies (Berthoud and Sabelli 1979). Even within our own society it may be wrong to place too much emphasis on the alienated consumer. Miller (1987) has shown how the products of mass culture can be used in extremely creative ways. In his view there is scope for a more searching analysis of the social strategies in which they are employed.

If production is emphasised at the expense of consumption, exchange is looked upon as a primarily economic transaction. This view may also be mistaken, as objects can almost take on a life of their own. In Appadurai's striking term we have to study 'the social life of things'. Kopytoff has enumerated some of the questions that can be asked:

Where does the thing come from and who made it? What has been its career so far, and what do people consider to be an ideal career for such things? What are the recognised 'ages' or periods in the thing's 'life', and what are the cultural markers for them? How does the thing's use change with its age, and what happens to it when it reaches the end of its usefulness? (1986, 66–7)

The emphasis is on diversity, and in tracing the biographies of different artefacts we can consider the ways in which their values and associations changed. At the same time, since exchange involves a relationship between specific people, the properties of any artefact could be manipulated through their use in specialised transactions.

Taken together, these observations raise problems for the archaeological analysis of production and exchange. Much of the difficulty is created because only two stages in the life cycle of an artefact can actually be observed: its production and its final deposition. What happened in between has to be inferred. The analysis of hoards has often emphasised the role of the producer, and, as we have seen, archaeologists working in the Western European tradition have commonly used these deposits as clues to craft organisation. In doing so they have been unduly influenced by their experience of 'industries' in the modern world. There is a further problem when we discuss the exchange of different artefacts. Since this process is archaeologically invisible it must be approached obliquely. Usually this has been done on the basis of studies which consider their changing frequency with distance from the source (Renfrew 1977). Understandably this approach is not very sensitive to the social processes that feature in the anthropological literature, and even in archaeology itself, simulation studies have shown how the same fall-off patterns can be created by several quite different processes (Hodder and Orton 1976, 126–53).

A second strand in the recent literature concerns the ways in which material culture is used within particular societies. This work suggests that it should be credited with a more active role. It can be employed to symbolise important distinctions within society. Thus it may be used to express differences of status, ethnic differences and differences of age or gender. These are all elements that can be recognised from the archaeological record. Usually this is most apparent in the study of burials, but Sørensen's recent analysis of Bronze Age metalwork in Scandinavia has broken new ground by investigating the contents of hoards. She has shown how this material was organised about three axes: the contrast between exotic and locally produced artefacts; the distinction between unique and standard objects; and the separate groups of material associated with men and women. All of these features combined to determine the contexts in which different artefacts entered the archaeological record (Sørensen 1987).

Such distinctions would have been crucially important in everyday life. As Bourdieu (1977) has shown, constant exposure to such features as dress styles, house plans, monuments or body decoration will reinforce the norms on which the continuity of society depends. Material culture defines the field of social experience and it sets its limits. In this way apparently mundane transactions help to uphold a particular view of the world. At the same time, symbols are essentially arbitrary and the categories employed are never fixed. If the original meanings of symbolic systems can never be brought to light, we can examine the changing contexts in which they were used. It may be possible to recognise the transactions in which they were deployed, the place of such transactions in the life cycle of the community and the kinds of location selected for the purpose. Together these constitute what John Barrett (1988) calls 'fields of discourse'.

At the same time, material culture changes. It is produced by knowledgeable actors, and so it can be manipulated. An obvious example is the creation of value. In Western society this is largely controlled by the laws of supply and demand, but again it would be wrong to project this system into the past, where access to particular objects, or the transactions in which they were used, might have been socially determined. It is the manipulation of meaning and value that creates the archaeological sequence on which our understanding of the past depends. We can illustrate that process by three ethnographic examples. These have the additional advantage of introducing ideas that will be used in later chapters.

Emulation is one of the processes that contribute to the instability of symbolic systems (Miller 1985, 184–96). Particular artefacts or styles may change their associations as lower-ranking groups imitate their peers. When this happens, objects that were formerly the prerogative of an élite may become so widely available that they lose their status and have to be replaced. A good example of this process is provided by the recent history of Papua New Guinea (Burton 1987). Here stone axes were produced in a number of restricted areas and played a central role as bride-wealth until metal axes became widely available. Stone artefacts lost their original value to objects made from the new material, but because the latter were easier to come by, they no longer played a specialised role in marriage payments, and pearl-shells were employed in the same transactions. In this case the value of each of these artefacts depended less on questions of supply and demand than on the social strategies of the people who were using them.

Similarly, artefacts or styles may change their symbolic associations as they move from one region to another. This is a field that has been studied by Helms (1988), who emphasises how access to foreign goods or esoteric knowledge may provide one route to social advancement. Again the colonial period supplies an obvious example of this process. Worsley (1968) has discussed the extraordinary 'cargo cults' of Melanesia, where millenarian beliefs have developed, connected with the influx of goods from outside the local system. Since it was believed that wealth derived from the correct manipulation of the spirit world, European customs were widely copied, and as European trade goods came into this region they were imbued with sacred properties. This would never be apparent from a purely typological study of this material. For an archaeologist the various *contexts* in which imported objects were employed would provide the only clue to their changing character.

Lastly, the practices involving different artefacts can also change through time or as they pass from one cultural setting to another. An excellent example of this process is provided by another case of colonial contact – the potlatch of the north-west coast of America (Rosman and Rubel 1971). Although the situation is extremely complicated, it seems likely that before the period of European colonisation, the potlatch had served a number of functions. It celebrated a rite of passage and often the succession to office. It was the prerogative of lineage-heads or elders, and involved the provision of food and also of certain valuables. Hosts employed the potlatch as a way of building alliances with other groups, who were obliged to respond in kind if they were to keep the alliances in being. During the colonial era, when warfare had been proscribed, this institution changed its character, whilst still maintaining some of the older forms. With the influx of wealth that resulted from the fur trade, it became a form of surrogate warfare, entailing a greater number of participants and a larger quantity of goods. Potlatches took place more frequently and now they involved the lavish consumption – even the destruction – of property. A ceremony which had originally been concerned with the formation and nurturing of alliances saw increasingly aggressive competition for prestige.

These are just three examples of the ways in which material culture can play a vital part in our reconstruction of the past, and they have been selected because each process seems to be evidenced in the archaeological analysis of hoards and votive deposits. At another level, the deliberate offering or concealment of valuables illustrates the same basic point: material culture is used in an active manner (Shanks and Tilley 1987a, ch. 4). It will be some time before these changes of attitude amongst archaeologists have much impact on the way in which such deposits are interpreted, but already it does seem possible to discern some possibilities. These will be taken up in later sections of this book.

From accident to intention

We have considered the ways in which property could be concealed and lost, and shall do so again in other contexts. There are also a number of suggestions as to why it should have been discarded freely.

At the outset we must distinguish between two processes which are often treated together in the archaeological literature, as they had been in early anthropological sources. These are *offerings* and *sacrifices*. The fundamental statement is by Hubert and Mauss (1964, 11–12). Sacrifice *changes the nature* of the thing being sacrificed; it makes it sacred. Sacrifice requires a living *victim*, which must pass into 'the religious domain'. Humans, animals and even vegetable matter meet this requirement, but since an artefact is inert, it cannot change its nature. That is why it can only be an *offering* (*pace* Kiernan 1988).

There have been various attempts to arrive at a classification of sacrifices. They may be either *regular* or *occasional* and may be carried out for different reasons. Among these categories are expiatory sacrifices (*Sühnopfer*), sacrifices of thanksgiving (*Dankopfer*) and sacrifices of request (*Bittopfer*). Occasionally these distinctions have been employed by archaeologists (e.g. Kyll 1966), but it is hard to see how they are to be applied to the surviving evidence, or why similar motives should not have underlain votive deposits of *artefacts*. The same applies to the still finer distinctions present in the anthropological and theological literature (Bourdillon and Fortes 1980; Gladigow 1984; Linders and Nordquist 1987), and for the purposes of this account we shall limit ourselves to the basic contrast between offerings and sacrifices described by Hubert and Mauss. It is easy to recognise archaeologically, and we shall find that deposits of these different kinds do occur in different cultural settings.

Having begun with these transactions in their simplest form, we must consider some developments of this theme. The first studies their effects at the level of the community, and the second their importance for the status of the individual.

Within the community offerings may have subsidiary effects. In a ranked society, such as seems to have existed in Bronze Age Denmark, the provision of votive offerings is thought to promote social solidarity by preventing too much wealth from falling into the hands of too few people. Thus religious ritual acts as 'a regulatory factor in social and economic organisation' (Levy 1982, 117).

The ritual deposits ... assured the general population that individuals (or families) could not accumulate wealth and prestige indefinitely. At the moment of expressing their power and wealth, the Bronze Age elite were also disposing of it by depositing the wealth and symbols of authority irretrievably in a well or bog. The elite returned from the offering place materially more like the general population, thus ameliorating social tensions due to inequality. *Yet, their mere ability to undertake this ritual action re-emphasised their elite status.* (*ibid.*, 108–9) [my emphasis]

If they were able to display their status so effectively through the offerings that they provided, it is hard to see quite how any 'levelling' mechanisms can have operated. And if the population was equally reassured by their leaders' knack of accumulating wealth and by their willingness to let it go, it is hard to see why this charade was so beneficial.

In fact this entire line of argument is curiously ambivalent. It looks in one direction towards the Marxist orthodoxy that ideologies misrepresent reality in the interests of a restricted group: ritual activity is manipulated in order to maintain inequality. In the other direction it is clearly indebted to a view of culture as a 'regulatory mechanism' – an adaptation which attempts to counter the perils of sudden change. In one case the actors and their motives are clearly identified; in the other it is the system itself that seems all-powerful (see Friedman 1979). The two positions are impossible to reconcile (see Bloch 1986, 4–9).

There may be a way out of this difficulty. So far our problem has been to understand the relationship between the provision of lavish offerings and the creation or maintenance of ranking. In fact the provision of votive offerings *can* benefit the individual. It has always seemed paradoxical that in some societies great prestige is attached to the acquisition of fine artefacts, whilst in others this is gained by their destruction. Gregory has suggested that both situations could be variants of a single phenomenon (1980 and 1982). Alliances may be formed and political strategies played out through the mechanisms of gift exchange. It is better to give than to receive, for every gift creates a debt that must be discharged, and the greater the debt the more pressing the obligations that are created. The system lends itself to frenetic competition as debts are constantly created and discharged. In such a system it is possible to build up an advantage but very difficult to maintain it over a long period. The resulting pattern is one of 'alternating disequilibrium' (Strathern 1971, 222).

Gregory's solution to our problem is to suggest that gifts to the gods provide a more satisfactory method of building prestige. These are not provided in the expectation of a counter-gift: they are directed towards the living. Votive offerings provide an unparalleled theatre for competitive consumption through the simple fact that the valuables that are offered are taken out of circulation. This has a marked advantage over competitive gift exchange, which permits the same wealth items to move back and forth among the contending parties, until the stakes are raised so high that some of them are ruined. Votive offerings still allow lavish displays to take place, but each time an offering is made, it reduces the pool of valuables available to the other contenders. Unlike competitive exchange in the everyday world, it can permit the continuous accumulation of prestige.

Gregory's own discussion concerns gifts to gods, but exactly the same logic should apply to the provision of grave goods, since this would normally be attended by an embargo on recovery. This may seem paradoxical, as it is often supposed that the character of this material reflects the social position of the deceased, so that in principle grave contents can be used as an index of social rank (O'Shea 1984). This is unjustified, since the provision of this material would have been in the hands of the mourners. Perhaps funerals are used for social display mainly during periods of instability when the status of the deceased needs underlining (Parker Pearson 1982). Equally important, the provision of elaborate funeral ceremonies allows the survivors to emphasise their own claims to social position. Indeed one recent study shows how often the provision of funerals may be subject to competitive pressures over time, so that they become increasingly lavish as lower-ranking groups imitate the practices of a social élite (Cannon 1989). Ultimately the process is self-defeating; as Cannon says, 'it is an inevitable consequence of competitive mortuary display that status expression eventually reaches either a magnitude that cannot be exceeded or a diversity that obscures further divergence' (1989, 447). At this stage we might envisage two alternative courses of action. One is a period of restraint, such as Cannon describes in his paper. The other is for conspicuous consumption to shift into another field where there might be fewer constraints on the frequency or magnitude of activity. Gregory's work suggests that offerings to the *supernatural* provided the ideal alternative. As we shall see in Chapter 3, much depends on how we understand the relationship between grave goods and votive deposits.

Now we must address a different question. How were specialised artefacts to retain their restricted roles? Let us return to Sir Bedevere's dilemma in the passage from *Le Morte D'Arthur* quoted at the beginning of this chapter. Should he follow the king's instructions and cast Excalibur into the water, in which case its remarkable powers would be extinguished with its owner? Or should he keep the sword in circulation, so that it could bring him wealth and prestige?

Meillassoux (1968) has suggested a novel interpretation of the ways in which valuables are consumed and destroyed. Many of these, he argues, are special-purpose artefacts, used in restricted transactions like marriage payments. Their essential feature is that they lie outside the normal sphere of circulation. If they were able to enter the general economy, their whole existence would be jeopardised, and for this reason they must be removed from circulation once the particular relationships that they express are at an end. The destruction of such artefacts solves the basic problem, which is 'to eradicate incipient value from objects expected to remain neutral and economically dormant' (Meillassoux 1981, 72). It is the problem that Sir Bedevere resolved as he threw Excalibur into the water.

If that problem could be solved by removing special-purpose artefacts from circulation, it would have been harder to control the value of types with a more general currency, but in certain cases a similar interpretation has been suggested (Kristiansen 1978; cf. Dupré and Rey 1978, 193–4). Some of the more elaborate artefacts in circulation in prehistoric Europe travelled over such long distances that it would have been virtually impossible to exercise control over their supply. For this reason it has been claimed that material was taken out of circulation in order to create scarcity. This interpretation has been especially popular for the Late Bronze Age/Iron Age transition when large amounts of bronze metalwork were buried and never recovered, and some writers have suggested that this was done in order to increase its exchange value in relation to the new raw material (Rowlands 1980, 44). We shall return to that example later, but it does seem rather unlikely that prehistoric societies possessed sufficient co-ordination to attempt a manoeuvre which would need careful planning today.

Summing up

This chapter has provided an introduction to the main issues investigated in this book and a review of the principal topics treated in the literature. It has also introduced some of the kinds of archaeological material that we shall be studying. The extent of the existing literature is enough to deter anyone from joining the debate. The variety of material to be considered can seem overwhelming, but this very diversity also allows a certain latitude. Since it is no longer possible for one author to assimilate all the relevant material – still less to synthesise it – there is scope for a more thematic approach to the subject. For this reason the book considers the evidence in a much wider chronological and cultural context than is usually the case. This is not necessarily a virtue, for any added breadth must entail a corresponding loss of depth. On the other hand, it may be no bad thing to stand back from the details of existing studies in order to contemplate the few clear outlines that can be seen.

The main analysis of the evidence is presented in the next three chapters, each of which is concerned with a major theme in the archaeology of hoards and votive deposits and with a specific period in their development. Thus Chapter 2 is a study of the changing significance of one major artefact type – the axe – and the ways in which it is represented in the archaeological record of the Neolithic and the earlier part of the Bronze Age. This chapter considers Neolithic developments in several different areas of Europe and their sequel in the third and second millennia BC, as stone axes were replaced by metal tools. In particular, it studies the growing division between the burial record and the artefacts deposited in hoards.

Chapter 3 is an account of the changes that occurred in both these parts of the archaeological record between about 1300 and 700 BC, during the Later Bronze Age. It considers the close interplay between grave goods and votive deposits, and the complex relationship between the contents and composition of votive deposits and those of the 'utilitarian' hoards identified in the archaeology of this period. It compares the archaeological sequences from Britain and Scandinavia, and concludes with a discussion of the massive recycling of metalwork that happened late in the Bronze Age, and its relationship to the adoption of iron.

Chapter 4 considers the rather different character of votive deposits after that change of technology, and, in particular, the renewed deposition of weaponry in rivers seen during the later years of the Iron Age. It compares these finds with the dry-land deposits associated mainly with temples and shrines, and suggests an interpretation of their changing composition as religious practices came under the influence of the Roman world. It is this transformation that signals the end of the prehistoric sequence.

Although strikingly similar practices to those described in these chapters can be recognised in the post-Roman period, these are not considered in detail in this book, since to a large extent they bear on issues that can be discussed using material from the prehistoric period. Some of these broader questions are brought together in the final chapter, which considers the deposition of valuables as an instance of 'long-term history', and reviews the main lessons to be learnt from material of this kind. It also discusses the particular approaches that have been summarised in this opening section. We shall return to them, no doubt chastened, in time for the final curtain.

Chapter 2

Train of an emblem

The axe leaps!
The solid forest gives fluid utterances,
They tumble forth, they raise and form
Hut, tent, landing, survey,
Flail, plough, pick, crowbar, spade,
Shingle, rail, prop, wainscot, jamb, lath, panel, gable . . .
The shapes arise!
Shapes of the using of axes anyhow, and the users and all that
 neighbours them . . .
Strong shapes and attributes of strong shapes, masculine trades, sights
 and sounds,
Long varied train of an emblem . . .
Walt Whitman, 'Song of the Broad-axe'

This chapter investigates the ways in which offerings of fine objects became established during the Neolithic period and their transformation as stone was replaced by metal. It builds on some of the points made in Chapter 1, but can consider only a sample of a vast archaeological literature. In order to keep the discussion to manageable proportions, it concentrates on the changing significance of just one type of artefact – the axe. In treating the contexts and associations of these objects, however, a wider range of material will be reviewed. In Whitman's words we shall discuss 'the using of axes anyhow, the users and all that neighbours them'.

The shapes arise

The axe is not a Neolithic invention. In Europe it can form part of the tool kit of Mesolithic hunter–gatherers. As the proponents of the Three Age Model recognised, the important development is the adoption of ground and polished tools. Although these do occur in Ireland during the Mesolithic period (Woodman

1978, 108–14), in most areas they are a new development at the time of the first farmers. Their implications are considerable.

The production of polished artefacts requires much more time and effort than the flaking of stone tools. Suitable raw material must be chosen with some care, and mistakes made during the preliminary working of the stone may take a long time to correct. Often different stages in the production process were carried out at different places: the preliminary shaping of the artefacts at the stone source and their final grinding and polishing in the settlement (Bradley 1984, 53).

This treatment of stone axes seems to improve the mechanical performance of their cutting edges and removes incipient platforms which can cause the blade to flake during use. It also allows the axe-head to be held firmly in its haft (Edmonds 1987, 170–1). These may not be the only reasons for such complex treatment of axes, for the extent of the polished surface often goes beyond what is needed in functional terms (*ibid*.). Less utilitarian considerations must also be mentioned here. It takes a long time to polish the entire surface of an axe, but this process gives it a distinctive appearance (Pl. 7). The polishing of stone tools makes them an ideal medium for the display of stylistic information. At the same time, because suitable materials would require such careful selection, axes might need moving over considerable distances, and the products of separate quarries should be readily distinguishable from one another. Such exotic items would stand out clearly from the range of local products. It may be no accident that the adoption of polished axes happens alongside the development of decorated pottery and the building of complex monuments. All these features are typical of Neolithic society, but none fulfils a purely 'economic' role (cf. Thomas 1988). This becomes even more apparent when we realise that polished axes of essentially similar type are found in areas with quite different natural environments. They are not simply work tools.

Stone axes in three regions of Europe

Another indication that polished axes had an added, social, importance is that they occur in such a wide range of sizes. Indeed,

Plate 7 Flint axe hoard from Hagelbjerggård, Jutland. Photograph: Nationalmuseet, Copenhagen.

the largest could not have been used for everyday tasks. Andrew Sherratt has commented on the unusually wide range of axe-heads found in Northern Europe (1976, 567), and to some extent the same is true in the British Isles (Chappell 1987, ch. 12). This may well be part of a much wider phenomenon; on a broader scale it seems as if the consumption of fine stone axes was often a feature of those areas in which hunter–gatherer groups had already developed complex social and economic institutions, before they felt the impact of an expanding agricultural economy. Such regions possessed a productive economic system of their own, and domestic plants and animals were introduced only gradually, where they were adopted at all. Areas like southern

Scandinavia remained outside the reach of agricultural colonisation for a thousand years before the traditional economic system began to break down. Some writers argue that the adoption of a 'Neolithic' economy and material culture in such regions results from competitive pressures within the local social system (Bender 1978; Thomas 1988), whilst others believe that this development was precipitated by crises within the local economy. For example, in southern Scandinavia the loss of oysters as an emergency food, used for one short period of the year, may have helped to bring changes in the system as a whole (Rowley-Conwy 1984), whilst in southern Brittany the loss of high-quality grazing land to the sea could have had a similar effect (Hibbs 1984, 274–5). We can illustrate the growing importance of the polished stone axe by studying the archaeological sequence in both those areas, and also in the British Isles, where the Mesolithic/Neolithic transition may have had a rather similar character. Although there are many contrasts between these three study areas, in each case monumental tombs were of special significance. Britain and Scandinavia share another distinctive monument – the causewayed enclosure.

Before discussing these sequences in detail, it may be helpful to illustrate the character of the material to be studied in each area. Around the coastline of southern Brittany there is some evidence for the existence of what have been termed 'complex hunter–gatherers', in particular the two excavated cemeteries at Hoëdic and Téviec, which provide clear evidence of social differentiation (Bender 1985; Clark and Neeley 1987). The region around the Gulf of Morbihan contains many finds of Neolithic axes, some of exotic origin and others of unusual type. A number of axe-production centres have been identified, and one of these, at Seledin in central Brittany, has been excavated (Giot, L'Helgouac'h and Monnier 1979, 359–66). The finds of axes – in dry-land hoards, in burials or as single finds – are complemented by large stone monuments where similar objects are depicted in megalithic art. The changing composition and contexts of that art will be central to our case.

By contrast, the end of the British Mesolithic is poorly understood, although there is reason to suppose that the latest sites were clustered around the shoreline (Bradley 1984, 9–10), and in Ireland and western Scotland they may have been occupied all year round (Woodman 1978; Mellars 1987). To this extent the settlement pattern may have been similar to that in Brittany and southern Scandinavia. The British Neolithic, however, is an amalgam of foreign elements whose closest parallels are to be found in widely separated areas of Europe, from Denmark to the Atlantic coast of France. There is no indication of a single source area, and for this reason it seems increasingly improbable that a 'Neolithic' way of life was introduced by large-scale colonisation. Domestic plants and animals could have been obtained by exchange, but the most striking foreign elements in the British Neolithic were actually styles of monument, which were linked with long-standing European ideologies rather than with farming *per se* (Thomas 1988). For our purposes these enclosures and funerary monuments play a more prominent role than the minimal evidence that exists of settlement and agriculture. A series of contemporary deposits includes stone axes and other objects, and the changing contexts of such finds will be considered in relation to these monuments.

Finally, there is the evidence from Scandinavia, in particular Denmark and southern Sweden. Here the last hunter–gatherers have been documented in much greater detail, if only because so much evidence survives along raised shorelines; by contrast, the contemporary coastline in Brittany and lowland England has been largely lost. Detailed studies of the economy and settlement pattern suggest a largely sedentary pattern of occupation in a remarkably productive ecosystem (Rowley-Conwy 1984). This seems to have continued substantially undisturbed even when neighbouring areas took up agriculture. It was only after a prolonged period, in which domesticates had been available but little used, that changes finally occurred (Zvelebil and Rowley-Conwy 1986). Even then the evidence for settlements and cereal farming remains as limited as it is in Britain. The main elements to claim our attention here are the contents of a series of funerary monuments and large earthwork enclosures, and a distinctive group of deposits, including stone-axe hoards, many of which were deposited in bogs. Changes in the location and character of these finds are the main subject of our discussion.

In the next section we shall consider the importance of stone axes in all three of these areas, together with the very different ways in which they were consumed. We shall also investigate the contrasting evidence for the introduction of *metal* axes into two of these systems.

Southern Brittany

There is much to be learned from Whitman's poem, quoted at the beginning of this chapter. For him the broad-axe is *the* symbol of agricultural settlement as it provides the means of clearing the land and building houses. Communities living on the Atlantic coast of Brittany may have taken a similar attitude.

This is a region which is better known for its large stone monuments, and in Colin Renfrew's formulation these also played a major symbolic role (Renfrew 1976). They may have acted as territorial markers for early agricultural populations living around the Atlantic coast, for it was here that the opportunities for expansion into new areas would have been checked. That is why there was a greater need to demarcate territory and to legitimise claims to the land through the physical presence of the ancestors. Although his argument was couched in terms of colonisation from other areas, the pressures would have been just as severe among the local hunter–gatherers. Many of the more productive resources around the Gulf of Morbihan had been lost in a marine incursion which culminated around 4800 BC, whilst opportunities for expanding settlement into inland areas were restricted by the less favourable terrain. Although that rise in sea level had covered a wide area of north-west France, the Morbihan had experienced the largest loss of productive land (Fig. 6; Hibbs 1984).

The chambered tombs considered by Renfrew are not the only stone-built monuments to survive from the early years of the Neolithic. Of equal relevance is a series of free-standing stone uprights known as menhirs. For the most part these are decorated in the same style as the early megalithic tombs (Shee Twohig 1981, 54–64). This art is mainly naturalistic and contains a number of motifs which could be expressions of the developing relationship between the population, the land and the food supply (Fig. 7). For our purposes the most important images are hafted and unhafted axe-heads, as well as bows and arrows, 'shepherds' crooks' and possible 'axe-ploughs'. Boats may also feature in

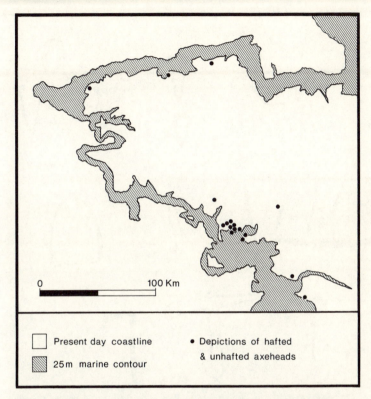

Fig. 6 The likely extent of land loss in Mesolithic and Neolithic Brittany, compared with the distribution of axe carvings in megalithic art. (Coastline after Hibbs 1984; distribution of carvings after Shee Twohig 1981)

the art, although this is controversial, and there has been a suggestion that images interpreted as 'yokes' may represent the horns of a large bovid – at all events carvings of two such animals have recently been identified on a menhir (Le Roux 1984). Although other signs are not naturalistic, the list provides a good approximation to the material equipment of a population making its first experiments with domesticates.

Depictions of sheathed axe-heads and axe-ploughs may be a particular feature of the menhirs, but otherwise there are similar

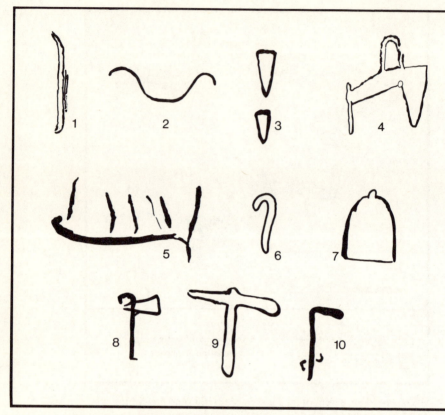

Fig. 7 Naturalistic symbols dating from the first phase of Breton megalithic art. 1: bow; 2: 'yoke'; 3: unhafted axe-head; 4: 'axe-plough'; 5: ? boat; 6: 'shepherd's crook'; 7: anthropomorph; 8–10: hafted axe-heads. (After Bradley 1989a and Shee Twohig 1981)

motifs inside the early group of chambered tombs, where they occur both in the burial chamber and the passage which communicated with the world outside (Shee Twohig 1981, 54–64). In a sense these carvings are 'hidden', in contrast to the 'public' symbols on the menhirs. There is no art on the kerbs that surround such monuments, and, as present-day visitors to the sites will know, the art inside the passage tombs was located in positions that would need careful lighting (Bradley 1989a). This surely indicates that such images were imbued with a special importance.

There are other reasons for suggesting that they were more than simple decoration. The small area around the Gulf of Morbihan has one of the highest densities of Neolithic axes of any part of Brittany (Fig. 8; Cogné and Giot 1952), as well as most of the depictions of axes in megalithic art (Shee Twohig 1981, 38–75; Fig. 6). The portrayal of unhafted axe-heads emphasises that these objects were not just simple work tools. The same applies to carvings of individual axe-heads inside elaborate sheaths. Some of the axes are found together with a striking anthropomorphic design.

Despite so much evidence for the special significance of axes, all too little is known about the contexts in which they were deposited. A number have certainly been discovered in small hoards (Le Rouzic 1927), or in the chambered tombs themselves. Of potentially more significance are those finds from a second type of monument. *Tertres tumulaires* are elongated mounds built over a series of small stone cists which are thought to have held human remains; although bones would not survive the acid subsoil, they do contain a small number of axes, which may have been intended as grave goods (Giot, L'Helgouac'h and Monnier 1979, 212–18). Such miniature chambers were completely undecorated, and were inaccessible once the mound had been built. The positions of some of these mounds were marked by menhirs, and around the base of one such menhir was placed a series of stone axe-heads, set in the ground with their blades uppermost (Le Rouzic, Péquart and Péquart 1923, 68–70).

In this early phase stone monuments seem to have been decorated with symbols that were apparently linked to the new mode of production. Some, like the bows and arrows or the possible boats, refer to traditional resources, whilst others – the axes and axe-ploughs – could be more closely connected with new forms of food production. These are associated with menhirs that could have acted both as totems and territorial markers. In some cases they may also have indicated the positions of the *tertres tumulaires* where the axe-heads themselves were probably used as grave goods. Other objects of the same kind were deposited in the vicinity of menhirs. All too little is known about

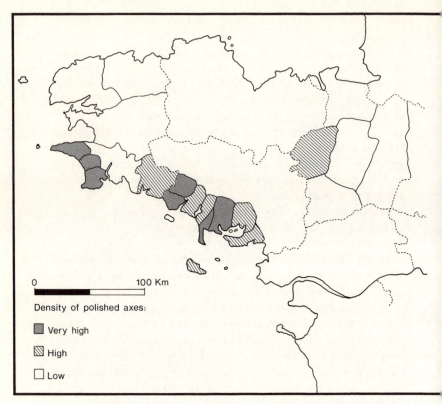

Fig. 8 The relative density of polished axes in Brittany. (After Cogné and Giot 1952)

the contemporary pattern of settlement, but in a region in which sedentary hunter–gatherers may have come under pressure from early farmers on one side and from a changing environment on the other, the choice of symbols for depiction on these monuments seems to be especially appropriate. At this stage, at least some of the images – those carved on the menhirs – still have a 'public' air, but the axes found in the *tertres tumulaires* already show how the objects themselves could be appropriated as grave goods. That process gathered momentum in the second part of this sequence.

By that stage, around 4000 BC, the demand for stone axes

around the Gulf of Morbihan seems to have influenced developments over 60 km away in central Brittany, which was still outside the main area of settlement. It was at this point that the Seledin quarries began operation, and many of their products have been identified on the coast (Le Roux 1979). At the same time, there is evidence for dramatic changes in the ways in which these objects were perceived.

At about this point in the sequence we find significant developments in the layout of the chambered tombs, which became generally bigger and more monumental. The chambers were more extensive and sometimes show evidence of subdivision; side cells could also be added to the passages (L'Helgouac'h 1965). The art inside these structures became increasingly complex, and the designs were sometimes larger and more prominent (Shee Twohig 1981, 53). Naturalistic likenesses still appeared, but now they were encapsulated in a range of non-representational patterns, which bear a close resemblance to the images recorded during states of altered consciousness (Fig. 9; Bradley 1989b). Such patterns are remarkably similar to the 'phosphenes' created under trance conditions. These occur in a number of different cultures and may be created by the nerves in the human eye. For this reason they are described as 'entoptic' phenomena (Reichel-Dolmatoff 1978; Lewis-Williams and Dowson 1988). In some cases existing designs might be incorporated into these decorated panels. Anthropomorphic images also play an increasingly prominent role during this phase.

On a few sites these developments were closely linked to the renewed use of earlier monuments. This is because these tombs seem to have incorporated fragments of existing menhirs, some of which had already been decorated (L'Helgouac'h 1983; Le Roux 1984). In such cases it seems as if the symbols of place established at the start of the sequence were broken up and built into more complex monuments to the dead. The same may also apply to the types of object depicted in the earliest art. The tomb at Gavrinis, for instance, includes carvings that portray a distinctive type of axe-head which had been perforated for suspension. Artefacts of exactly this form have been discovered in a second series of monuments around the Gulf of Morbihan, where they were often made in attractive non-local materials, including

Fig. 9 Entoptic phenomena and axe carvings at Gavrinis, Brittany. (After Bradley 1989a and Shee Twohig 1981)

jadeite. These are found in quantity beneath a series of enormous mounds, where they occur together with a large number of personal ornaments (Giot, L'Helgouac'h and Monnier 1979, 218–25).

Such *grands tumulus* may be elaborate versions of the *tertres tumulaires* considered earlier, but they are of exceptional size. Again they differ from the normal pattern in containing a series of closed chambers, with no connecting passage to the outside world. Art is virtually absent from these sites, which sometimes incorporate the remains of existing passage graves into their design, in rather the same way as the chambered tombs included older menhirs. It is usually assumed that the *grands tumulus* were funerary monuments, although the acid conditions prevailing on these sites mean that there is little evidence of human remains, and the collections of fine stone artefacts exist in virtual isolation. Even so, it is tempting to consider these as personal valuables, especially those axe-heads which had apparently been used as pendants.

Some of the *grands tumulus* may have been marked by menhirs in the same way as the earlier *tertres tumulaires*. One example stands out from all the rest. This is Le Grand Menhir Brisé, which

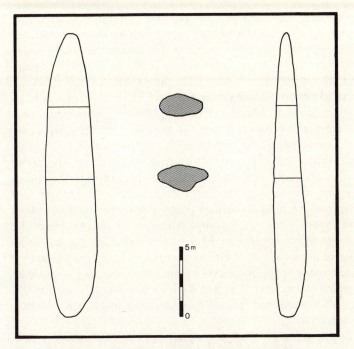

Fig. 10 Profiles and cross sections of Le Grand Menhir Brisé, Locmariaquer, Brittany. (After Hornsey 1987)

would originally have stood to a height of 20 m. The stone weighs over 300 tons and probably broke during its erection (Hornsey 1987). It was located at the southern end of the large mound of Er-Grah. The surfaces of this stone had been carefully dressed, and the monolith has a particularly regular outline (Fig. 10). Apart from its base, which would have been buried in the ground, it has the same profile, the same cross-section and even the same tapering butt as the finest axe-heads found in this region of France (Bishop, Woolley, Kinnes and Harrison 1977, figs. 1 and 2). This can hardly be coincidental, for it occupies a critical position in the local sequence. At one level it is the ultimate successor to the public symbols that mark the *tertres tumulaires*, whilst at another it refers to the more private symbols buried beneath the largest mounds.

Polished axes seem to have assumed a more specialised role during this period. No longer were they so closely associated with the 'public' art of the menhirs. The chambered tombs where they *were* still a major feature now had a more complex plan, and the art itself was hidden from the daylight (Bradley 1989a). Some of the surrounding imagery is very like the entoptic patterns associated with trance conditions. Strange anthropomorphic designs play a prominent role, and even the axes themselves may have been associated with supernatural powers. At the same time, some of the specific objects depicted on the tomb walls were being deposited in large numbers beneath the *grands tumulus*. These were probably burial mounds, but for our purposes the most important point is that the small chambers underneath them were completely inaccessible. In effect the passage tombs could have been used as sanctuaries, with a distinctive art style that referred to states of altered consciousness, whilst some of the finest axes became the insignia of a restricted segment of society. It is not too much to suggest that in this way they were transformed from *symbols of place* to *symbols of power*.

In one sense the changing layout of megalithic tombs in Brittany may have been intended to exclude all natural light, and by this means to conceal the art from casual scrutiny (Bradley 1989a). This may account for the changes of tomb design considered in this section, and must surely be the explanation for their sequel, the distinctive *angled passage graves* (L'Helgouac'h 1965, ch. 10). Here the passage is deflected so that the chamber walls are in perpetual darkness. These tombs are found mainly around the Gulf of Morbihan and perhaps represent the culmination of some of the processes described so far. Some may still contain 'trance' imagery, but now identifiable artefacts are excluded from the repertoire, and over 75 per cent of the decorated stones depict a strange anthropomorphic figure (Shee Twohig 1981, 68–70). Most of these images were placed in the 'darkened' section of the tomb, and were roughly twice the size of those in areas with any access to daylight (Bradley 1989a). By this stage the axes that were once portrayed alongside this figure on the walls are found among the contents of these monuments. The transition was complete. These objects may be grave goods, or they may be offerings to a deity. In either case their symbolic importance is assured.

Southern Scandinavia

Our other two examples have rather more features in common. In each case it is the association between deposits of axes and special-purpose enclosures that is most informative. Although the two study areas share rather similar forms of monument, there remains a fundamental difference between these two sequences. Such differences become still more pronounced when we consider the adoption of the first metal axes.

The evidence from southern Scandinavia has two particularly distinctive characteristics. It is in this area that the delayed reception of agriculture is evidenced in most detail. Again, it seems as if agriculture was adopted only after a prolonged period in which domesticates were available but little used (Rowley-Conwy 1984). This change involved a movement away from marine and coastal resources, towards the greater use of the *land*. This is shown extremely clearly by C-13 analysis of human bone, which reveals a change from a predominantly marine diet (Tauber 1982), and it is perhaps in this context that the axe became such an important symbol. At the same time, it was in this region that axes were made in a wider range of sizes than in other parts of Europe, suggesting that non-utilitarian considerations may have been important in the development of this artefact (cf. Sherratt 1976, 567).

In the period during which domesticates were first adopted there is much in common between the sequence in this area and that in southern Brittany. Both involved the choice of the polished axe as a special type, and both regions saw the development of monumental tombs. Although the use of these structures may be associated with a wider European ideology (Thomas 1988), in neither area does this development provide the earliest evidence of social differentiation.

Over an area extending from north Germany to southern Sweden there is evidence for isolated deposits of axe-heads and other stone artefacts in bogs and dry-land hoards (Nielsen 1977; Rech 1979). Evidence of contemporary settlements is limited, but comparable finds are recorded from some of the early

funerary monuments. As we saw in Chapter 1, North European
scholars have always been prepared to countenance a class of
'ritual' hoards. In this case there are persuasive arguments for
treating these collections as votive deposits.

The locations of these finds are revealing, for large numbers
were deposited in bogs or other wet places, from which it would
have been difficult to recover them. In any case the size and
fine condition of many of the axes makes it unlikely that these
were everyday tools. There are further reasons why that interpretation would be improbable. These axe hoards form only part
of a wider distribution of deposits from watery locations (Fig.
11; Rech 1979). During the Early Neolithic period collections
of amber (Pl. 8), animal bones, decorated pottery and human
remains were also placed in bogs; and even if the groups of amber
or fine axes could have been hidden there and lost, this cannot
be true of the other finds. Quite clearly, food could not have
been stored in this environment. Nor can we devise a 'rational'
explanation for the finds of human bodies, some of which were
partially dismembered (Bennike and Ebbesen 1986).

So far these groups have been considered separately, but in
fact their contents show a certain overlap, and material from
more than one of these classes can be found together in the same
deposit. In particular, stone axes can be associated with each
of these types of material. At the same time, some of the groups
have more restricted distributions than others. Thus axe hoards
and finds of pottery occur over large parts of southern Scandinavia, but with more deposits in some areas than others. Those
same concentrations can be observed in the distributions of the
remaining finds. Thus amber hoards are largely confined to the
main area with deposits of ceramics and stone artefacts in Jutland,
and on Funen and Zealand discoveries of human and animal
remains occur over the same areas as axe hoards and pottery
vessels. Taken together, these groups may represent variations
on a wider tradition of intentional offerings (Rech 1979). To
some extent this may have run in parallel with the use of axes
as grave goods. Burials containing these artefacts are most common in north Jutland, but are less often found where the other
kinds of deposit predominate (Nielsen 1977). Even the pottery
vessels found in Danish bogs are of different types from those

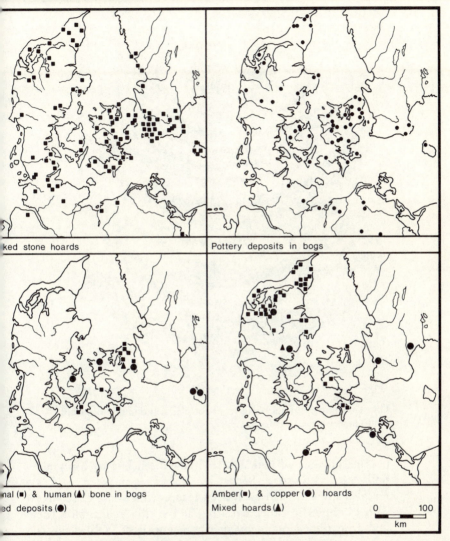

ked stone hoards

Pottery deposits in bogs

nal (■) & human (▲) bone in bogs
ed deposits (●)

Amber (■) & copper (●) hoards
Mixed hoards (▲)

0   100
km

Fig. 11 The distribution of Early Neolithic deposits in southern
Scandinavia. (After Bradley 1987 and Rech 1979)

found with funerary monuments (Bennike and Ebbesen 1986,
99). It was only in the Middle Neolithic that such monuments
became a major focus for intentional deposits. Two types of site,

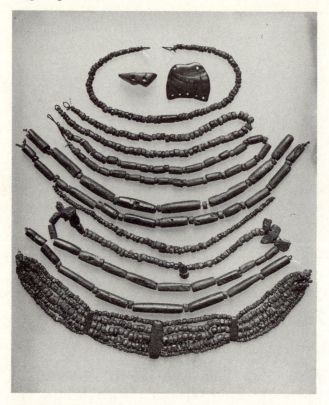

Plate 8 Hoard of amber beads from Sortekaer, Jutland. Photograph: Nationalmuseet, Copenhagen.

passage graves and 'cult houses', have been known for some time (Strömberg 1971; Becker 1973), but recent fieldwork has revealed a series of causewayed enclosures which have close links with examples in other parts of Europe (Madsen 1988). The finds from these monuments shed even more light on the deposits considered so far.

These enclosures are generally situated on spurs, and are found at fairly regular intervals (Fig. 12), accompanied by clusters of funerary monuments (Andersen 1980; Madsen 1988). Some were used over a short period, whilst others see a more complex history of construction and reconstruction. There is no reason to suppose that these sites could have been defended, and the only convincing evidence for domestic activities comes from other phases in their use, generally when the earthworks were no longer maintained. The deposits found on these sites come from two distinct locations, although they have common features. Careful excavation has emphasised the special importance of the different segments of ditch, some of which were completely enclosed by fences (Andersen 1980, fig. 8). These provide evidence of *in situ* burning and sometimes seem to have been refilled deliberately. They contain a number of structured deposits, which closely resemble the bog finds described earlier. Thus there are finds of complete pots with elaborate decoration and vessels which had been intentionally smashed – at Toftum, where the earthwork was dug through sand, this happened where stones protruded from the sides of the ditch (Madsen 1988, 314). There were also distinctive deposits of animal bone. Some were concentrations of material that stand out from the general paucity of such finds in the ditches, and others consisted of placed deposits of particular bones. A group of dog skulls from Bjerggård provides an example of this practice (*ibid.*, 310). In addition, human skull and jaw fragments were found in the earthwork at Sarup (Andersen 1980). Stone artefacts, including axes, can also be found in these ditches.

Inside these enclosures there was sometimes a series of pits, which seem to have been filled with a certain formality. Among the most striking of their contents are deposits of complete decorated pots, but other finds include stone axes and groups of human and animal bones. It hardly needs to be added that these enclosed sites bring together most of the categories of material known from bog deposits (Madsen 1988). In fact the frequency of 'wet' finds declines during the period in which these enclosures were being used (Rech 1979).

Other changes happened during the Middle Neolithic. There are signs of a more concerted onslaught on the landscape (Madsen 1982, 227), and intentional offerings also become more frequent at funerary sites. Here there is a change from the local form of dolmen, which sometimes contained articulated bodies, to the adoption of an exotic type of monument – the passage grave – in which the bones of more individuals were introduced after their bodies had received preliminary treatment elsewhere

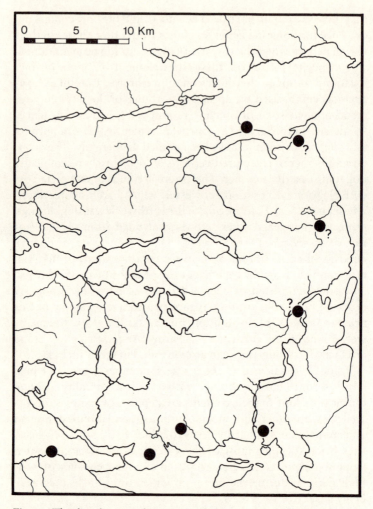

Fig. 12 The distribution of causewayed enclosures in east Jutland, Denmark. (After Madsen 1988)

(Thorsen 1980). These sites saw the deposition of large amounts of decorated pottery, somewhat different in character from the ceramics found at settlements of the same date. This particular episode was fairly brief, but its effects were far-reaching. From this time onwards there is the first evidence of large open settlements, some of which may have developed directly from causewayed enclosures established on the same sites (Madsen 1988). This change from 'public' monuments, associated with specialised deposits, to a group of larger residential sites suggests that, as in Brittany, a restricted section of the population was reserving traditional ritual practices and ritual places to itself (cf. Hodder 1988, 69).

Several of these developments share a common feature; they provide evidence of the adoption of ceremonial monuments and practices that ally them to a wider ideology. The passage graves belong to a long tradition of funerary architecture seen along the Atlantic coast from about 5000 BC; indeed, it was tombs of this type which contained the decorative devices considered earlier in this chapter. In the same way, the causewayed enclosure is a major type of European monument which had first developed a thousand years or more before. The association of such sites with deposits of elaborate artefacts and of human and animal bone is found in other regions. The same applies to the circulation of unfleshed human remains, which links the funerary monuments and enclosures in Scandinavia with similar processes elsewhere. If certain communities or individuals were in contact with other parts of Europe, it is not surprising to discover a small number of copper objects in the Scandinavian Neolithic (Randsborg 1978). These must have originated far to the south in Central Europe, and their discovery is tangible evidence of the extent and power of such connections.

It is unfortunate that we do not know the relationship of these finds to the introduction of causewayed enclosures into Scandinavia, and it seems as if metalwork was imported towards the close of the Early Neolithic period, rather than the succeeding phase (*ibid.*). Although the number of finds is rather limited, the character and contexts of this material are most revealing. The main type to be represented is the copper axe, with smaller numbers of ornaments; one hoard also contained a dagger blade. Few of the finds have any associations: there is only a limited number of hoards or grave finds, and not many of the copper axes come from any clear context. The hoards and single finds of copper axes have a similar distribution to the stone axe hoards of the Early Neolithic, with the highest density of finds in the same regions (*ibid*., fig. 2). In contrast to the finds of ornaments, no metal axes have been recovered from graves. Although the evidence is very limited, it seems likely that copper axes were employed in the same way as locally made stone axes, and were deposited in similar contexts.

In one case it may be possible to take these connections further. Among the most distinctive deposits with copper artefacts was a hoard found during mineral extraction at Årupgård (Sylvest and Sylvest 1960). This consisted of a ceramic vessel containing eight copper ornaments, 271 amber beads and 177 other fragments of amber. According to one suggestion the findspot may be located within another enclosure, and certainly it shares the characteristic siting of these monuments. In addition, pits containing complete pots like those at Sarup are known to occur on the site (Madsen 1988, 309). The area is too badly damaged for this idea to be tested, but it would draw the early appearance of copper in Scandinavia into the web of connections that we have traced in this case study. We shall consider this point again when we discuss the first appearance of metalwork in Britain.

The British Isles
The sequence in Britain is difficult to define in its earlier stages, although developments from the building of causewayed enclosures onwards can be followed with some clarity. For that reason this account focuses on the period when enclosures were in use on both sides of the North Sea and traces their sequel in Britain through to the introduction of metals.

There are two main areas of uncertainty that have to be confronted. First, the Mesolithic/Neolithic transition has proved to be very elusive, and there seems to be a hiatus of nearly a millennium between the latest radiocarbon dates for Mesolithic sites in lowland Britain and those for samples associated with a Neolithic material culture (Bradley 1978a, 7–8). There are perhaps two solutions to this problem, although both are certainly contentious. One way out of our difficulty is to separate the discussion of environmental evidence from any consideration of styles of artefacts and monuments. If we do so, we find that there are cereals in the pollen record almost a millennium before we have pottery or monumental structures of 'Neolithic' type (Edwards and Hirons 1984). A significant proportion of the clearance episodes associated with these cereals is found near to the sea, suggesting a prolonged period in which crop cultivation may have supplemented the lifestyle of coastal hunter–gatherers. The second approach to this problem focuses on changes in sea level. It is striking that the hiatus in the radiocarbon chronology occurs in southern Britain but not in regions of isostatic uplift, where Mesolithic sites are found on the relict shorelines of north-west England, Scotland and Ireland (Bradley 1984, fig. 2.2). This is not to say that inland areas were completely unoccupied, but fieldwork in those regions that do have a complete archaeological record suggests that during the fifth millennium BC settlement of coastal areas may have been fairly stable. The adoption of farming could have followed a similar sequence to developments in Brittany and Scandinavia.

Again the stone axe has both a functional and symbolic import-ance, but until quite recently British archaeologists followed the Western European tradition of explaining the archaeological record in terms of everyday experience. Thus axes were made in 'factories' and distributed by traders or middlemen; axe hoards represented the stock-in-trade of merchants (Cummins 1979); causewayed enclosures were used for the exchange of goods (Megaw and Simpson 1979, 84); and those axes found in rivers were chance losses (Adkins and Jackson 1978). In the light of our discussion of two neighbouring parts of Europe, it seems unnecessary to insist on the symbolic importance of some arte-facts, or on their dual role as tools and as primitive valuables. Rather, three important points can be made concerning the con-texts in which the British axes are found.

First, it is quite clear that distribution of axes from known production sites does not follow an orderly pattern. By about 3500 BC it is known that stone axes were being exchanged over considerable distances and that often they circulated in areas which had equally suitable raw materials of their own. In some cases axes of exotic origin may occur in concentrations some distance from their source. Examples include the high proportion of Cumbrian axes in Yorkshire or East Anglia or the group of Cornish axes in the Thames estuary (Fig. 13; Cummins 1979).

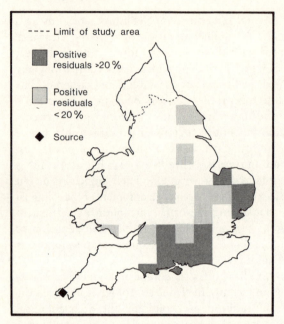

Fig. 13 The over-representation of Cornish Neolithic axes in eastern England. The map plots those areas in which the density of Group 1 axes is above the level predicted by the 'gravity model'. (After Chappell 1986)

Secondly, it is important to challenge the 'utilitarian' interpretation of some of these finds. Often this has become established in the literature despite the contrasting interpretations placed on similar evidence in Europe. There is no doubt that axes that had been imported from the Continent are sometimes found in specialised locations, but there is a reluctance to build on this conclusion. Thus jadeite axes – one of the types found in such distinctive deposits around the Gulf of Morbihan – are recorded from springs and other wet locations in Britain (Bradley 1987, 354). The best known example was found in mint condition beside the Sweet Track in the Somerset Levels, where a pot containing a deposit of food has also been discovered (Coles and Coles 1986, 59–60). Again the small corpus of Scandinavian flint axes in Britain includes further river finds (Bradley 1987,

354; Holgate 1988, 334–5). At the same time, a considerable number of stone axes have been found in the Thames, the British river which has experienced most dredging. Like the few hoard finds from Britain, these axes tend to be larger than the examples found on dry land in the same area, but rather than accept that these had been deposited intentionally, Chappell's recent study suggests that they were chance losses: 'the sizes of these implements probably reflect ... the sizes of axes generally carried by people using the Thames as a transport route' (1987, 339). This seems most unlikely when we consider the high proportion of exotic axes in the Thames. This can only be matched in the upper levels of the Windmill Hill causewayed enclosure (Bradley 1984, 56–7).

That brings me to my third point. There can be little doubt that some of the axes introduced to major monuments had been treated in special ways. Their very presence is intriguing, as axes are over-represented at certain causewayed enclosures, compared with settlement sites of the same date (Bradley 1982a). Again foreign axes play a striking role in monuments. A Scandinavian axe was deposited in the mound of Julliberries Grave, a late long barrow which had no burials (Jessup 1939). Similarly, among the small number of jadeite axes imported to this country are examples from two causewayed enclosures and a chambered tomb (Mercer 1980, 23). Axes originating in other areas of Britain were also singled out for special treatment. Some were buried ceremoniously in pits or ditches, as happened at Hamble-don Hill (*ibid.*), whilst others could be reduced to fragments and deposited with human remains, as they were at Etton (Francis Pryor, pers. comm.).

At one level the British causewayed enclosures were used in rather similar ways to those in southern Scandinavia. Again, they may be found near to groups of funerary monuments, although there is little indication that the sites were regularly spaced. There is evidence for large-scale food consumption and for extensive deposits of animal bones (Bradley 1984, 28). Large amounts of pottery were placed in the ditches or internal pits, and some of the sites contain human burials, whilst others show evidence for the circulation of unfleshed bones (Mercer 1980). Sometimes the ditches were refilled to cover formal deposits of artefacts or bone, and were recut in exactly the same places. The positions of the separate causeways were carefully emphasised, both by the practice of recutting and by deposits in the ditch terminals (e.g. Pryor 1987). In Britain, and probably in Scandinavia, some of these sites developed into large settlements, but here there is a most important contrast. In Scandinavia this appears to have been accomplished peacefully, and the original circuit of earthworks fell into disrepair (Madsen 1988). In Britain, however, those sites which show strong evidence of domestic activity were drastically remodelled. The interrupted ditches were replaced by continuous earthworks and the banks may have been turned into defensive ramparts. Sites which had been used as ceremonial centres became defended hill forts, and there are signs that some of them were attacked and destroyed (Darvill 1987, 76). After 3300 BC, there is little evidence for the continued use of this kind of monument, and we see the establishment of sharply contrasting systems in different parts of the country.

At the risk of over-simplification, those developments took two alternative courses, although in practice the division was sharper in some areas than in others. One tradition may have involved a return to the construction and operation of large ceremonial monuments (Bradley 1984, 42–4 and 75–84; Darvill 1987, 79–82). This included the later use of cursuses and the development of henges. Both types appear to be peculiar to the British Isles, although the stone settings that accompany members of the latter group are not unlike a series of poorly dated monuments in Brittany (Burl 1976). In this tradition attention seems to have focused on the use of large earthwork enclosures and the stone and timber settings sometimes found inside them. Although a few of these earthworks could have been inhabited, for the most part they dominate the archaeological record at the expense of contemporary settlements, which have left little trace. Such monuments tend to occur in groups that can be considered together as component parts of larger 'ceremonial centres' (Bradley and Chambers 1988). There may be evidence of occupation in their vicinity, and for this reason it is a misnomer to describe these complexes as *ritual* landscapes. Some of the earthworks in this group were built on a far larger scale than the earlier causewayed enclosures, and in a few cases they incorporated basic astronomical alignments (Bradley 1984, 75–84).

These sites and the areas in between them undoubtedly formed the focus for a series of specialised deposits. A number of the major ceremonial centres are connected by a distinctive ceramic tradition (Grooved Ware) and its associations, although this is also found on some of the contemporary occupation sites (Wainwright and Longworth 1971, ch. 6). These ceremonial complexes may include human remains, but it does not seem as if their main function was as cemeteries. They may also contain large deposits of faunal remains, especially groups of pig bones that could be evidence of feasting. In addition, lavishly decorated pottery was deposited in certain of these sites, apparently in a highly structured manner (Richards and Thomas 1984). For our purposes it is most significant that they contain exotic stone artefacts, among them polished axes (Houlder 1976). These can form part of the complex deposits described already, but they can also be found in unusually large numbers in the areas around these monuments. In the latter case less is known about the circumstances surrounding their deposition.

In some respects the deposits recall those found with earlier causewayed enclosures, where again there is evidence of large-scale consumption and the deposition of complex artefacts. It is unlikely that a direct link exists between these two traditions because they may be separated by several hundred years, but they can perhaps be understood in terms of similar processes. They may be the work of a society in which overt social distinctions were muted and where relations with the supernatural played a major role in the political structure.

The alternative development emphasised the role of the individual through the provision of grave goods and the construction of circular burial mounds (Kinnes 1979). It is likely that this tradition had already begun to emerge in northern England before the causewayed enclosures went out of use, and certainly it gained in importance during the Later Neolithic. Like the distinctive social network associated with the use of Grooved Ware, this tradition emphasised its separate identity through the use of material culture. Grooved Ware played no part, and a contemporary pottery style (Peterborough Ware) is sometimes found in association with funerary monuments and with poorly preserved occupation sites in their vicinity (Thorpe and Richards 1984). More important, the graves of this tradition include a wide range of specialised artefacts, which to some extent are absent from henges.

The main types of artefact in these graves are belt fittings, beads, pins, maceheads, arrowheads and polished knives (Kinnes 1979). A proportion of the finds were made out of raw materials which were not widely available. Axes play a distinctive role in these graves. Most of the satisfactory associations are found in northern England, where specialised forms of axes and adzes were being made, but most of the grave finds were of flint, rather than non-local stone. Imported axes are uncommon as grave goods, and almost all the examples are from areas where the tradition of early single burial was strongly established (Chappell 1987). This contrast is important since at a national level non-flint axes are more often associated with Grooved Ware than with Peterborough Ware (Bradley 1984, table 3.5). Moreover, the kinds of flint axes found in the graves are not part of the assemblage that is found with major henges.

To summarise, although the British causewayed enclosures do have much in common with those in southern Scandinavia, their development into large domestic sites was not accomplished smoothly, as it was in the latter area. After a period of conflict we find great changes in the archaeological record, with the emergence of two contrasting traditions in different areas, one associated with fresh types of ceremonial monument, and the other with a series of single graves (Fig. 14). These two traditions are both widespread, but their archaeological manifestations tend to avoid one another, even within the same areas of the British Isles. They were distinguished by striking contrasts in material culture, and, in particular, by separate ceramic styles. This contrast even extends to the use of axes. In the single burials specialised forms of axe and adze were selected as grave goods, but these were made of flint of fairly local origin; exotic axes are rarely found in the same contexts. By contrast, the ceremonial sites were chiefly associated with Grooved Ware, which tends to be found with non-flint axes. Finds of this type appear in specialised deposits inside henges and frequently they are also recorded as single finds in the vicinity of these enclosures. In addition, axes are also found in hoards and, more often, in wet locations.

These contrasts are important for our understanding of the British sequence, for they seem to shed light on the adoption of Beaker artefacts in this country. It is certainly true that the two traditions described above have quite different emphases; recently it has been suggested that they were also in competition with one another (Thorpe and Richards 1984). In one case social relations may have been mediated through access to the supernatural, whilst in the single-grave tradition position may have depended more on achievement or descent, and possibly on access to prestige goods. If one tradition located social distinctions in the supernatural, it could hardly be challenged on the basis of worldly deeds, and the two systems would be incompatible. This is a provocative hypothesis, but one which will be difficult to test. Its strongest point, however, is that it does seem to account for the rapid assimilation of artefacts belonging to the Beaker network into the tradition of individual burial. Similarly, these artefacts are rare or absent at henges during the earlier part of the sequence. In this sense the reception of Beaker material varied from one region to another according to the kind of system that was already established.

This distinction is of immediate relevance to our argument, since Beaker ceramics seem to be associated with the earliest metalwork in Britain (Burgess 1978). How far was this material assimilated into the local context, as it had been in Scandinavia? And does its adoption mark a radical change in patterns of deposition? As Burgess has pointed out, Beaker pottery is associated with copper and bronze in the form of weapons, tools and ornaments. Gold ornaments are also known, but 'there is not one association of a Beaker with any form of axe in these islands' (*ibid.*, 210). Quite simply, two separate traditions of early metalwork can be recognised in Britain. One contains daggers, small tools and most types of ornament, and these occur mainly in burials, often with decorated pottery. The second group comprises hoards and single finds, and contains halberds, spearheads, gold lunulae and, far more frequently, axes (Needham 1988). These separate types are rarely associated with one another and can be found in watery locations.

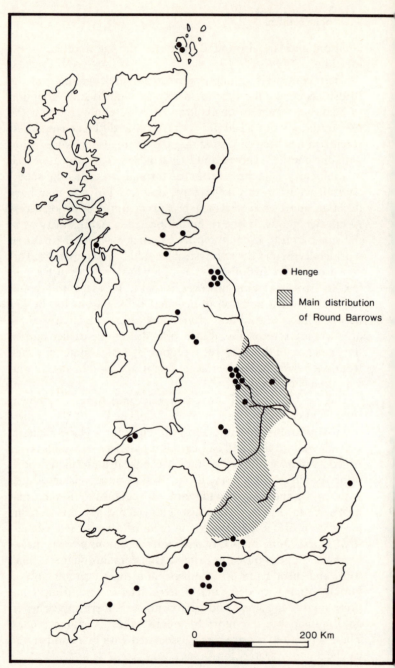

Fig. 14 The greatest concentration of Neolithic round barrows in Britain, compared with the distribution of 'classic' henge monuments. (Round barrows after Kinnes 1979; henge distribution after Harding 1987)

If we accept that Beakers and some of their associations were introduced into an already existing tradition of single burial, there seems every reason to accept the corollary that other metal types, axes in particular, were incorporated into an established tradition of votive deposition. This does not preclude their use as work tools any more than it does with stone axes, but it would mean that the reception of metalwork shows at least as much continuity as it did in the Scandinavian example. For that reason it may be no coincidence that the two 'Early Bronze Age' axes to be found by recent excavation both came from henge monuments: Mount Pleasant (Wainwright 1979, ch. 10) and Newgrange (O'Kelly and Shell 1978; Sweetman 1985).

Discussion

We have now traced the changing roles of polished stone axes in three areas of prehistoric Europe, and in two cases we have also investigated their relationship to the earliest appearance of metal. Before moving on to discuss the importance of the new raw material, it may be useful to consider the main observations made so far.

In all three study areas the axe took on an added significance early in the Neolithic period, as the lifestyle of sedentary hunter–gatherers changed and attention shifted from a largely coastal economy to a greater commitment to the *land*. The same process may also lie behind the development of ancestral monuments, including long mounds, chambered tombs and, possibly, menhirs.

Although stone axes were sometimes deposited with the dead, the main evidence that they possessed an added importance is found in other spheres. In southern Brittany this comes mainly from their depiction in megalithic art, as well as from hoard deposits and the enigmatic collections from the *tertres tumulaires*. As we have seen, the art became more elaborate and the tombs developed a complex ground plan in which the decorated stones were increasingly distanced from any source of natural light. When axes were depicted on the walls, they were incorporated into complex panels which may include references to the kinds of patterns experienced under trance conditions. At this stage anthropomorphic images played an increasingly prominent role, and by the time that angled passage graves were built these figures came to dominate the art entirely. As depictions of stone axes moved from the 'public' art of the menhirs to the 'private' art of the passage tombs, the axes themselves, and the fine artefacts associated with them, were also distanced from the world of everyday experience and were deposited in great numbers beneath the *grands tumulus*. They may well have been grave goods, but this cannot be proved. In the Breton sequence we see the assimilation of public symbols into the private domain and the accumulation and consumption of axe-heads made of exotic materials. This took place within a specialised group of monuments. In this case they could have become the insignia of a social élite. If so, that group perhaps owed its position, not just to control over the circulation of these objects, but also to the cosmic references with which such artefacts came to be associated.

In southern Scandinavia the stone axes were deliberately deposited in watery locations from which they would have been difficult to recover. For this reason they can justifiably be regarded as votive offerings. These were not the only types of material to be treated in this way, and stone axe hoards form only part of a more varied series of offerings which also include decorated pottery, amber, human bones and animal remains. Despite a certain overlap with the finds from funerary monuments, these deposits often complemented the burials of the same period.

With the expansion of settlement and food production during the Middle Neolithic, most of these practices became more institutionalised and seem to have taken place within special-purpose enclosures, each of which may have occupied a distinct territory. Here there is evidence for consumption on a larger scale, augmenting the practices evidenced from cult houses and passage graves. Although these enclosures were used over quite a short period, their construction and operation came at a period of major change. A few of these sites went on in use as very large settlements, whilst some of the artefacts that had been deposited there, including axes, are found in the hoards of the following phase (Rech 1979). By that stage they are rather less frequent and their distribution largely complements that of flint daggers, which are associated mainly with single burials (Lomborg 1973).

In this case the offering of fine artefacts may have been one of the processes through which certain individuals or groups distinguished themselves from their competitors. Not only were certain of the ceremonial centres transformed into major settlements: the stone axes which had played such an important role in Early Neolithic deposits are now to be found on these sites. At one level a restricted segment of society may have appropriated the ritual practices associated with the community and may have turned them into an arena for competitive consumption. At quite another level, they may have appropriated to themselves some of the symbolically charged artefact types that had previously been dedicated to the gods.

The British evidence provides a further contrast, for if the Scandinavian sequence shows a change of emphasis from votive deposits to individual burials with grave goods, in Britain the two traditions existed in opposition to one another for over 500 years. Stone axes, however, were firmly associated with the tradition of ceremonial monuments and feature only occasionally in the burial record, although axes made of local flint have different associations. Hoards are uncommon in Britain, but non-local axes are found in rivers and springs. In this case neither tradition gave way to the other one. When some of the British enclosures took on domestic attributes, as they seem to have done in Scandinavia, that development was short-lived. And when the first metal objects were buried in British graves, they were matched by deposits of axes on other sites. It is the significance of those changes that we must consider next.

The users and all that neighbours them

Introduction

There is an important difference between the first appearance of metalwork in Scandinavia and its introduction into the British Isles. In both cases it is true that its adoption can be understood only in terms of existing patterns of circulation and consumption. Thus most of the copper axes in southern Scandinavia occur as hoards or single finds, whilst the earliest metal objects in Britain are divided between deposits of a rather similar kind and those found with individual burials.

On the other hand, the archaeological sequences in those two areas differ radically. The use of copper objects in Scandinavia was only an episode within a longer Neolithic sequence, and metal had to be re-introduced some centuries later. In the meantime, the hoarding of axes became less important, and burials with fine flint and stone artefacts assumed a more prominent role. Indeed, the earliest Bronze Age 'ritual hoards' claimed in Levy's monograph contain ornaments and weapons more often than tools (Levy 1982, 26–8). Probably the hiatus occurred because this area was so far away from the sources of the raw material. It would always have been vulnerable to fluctuations in supply.

By contrast, the British Isles may not have received any metalwork before the Beaker period (Harbison 1978; Burgess 1978), but from that time onwards there are no breaks in the sequence, even if different amounts were in circulation. There is a further contrast with the evidence from Scandinavia, as certain areas of Britain and Ireland include deposits of copper, tin and even gold. Although these were not used to the same extent from one period to another, their exploitation from an early stage may help to account for the distinctive character of the archaeological record.

At a still broader level our comparison between these two areas highlights several contrasts that permeate the archaeology of the European Bronze Age. First, there is a fundamental distinction to be made between those regions which saw the occasional use of metals in an essentially Neolithic setting (Ottaway 1973; Ottaway and Strahm 1974) and others where it was introduced more abruptly, centuries later. In one case metal was assimilated gradually into contemporary material culture and for a while played much the same roles as other exotic or unfamiliar items. This is a feature of the Pfyn and Cortaillod Cultures in the early fourth millennium BC and occurs to an increasing extent from that time onwards. This development is particularly characteristic of West Central Europe (ibid.).

The alternative course was the fairly rapid introduction of a metal technology into areas in which it had no local precedent, and in these cases the metal objects might be treated in a highly structured manner. Here they really were a new development and may have had a rapid and substantial impact. In most cases they are associated with the Bell Beaker phase, a period that saw other radical changes in material culture. The introduction of the new technology often occurred alongside the appearance of fine pottery, specialised archery equipment and possibly the riding of horses (Shennan 1976).

This does not mean that by the Early Bronze Age the actual uses to which metalwork was put need have differed greatly between Central, Western and Northern Europe. The important contrast was in the *earlier history* of these three areas, and in the degree to which metals were a new development. To a large extent this may be related to the proximity of suitable ores in Central Europe and their rarity in the West. The important contrast already seen between Britain and southern Scandinavia can be extended to a much larger area. Western Europe is ringed by metal deposits but has few of its own. This striking pattern can be illustrated (Fig. 16) by comparing Renfrew's map, which summarises the inception of metalworking in different areas (1979, fig. 10), with the distribution of European copper ores (Tylecote 1987, fig. 1.1).

A final important contrast arises from our Scandinavian and British case studies. This is the distinction between grave goods and the objects deposited in hoards. In Scandinavia this contrast can be exaggerated, but in Britain we find sharply contrasting artefact assemblages throughout the Later Neolithic. In this case these distinctions are strongly reinforced by the adoption of metals.

The same contrast has been recognised in areas which have not entered the discussion so far. In large parts of Western, and particularly Northern, Europe the contents of graves and hoards show little overlap. In other cases they may have complementary distributions, and sometimes particular artefact types transfer from one group to another during the local sequence (Aner 1956; Randsborg 1974, 58–60). In particular, finds from watery locations can often complement the burial record on dry land. Two examples illustrate these points especially clearly. In the southern Scandinavian Early Bronze Age there is a clear division

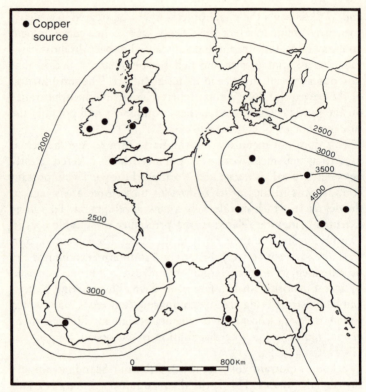

Fig. 15 The spread of metalworking in prehistoric Europe according to Renfrew (1979), compared with the distribution of the principal copper sources. (Sources of metal after Tylecote 1987)

between those types found mainly in burials and others which appear largely in hoards (Fig. 16). Here *chronological* patterning is all-important (Willroth 1984), as swords and spears become less common in hoards and occur with increasing frequency in graves. Finds of daggers, on the other hand, occur in both contexts in about the same proportion throughout the sequence.

A good illustration of *spatial* patterning is provided by Schubart's work in north-east Germany (1972). In Period 2 that area shows some division between two major groups of burial finds, largely separated by a distinct concentration of hoards (Fig. 17).

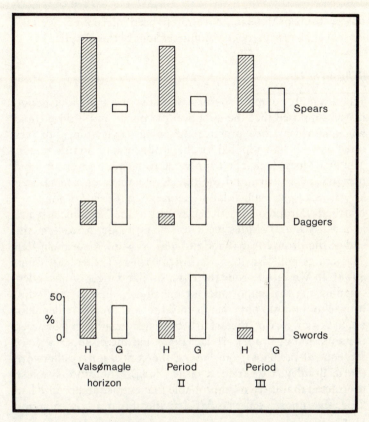

Fig. 16 An example of the way in which specific artefact types may change between hoards (H) and graves (G) during the archaeological sequence. This figure illustrates the chronological distribution of three weapon types in the Early Bronze Age of southern Scandinavia. (After Willroth 1984)

Both groups of material involved a different selection of artefacts. In Period 3, however, the distributions of graves and hoard finds was the same, and their contents also show a greater overlap. Only the male graves contain a distinctive group of artefacts, whilst the female graves have rather similar contents to the hoards. These are examples of a much wider phenomenon, but observations of this kind have rarely been interpreted. We take up that challenge in the remaining sections of this chapter.

Why metal?

This is a more complex question than it seems. For a long period it was supposed that the adoption of copper and bronze could be explained by their practical advantages over stone, but very often metal is first adopted for the production of prestige goods. The first types to change from stone to metal are weapons and personal ornaments, and the full development of a metal tool kit can take place much later (Renfrew 1986). For example, in Northern Europe such central elements of the Neolithic assemblage as axes and sickles were still being made in stone at the end of the Bronze Age (Baudou 1960, 139–46; Groenman Van Waateringe and Van Regteren Altena 1961; Tackenberg 1974, 47–8). In Western Europe there is a similar danger of misunderstanding the real importance of metallurgy. In this area a full bronze tool kit did not emerge until the later second millennium BC. In Britain we can trace a fairly consistent relationship between the adoption of bronze artefact types and the disappearance of the equivalent items from among the contemporary flintwork (Ford, Bradley, Hawkes and Fisher 1984). The process was so protracted that it seems improbable that copper and bronze had a decisive impact on everyday activities for nearly a thousand years.

Nor is it clear that the adoption of metals brought significant improvements in the performance of personal weapons, although there certainly have been claims to this effect. Some of the new types of weapon – in particular daggers, swords and spears – could be so elaborate that they may not have been used. Wear analysis can be informative in these cases. In Britain it is clear that the more complex daggers, some of which were decorated, had been carefully maintained and repaired, whilst the simpler forms could be buried before they showed much sign of use (Wall 1987). Similarly in Period 2 in Scandinavia the highly decorated swords found in complex grave groups show little sign of use, whilst a second group, which is known from simpler burials, reveal traces of combat damage and even of resharpening. The

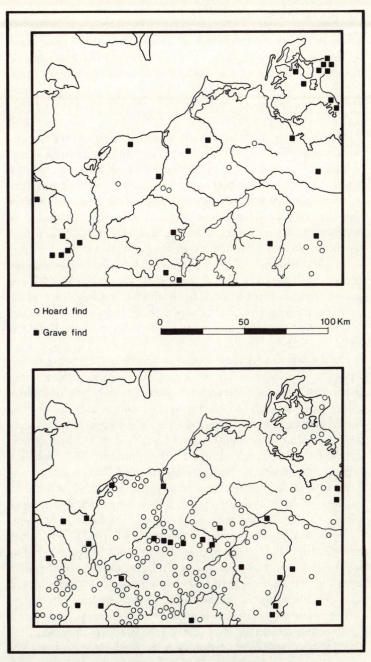

○ Hoard find

■ Grave find

0   50   100 Km

Fig. 17 An example of the changing spatial relationship of hoard and grave finds, illustrated by two distribution maps from north-east Germany. The upper map shows the situation in Period 2, and the lower that in Period 3 of the Early Bronze Age. (After Schubart 1972)

latter have been interpreted as warriors' swords (Kristiansen 1984b). A similar approach can be taken to the goldwork of this period, and Coles and Taylor have drawn attention to ornaments in such fresh condition that they may have been made specifically for deposition in the grave (Coles and Taylor 1971, 13).

Metal may be more important because of non-utilitarian considerations. We have already seen the emphasis that Neolithic society had placed on the movement of exotic artefacts, and the ways in which such objects could be accumulated in regions that had adequate raw materials of their own. It seems likely that the importance of these finds depended on the fact that they were obviously not of local origin; the same seems to apply to the adoption of ritual practices, art styles and even styles of monument from distant areas (cf. Helms 1988). For obvious reasons metal is well suited to play this role since the raw materials have such a limited distribution. This is almost certainly the explanation for the appearance of copper in the Scandinavian Neolithic, and there is every reason to suppose that this attitude continued to be important.

On the other hand, metalwork has great advantages over stone artefacts. First, it is a far more malleable medium than stone. Stoneworking is a subtractive technology and does not allow major modifications to be made to the forms of existing objects. Sometimes pieces of existing axes were reused, but in other cases axes were flaked or smashed to ensure that they could not be employed as ordinary tools (Mark Edmonds, pers. comm.). Metal, on the other hand, can be recycled and, unlike stone, raw material from different artefacts can be pooled in order to make new ones (Tylecote 1987). This is a practice that is most obvious in the Late Bronze Age 'founders' hoards', but metal analysis reveals that raw materials were being recycled from a much earlier stage. Thus exotic objects could be reworked into local types, or locally produced artefacts could be modified to copy the characteristic forms taken by imports. It is for this reason that the dissemination of metals led to such striking similarities between artefacts across wide areas of the Continent.

A second advantage that metals have over stone is that they can carry complex decoration, a feature which had previously been confined to pottery and rock art, among those forms for which archaeological evidence survives. It is not surprising that early metalwork shares so many decorative devices with other media. Thus lunulae share motifs with Beaker pottery, although the two never occur in direct association with one another (Taylor 1970), and decorated axe-heads exhibit some of the same devices as the ceramics in contemporary burials (Megaw and Hardy 1938). This is particularly striking when we recall how rarely such axes are found with the dead. Apart from abstract motifs like these, more naturalistic images may be employed on metalwork. Since bronze is such a flexible medium, it comes as no surprise that some of the more complex decoration shows features that may link it with distant areas. Thus in Scandinavia, where the naturalistic devices on some of the early metalwork recall the rock art of the period, this decoration may refer to an iconography in use in the Mediterranean (Kristiansen 1987, 44 and 48–51).

There is a danger that the argument can become too subjective, especially as the original significance of metalwork is inferred from the ways in which it was deposited. Fortunately, there is an independent source of evidence. We have already mentioned the links between Scandinavian rock art and the designs on some of the bronzes. Rock art is informative in other ways (Abélanet 1986; Chenorkian 1988).

Apart from the rock art of Scandinavia, important evidence comes from Val Camonica in northern Italy (Anati 1976), Monte Bego in southern France (De Lumley, Fontvielle and Abélanet 1976), inland areas of Spain (Acosta 1968) and from scattered sites in the British Isles (Simpson and Thawley 1973). There are important differences in the evidence from these areas, and there is no reason to suppose that they represent a unitary phenomenon. Nevertheless, metalwork has a prominent role in every case.

It is revealing that in each area the art represents only certain of the metal types that were in existence at the time. Thus weapons predominate at Monte Bego, with numerous depictions of daggers and halberds, but only three representations of axes and one possible sickle (De Lumley, Fontevielle and Abélanet 1976; Abélanet 1986, ch. 6). This contrasts with the evidence

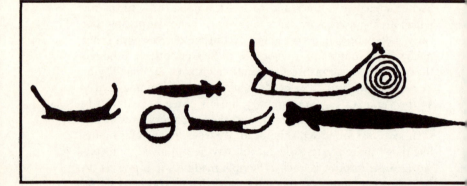

Fig. 18 An example of the connection between metalwork, ships and sun symbols in the rock art of Bohuslän, western Sweden. (After Gelling and Davidson 1969)

from Val Camonica, 350 km away. Here the weapons are found together with depictions of hafted axes (Anati 1976; Abélanet 1986, ch. 7), as they are in the poorly dated Spanish art (Acosta 1968). Monte Bego is some distance from a major metal source, so it is interesting that the weapons depicted there include types that usually occur in distant areas. The same may be true of the bronzes represented in Scandinavian rock art, since Northern Europe lies well outside the distribution of the necessary raw materials. Here the main types of weapons were swords and spears, while axes are nearly always depicted in their hafts (Malmer 1981, ch. 7). In this region there is a recurrent association between carvings of bronze artefacts and ships (Fig. 18). This may reflect the fact that all metal had to be imported, quite possibly by sea. The ships can also be associated with a 'solar' motif, which might represent the metal itself, but here it is unwise to speculate too freely.

In some respects the British evidence stands apart from the rest. In this case the art is largely abstract, but the only portable artefacts to be depicted are metalwork (Simpson and Thawley 1973). The repertoire is limited, being confined to the daggers and axes that epitomise the finds from graves and hoards respectively. A number of these carvings are associated with burial monuments, and the best-known collection comes from Stonehenge. These images lack the supporting detail found in other areas, but it may be revealing that all the axes were depicted without their hafts, suggesting that they were important *as metal*.

Taken together, the evidence from rock art can teach us certain lessons. Only a limited range of items is portrayed – weapons in every case and axes only in certain areas. The weapons at Monte Bego include exotic types, just as those portrayed in Scandinavian rock art must have been imported over considerable distances. This last observation is perhaps emphasised by the ship symbol that plays such a major role in this area, and conceivably by the solar symbol sometimes associated with these vessels. In Britain the metal axes are portrayed without their hafts, as they would appear when freshly cast. In all these ways the art bears witness to the special significance of early metalwork.

The sources of variation

Although there is reason to suppose that copper and bronze were first employed in a restricted range of transactions, the metal industry eventually transgressed those limitations. Just as the adoption of metalworking has a lengthy history, so does its extension into the utilitarian sphere. To a large extent such developments were influenced by two of the considerations mentioned earlier in this chapter: the circumstances in which metalworking was first adopted; and the locations of different communities in relation to the sources of raw material. Both these factors must be taken into account if we are to understand the wide variety of metalwork deposits that have come to characterise the Early Bronze Age.

We have already observed a fundamental division between the kinds of objects deposited in hoards and those buried with the dead. In some cases that division perpetuates a contrast that was already present in the Neolithic period; this perhaps accounts for the continuing importance of axes. Even so, there are indications of major contrasts between developments in different regions. These must now be considered.

We have already suggested that two features may have had an important influence on the ways in which metalwork was circulated and consumed. First, we must consider the importance of history. In some areas metalwork had been used for a considerable period before the Early Bronze Age and had become an essential part of contemporary material culture. During this early phase of use, copper artefacts had undoubtedly played an important role, and the new raw material was employed to produce elaborate copies of the stone objects that were so important in creating and maintaining social relations. A good example is provided by the copper shafthole axes made during this phase (Kibbert 1980, 23–54). Some of these occur in hoards or rivers and can be elaborately decorated. By the period in which metal-working had spread throughout North-West Europe, this experimental phase was largely over, and less complex forms of axe were being made in these areas. At this stage a clear contrast becomes apparent. In areas with a long history of metalworking, simple axes were widely distributed, but in regions in which it was a recent introduction these axes were imbued with special qualities. Such objects could be deposited with some formality in springs or bogs, and unhafted axe-heads could even be placed in special containers, which recall the sheaths depicted many years before in megalithic art (Barrett 1985; Needham 1988). Some of the early metal axes seem to have been deliberately broken, and in certain cases their cutting edges provide evidence of intentional damage (Coles 1969, 33–4; Needham 1988). These are just the types of axe depicted without their hafts in British rock art.

More importantly, quite a large number of these axes had been decorated (Pl. 9). This is particularly interesting as it is very much a feature of those areas in which such tools were a recent introduction, and is less common where metalwork had been used over a lengthy period. As we mentioned earlier, the characteristic decoration on the British and Irish axes shares elements with fine pottery which was employed in funerary ritual (Megaw and Hardy 1938). The presence of decoration also seems to have affected the circumstances in which these artefacts were deposited. In Ireland, for example, plain axes of Killaha type outnumber decorated axes by 56 per cent to 44 per cent, but the proportions are exactly reversed among the river finds, where decorated artefacts predominate (Harbison 1969). These features

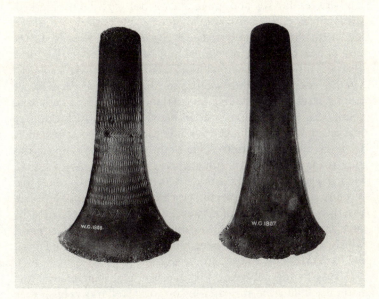

Plate 9 Two decorated axes from Willerby Wold, North Yorkshire.
Photograph: British Museum.

are not peculiar to the British Isles, but the evidence for decorated
axes during the Early Bronze Age falls off rapidly as we approach
those areas with a longer-established tradition of metalworking.

There is a second area in which that historical contrast may
have exerted a powerful influence. We have already seen how
sharp the distinctions may be between the contents of graves
and the material found in hoards. All our examples have been
taken from Britain and Northern Europe, however, and this is
largely because such divisions are not so clearly marked in areas
further to the south. Again, it would be wrong to impose a rigid
scheme when there was so much local variation, but there is
at least a tendency for less structured deposits to be found in
areas with a long history of metallurgy. This is best illustrated
by considering three studies of Early Bronze Age axes and their
associations. The first is concerned with an area of West Germany
centred upon Frankfurt (Kibbert 1980), and in this case the over-

lap between hoards and grave finds is not particularly marked. Although axes do occur in both contexts, few of the types associated with them in the burials are discovered in hoards. In the case of Mayer's study of axes from Austria, there is rather more overlap, although this should not be exaggerated (Mayer 1977). On the other hand, when we turn to Abels' study of the evidence from a large area including Switzerland, south-east France and south-west Germany the overlap between these categories is so marked that it is no longer possible to infer find circumstances from the metalwork itself; some of the associated groups in this corpus may come from either graves or hoards (Abels 1972). Here daggers and axes, the two artefacts most strictly segregated in parts of North and North-West Europe, are regularly found together in both types of context. The point is emphasised by such famous hoards as those from Dieskau in East Germany, which contain enormous collections of tools, weapons and ornaments (Von Brunn 1959, Taf. 12–23).

Access to the ore sources is another important feature and naturally influenced the early history of metallurgy. This is seen in two characteristics of these deposits: the great differences in the amount of material in some of the collections; and the extent to which they contain evidence of metalworking *per se*. We mentioned one of the great East German hoards. It has long been appreciated that some of the deposits found nearer to the sources of the metalwork in Central Europe include very large numbers of bronze artefacts (Harding 1983, 23–44). For the most part this is a new phenomenon and is not found in the Copper Age in this area, when the hoards were fewer and very much smaller. Those belonging to the later part of the Early Bronze Age period show much more variety, and some contain an enormous amount of metal; the artefacts from the Bresinchen hoard – 146 in all – weigh 30 kg. They can be found in ceramic vessels that could not have been used to transport them (Gimbutas 1965, 268–70), and sometimes, as at Dieskau, more than one such deposit may be discovered on the same site (Von Brunn 1959). Among their contents are axes, daggers, halberds, massive bracelets and neck rings. This can be compared with the small size of the average Early Bronze Age hoard in Britain. While the contents of the Central European hoards contained many different types of artefact, the British material has the narrow range of objects found in outlying areas of Europe.

In fact the hoard finds from such regions exhibit a number of largely new features. These will not be considered in detail here, as all anticipate the characteristic patterns of the Later Bronze Age, considered in Chapter 3. There is evidence for the circulation of standard units of metal in the form of ingot torcs (Menke 1979; Harding 1983, 30–41). These may have been produced to standard weights (Menke 1979, Abb. 9 and 10), and certainly they were based on a type of personal ornament, which can be found in finished form over a much wider area (Pl. 10). Close to the putative sources of the metal these tend to be discovered together in hoards, but at the outer edge of the hoard distribution they can be associated with other types of object. In some cases these collections also include metalworking residues, suggesting that some of the accumulations may come from the sites of workshops (Fig. 19; Menke 1979). There is similar evidence from Ireland, another source of metal at this time. Here some of the axes may have circulated in unfinished form and could have been treated as blanks or ingots (Harbison 1969, 22–4). In Ireland collections of artefacts can also be discovered together with metalworking residues (*ibid.*, 71).

Ingots and scrap metal tend to be found in areas close to metal sources, and in an obvious sense they have light to shed on the scale and organisation of metal production during the Early Bronze Age. There is also a sense in which they herald new developments that were ultimately to extend across most of Europe. The massive accumulations of metalwork are new, but are echoed by many deposits of the Later Bronze Age. The evidence for standardisation is such a striking development that it is still the subject of controversy, and the signs that existing objects may have been collected together for recycling provides support for an interpretation that is otherwise based on metal analysis (e.g. Needham, Leese, Hook and Hughes 1989). It seems to indicate that more concerted, or at least more archaeologically visible, attempts were being made to ensure a continuous supply of raw material. With only limited exceptions, these tendencies have not been recognised in the archaeology of areas that lay further from the sources of the metal. Much of the Later Bronze Age sequence

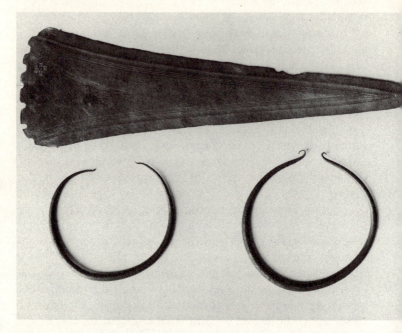

Plate 10 Ingot torcs in the hoard from Beitsch, East Germany.
Photograph: British Museum.

shows how that disadvantage was overcome. The distinctive
deposits found close to the metal sources are the start of a new
development, but they also emphasise the different character of
the archaeology of remote areas.

Interpretations

This chapter has investigated the circumstances in which axes
developed a dual role, both as work tools and as votive offerings.
We saw how during the Neolithic period axes came to be imbued
with special significance, basing our argument on the evidence
of megalithic art, bog hoards, river finds and grave goods. In
one case, stone axes had been portrayed on the walls of megalithic
monuments, together with what seem to be trance images, and

this could have invested these objects with supernatural meanings. In other cases the axes themselves could be consumed along with other forms of offering at special ceremonial centres, or they might be appropriated by one segment of society for burial with its dead. This, then, was the inheritance with which Bronze Age societies came to terms.

By the Early Bronze Age the significance of axes was assured, but with the development of a belief system which favoured individual burial with grave goods, often weapons, these objects were increasingly excluded from these burials and deposited in separate contexts. One of the recurrent elements in the early history of metalworking is the division that came to exist between the finds from graves, and the hoards and single finds of the same period. Each contained an extremely stereotyped assemblage, and at any one time they showed only a limited overlap. In some areas this distinction can be traced back to Neolithic practice, whilst in others it may have been a later development. In general terms the deposits of the Early Bronze Age seem to have been more rigidly categorised in those areas where metalworking was a recent introduction, and/or where the metals themselves were not of local origin.

This distinction between grave goods and other deposits is expressed in several ways. Most commonly, it is shown by contrasts between the types of artefact deposited in these different contexts, but in other cases it may also be expressed in spatial terms, so that hoards and burial finds have mutually exclusive distributions. Again, there are cases in which only one group of burials shares material with hoard deposits, whilst other classes of burial maintain a rigid separation. Although objects may make the transition between those categories through time, at this stage it is unusual for one group to replace the other entirely. Among the most important distinctions was that between wet finds and dry-land finds.

It is worth contemplating the possible meanings of these different deposits. Let us take the grave finds first. It may seem odd to describe these as 'deposits' in the same terms as hoard finds, but to suppose otherwise is to assume that the dead buried themselves. Apart from those items which were part of the costume of the deceased, the grave goods could represent funeral gifts

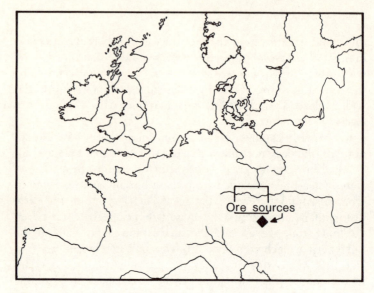

A

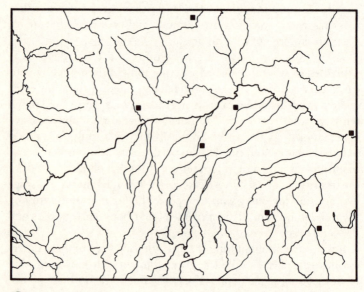

C

Fig. 19 The distributions of three groups of hoards in relation to the ore sources of the German–Austrian borderland. A: location of the raw material; B: *Ringbarren* hoards; C: mixed hoards containing axes and ornaments; and D: mixed hoards containing raw materials or casting debris. (After Menke 1979)

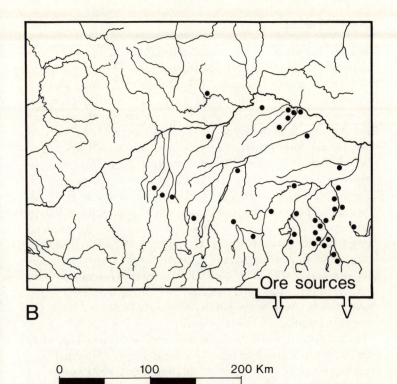

B

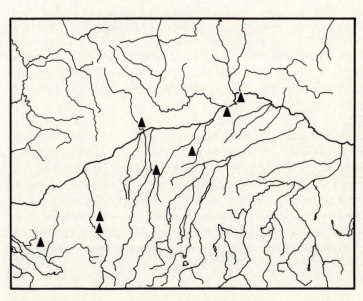

D

from the survivors. It is obvious that certain items were considered more appropriate than others, particularly the daggers in the male graves, but there need be no *direct* link between the objects deposited by the living and the status or achievements of the dead. As John Barrett says, we are seeing only those objects that accompanied the body in the final stage of the rites of passage, and the provision of such artefacts would have been controlled by the mourners (Barrett 1989b). It follows that the apparent 'richness' or 'poverty' of the grave assemblage may tell us most about circumstances at the time that the burial took place. In some cases the importance of the deceased needed no underlining, and the relationship of the survivors to the dead person would not have to be emphasised. At other times the funeral may have provided the occasion for the lavish consumption of wealth. No doubt certain artefacts were appropriate deposits in this situation and others were inappropriate, but the distinction between grave goods and hoard finds need not have been as marked as it sometimes seems.

Hoard finds, especially those deposited in watery locations, share with grave goods the distinguishing characteristic that they were not intended to be retrieved. In some areas the axe provided what John Barrett has called 'the core symbol about which the other objects came to be arranged' (1985, 103). Perhaps the major feature that distinguishes grave goods from hoard finds is that the artefacts with burials are linked to a specific individual, whereas those deposited in hoards lack this close identification with one person; thus Needham describes them as 'community deposits' (1988, 246). It is more difficult to suggest the contexts for these offerings. Like grave goods, they may be associated with rites of passage, even with death, but this cannot be demonstrated. It is clear, however, that they generally took place in quite different locations. They may consist of votive offerings made on other occasions, and they may be the work of different parts of the population (cf. Barrett and Needham 1989). It is even possible that the separation between these groups is so strongly marked because the two forms of consumption were used in competition with one another, funeral gifts expressing claims to the authority of the deceased, and the votive hoards providing another means of winning prestige. Again, this is speculation, and it is just as likely that these small deposits were intended to placate the supernatural powers.

We saw in Chapter 1 how offerings can assume a competitive character and provide one means by which contending parties may break out of the restrictive conventions of gift exchange and establish an unassailable position in relation to their competitors. There is a problem in applying this model in the present case, for in North-West Europe it is quite impossible to establish what were regarded as significant offerings. The quantities of metalwork deposited in many hoards are small, even compared with the contents of more elaborate burials, but since they are found so far away from the main sources of the raw material, they may still have had a significant impact. On the other hand, they are not at all comparable to the lavish deposits that are found in Central Europe.

It may be that the best approach is to compare the two extremes shown by this evidence: the highly structured but relatively parsimonious offerings in the graves and hoards of North and North-West Europe, with the more profligate consumption of metal that took place closer to its sources. Here there is less structure to the different deposits, but the quantities of metalwork involved are vastly greater. This is not just a reflection of the proximity of metal ores, for it is a feature that develops only gradually in this area. Andrew Sherratt has commented on this, and on the contrast that is seen between the small Copper Age hoards in this region and the massive groups of Bronze Age metalwork (1976, 579–80). He suggests that the smaller, more structured collections reflect a society with a well-defined social order, in his terms a 'chiefdom'. By contrast, he sees the lavish but essentially unstructured deposition of metalwork in the following period as evidence for the emergence of a much more competitive system, in which the squandering of valuables was a way of winning prestige. For Sherratt this is a 'big man' society.

There certainly is some evidence for increasing instability in this area, despite the prospects offered by control of the metal supply. During the Corded Ware and Bell Beaker periods there is little evidence of large settlements, and the fortified sites that had long been established here went out of use. It was in the later part of the Early Bronze Age that this pattern was re-established over a wide area. A number of these defended sites seem to have been engaged in metallurgy as well as other forms of craft production. They can include concentrations of apparently high-status artefacts, as well as imports from more distant areas. There is occasional evidence for centralised food storage at these locations, which seem to have dominated small networks of undefended settlements. Shennan (1986) has related the development of these sites to the unsettled conditions brought about by competition for status goods and control of the metal supply. It is tempting to relate these developments to the pressures that occasioned the lavish consumption of metalwork in the votive sphere.

By contrast, there is little settlement evidence from the more distant areas in which the hoards are so much smaller and more tightly structured. Nor is there any sign of fortifications on the Central European model. Rather, the landscape is dominated by burial mounds and the artefact record by grave goods and hoard finds. In Britain, and to some extent in Brittany and Ireland, the major concentrations of burials may be found around the ceremonial centres of the Neolithic period (e.g. Bradley 1984, ch. 4; Darvill 1987, ch. 4). It seems as if relations with the supernatural still played an important part in shaping the society of the living. This seems to be a very different system from the one in Central Europe, and that is why it may be unwise to interpret the metal deposits of both areas in the same terms. There were real differences of resources – and also of history – between these two regions.

We have already observed that in some respects the metal deposits of Central Europe anticipate features that were to become widespread during the Later Bronze Age, in particular the evidence of standardisation and careful recycling in the metal industry. In fact there are other ways in which these developments indicate the shape of things to come, for the fortified settlements and extravagant metal deposits in this area also anticipate characteristic features of the Later Bronze Age in Western Europe. If a real contrast existed between societies in these two areas during the period discussed in this chapter, the outlines will stand out in sharper relief when we have seen what was to follow.

Chapter 3

The cove of armoury

'Then Albion's Angel rose resolv'd to the cove of armoury;
His shield . . .
He took down from its trembling pillar; from its cavern deep,
His helm was brought by London's Guardian & his thirsty spear
By the wise spirit of London's river . . .'

William Blake, *America: a Prophecy*

Introduction

The Later Bronze Age is a major period of change (Coles and Harding 1979, 335–7, 459 and 491–3). It sees an expansion in the scale and archaeological visibility of settlement sites. We find the widespread adoption of the new funerary practices character- ised by the 'Urnfield' phenomenon. There is a quickening in the scope of long-distance exchange, and a corresponding increase in the scale of metal extraction. Over the same period we can recognise new developments in the organisation of food produc- tion and in techniques of farming and food storage. In some areas land was being enclosed, and many regions saw the adoption of hill forts. Such widespread processes were not entirely new, but the Later Bronze Age is characterised by different geographi- cal divisions from the networks established during earlier phases.

Equally important changes affected the deposition of valuables. In particular, there seems to have been a clear identification between finds of weaponry and watery locations. No doubt this grew out of some of the distinctions considered in Chapter 2, but now there was a much sharper division between dry-land finds and those from rivers or bogs. Weapons and ornaments predominate, and generally these changes involved the down- grading of the axe as a key element in wet deposits. Instead it is increasingly found in dry-land hoards, often in circumstances that suggest a connection with metalworking.

A further pattern is still more tantalising. This is the reduced frequency, and sometimes the disappearance, of complex burials. In many areas there are fewer large burial monuments, and often there is less evidence for the provision of elaborate grave goods. We see the widespread use of cremation, rather than inhumation, and sometimes the deposition of the dead in large collective cemeteries. These changes have been taken to indicate the spread of an 'Urnfield' ideology (Alexander 1979, 221–7), and for an earlier generation they represented mass migration on a similar scale to the movement of the 'Beaker Folk' (Childe 1950, ch. 9). This now seems unlikely, as the general pattern is crosscut by so much local variation. Within this detail, however, one tendency is clearly marked. Less emphasis seems to have been placed on the remains of the dead, and the graves themselves were no longer the focus for such elaborate offerings. Instead rivers and other watery locations saw the most lavish consumption of metalwork.

To a large extent these broad trends are crosscut by different regional histories, and it is during this period that a contrast may be found between developments in Northern, Western and Central Europe, and often between much smaller parts of these regions. At the risk of over-simplification, we can suggest that in Central Europe, close to the main sources of the metal in use during this period, greater emphasis was placed on the provision of grave goods than in other areas, and rather less on 'votive' deposits. In Western Europe, on the other hand, grave goods play a less crucial role, and river metalwork is of growing importance. The main distribution of river deposits is in areas distant from the metal ores, and a high proportion of the finds consists of weapons. Lastly, in Northern Europe, an area in which local sources of metal were entirely absent, wet finds were of great importance, especially compared with the finds from contemporary burials. These wet finds come from bogs rather than rivers and are complemented by similar finds from dry land. In this case the proportion of weaponry falls and the percentage of ornaments increases. Ritual objects, such as lures, also play a major part in these deposits. In all three areas, however, 'utilitarian' hoards are of some importance, and these do have strikingly similar characteristics to one another. The one major point of contrast is in the very high proportion of axes circulating in Western Europe and the equally high representation of sickles in Central Europe.

It is not possible for one chapter to accommodate every variation among these finds, for it is the extent of such contrasts that has inhibited attempts at synthesis. Here our main emphasis is on *the deposits of weapons in watery locations*. We shall begin by sketching the changing relationship between grave goods, hoards and river finds, before turning our attention to the problems of interpretation. We must restrict ourselves to the broad outlines, and to two major sources of variation in the archaeological record. We shall consider the influences that lay behind the sharp *regional* contrasts in the use and consumption of metalwork, and shall also study the evidence of *chronological* development. At one end of the sequence we need to specify the changes that affected metal deposits during the transition from an Earlier to a Later Bronze Age, and at the opposite extreme we must face the still more complicated questions of how and why this system came to an end. We shall see how the circulation and consumption of bronze metalwork became ever more complex processes and discuss the limitations within which the system was operating. In turn, this will involve some consideration of the circumstances in which iron was first adopted.

Observations

Burials and river finds

In 1971 Torbrügge published a fundamental study of the problem of river metalwork. This has had an enormous influence. It covered a vast chronological and geographical range, and its publication has been the main reason that such discoveries are accepted as a real phenomenon today. Because his analysis has been so influential, it will not be necessary to summarise all the evidence here.

In essence, Torbrügge identified two major relationships between grave goods and water finds, often those specifically from rivers. First, there were cases in which characteristic artefact types moved from the burial record to water deposits or vice

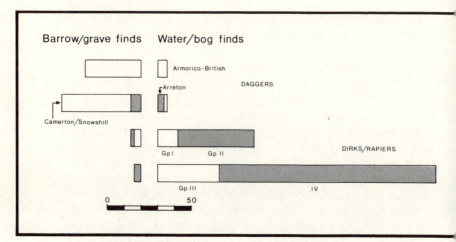

Fig. 20 The contrasting contexts in which daggers, dirks and rapiers are found in England, Wales and Scotland. Note that the chronology of late daggers and early rapiers may overlap (see Barrett and Needham 1989). (Based on data from Gerloff 1975 and Burgess and Gerloff 1981)

versa. For example, most of the daggers of the British Early Bronze Age have been found in graves, but the great majority of their immediate successors, the dirks and rapiers, are recorded from water locations and such weapons are very rare in burials (Fig. 20; Burgess and Gerloff 1981). In other cases the sequence could move in the opposite direction. Thus, in the middle Rhine, swords are well known as river finds in Hallstatt B3, but nearly all those dated to Hallstatt C come from burial mounds (Wegner 1976).

The second relationship is recognised at a regional scale. This is where the same classes of artefact are deposited in graves or water deposits, but in different areas. For example, Torbrügge himself shows how there is a long-running contrast between the deposition of weaponry in graves in Central Europe and its discovery in water deposits further to the west (Torbrügge 1971). This contrast extends from the first flange-hilted swords to those produced at the very end of the Bronze Age (*ibid.*, Beilagen 11 and 16; Fig. 21). It is mirrored on a local geographical scale.

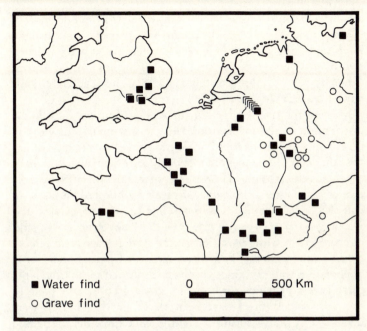

Fig. 21 The distribution of Hemigkofen and Erbenheim swords in North-West Europe, emphasising the contrast between water finds and those found in burials. (After Torbrügge 1971)

Thus in south-west Germany during Hallstatt A swords were deposited with burials in flat graves in some areas and in rivers in others (*ibid.*, Beilage 23).

Some variants of these patterns are worth mentioning here. If river finds and cremation cemeteries are found close to one another, there may be little or no evidence of rich burials during the same period. The British Middle Bronze Age provides an example of this pattern (Bradley 1984, 108–14). There are also areas in which river metalwork is found but where burials of any kind are virtually absent. An instance is provided by the Irish Later Bronze Age (Eogan 1964, 285). The sequence in the middle Rhine epitomises a number of these developments (Fig. 22). After a peak of barrow burials during Bronze B–C, swords are found mainly in rivers and flat graves, and to some extent the distributions of these deposits move apart from one another through time. The river finds seem to have played an increasingly important role, so that between Hallstatt B1 and B3 finds of swords in rivers gradually took over from those in flat graves. When barrow burial resumed in Hallstatt C, however, river finds almost ceased (Wegner 1976).

Most of the river finds occur in Western Europe, outside the distribution of the metal ores. They consist mainly of weapon types which would be found with graves in other periods; otherwise they can complement more poorly furnished burials in those areas. It is closer to the major sources of metal, in Central Europe, that we encounter a somewhat stronger tradition of burials with complex grave goods (Gimbutas 1965, 307–10; Coles and Harding 1979, 359–66). Otherwise the Later Bronze Age situation contrasts with the earlier system. At that stage areas remote from the metal sources had maintained a sharp division between grave goods and the kinds of object deposited in hoards. Now there is less evidence for complex grave groups, and some of the types which might have been placed in 'rich' burials were deposited in watery locations. At the same time, the specialised hoard deposits that had characterised Western Europe during that early phase lost their distinctive identity.

At an empirical level it has been tempting to interpret some of the river finds in terms of funerary ritual. They contain the kinds of artefact that had once been associated with the dead, and in some sequences burials with grave goods take over from water finds again at the end of this period. The distribution of wet finds can complement the distribution of grave goods, and in areas in which 'rich' burials are rare or absent, these may be the only complex deposits of any kind. Although it is customary to suggest a link between these categories, it is much more difficult to provide an interpretation.

Again we have to ask ourselves what were the roles of complex grave goods. As we have seen, these would have been provided by the mourners and need not have been the personal property of the deceased. Lavish grave offerings may be a feature of quite specific circumstances, as may the construction of large mounds. It seems possible that these are found mainly in periods of political instability, when funerary ritual provided an opportunity for lavish display among the survivors – we should not forget that this is one way in which the potlatch was first used. During the Early Bronze Age such grave finds had normally existed alongside, or even in opposition to, hoards that contained a different artefact assemblage. Some of those hoards were deposited in watery locations.

Later Bronze Age practice merged these two domains. To a large extent the tradition of making offerings in such locations continued with the deposition of weaponry, but some of the customary elements seem to have been dropped. In Western Europe the axe may have lost its status in favour of complex weapons – swords, large spearheads, shields and occasionally helmets. Where burials were still deposited, they were sometimes accompanied by smaller bronzes, some of them of the types found on settlement sites (Herrmann 1966; Dehn 1972). In some areas, then, these changes drew on elements of the Early Bronze Age burial rite, and in others they may have usurped its role as an arena for the deposition of fine metalwork.

The distinction between grave finds and water finds is lessened further once we appreciate that these changes were happening at the same time as other developments. Firstly, cremation was widely adopted. The burning of the body is particularly important here, as it distances the living from the dead in a way that need not happen in the complex rites of passage associated with inhumation burial (cf. Bradley 1982b, 118–20). A second, related change was the use of flat cemeteries rather than massive mounds (Fig. 23). Although small barrows continued to be built in some areas, there can be little doubt that the Later Bronze Age often saw the disuse of large funerary monuments, at least in those areas with substantial river deposits. This is hardly surprising since earthworks of this kind would form a lasting link between the dead and the living. Exceptions to both these statements can be found, but they are sufficiently widely scattered to do little to weaken the argument.

These developments do not necessarily occur together, but each reveals a break in continuity between the dead and their successors. The translation of traditional types of funeral offering to a distinct location might be yet another indication of that process. In some cases this may have been done in order to ensure

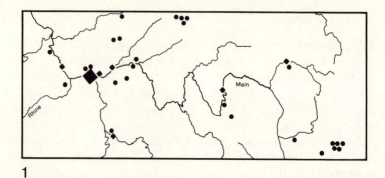

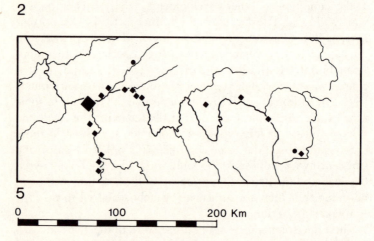

Fig. 22 The changing context of sword finds in northern Bavaria and in middle and south Hessen. 1: Bronze B–C; 2: Bronze D; 3: Halstatt A; 4: Halstatt B1; 5: Halstatt B3; and 6: Hallstatt C. (After Wegner 1976)

104

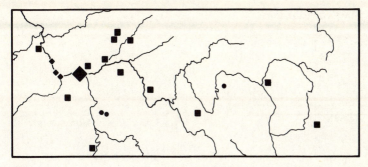

3

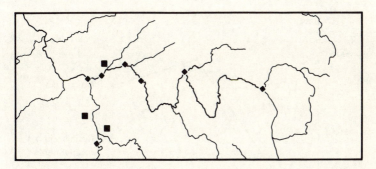

4

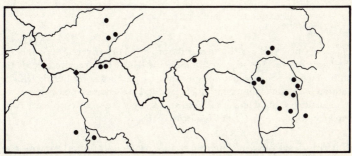

6
- ● Barrow
- ■ Flat grave
- ◆ River find
- ◆ Concentration of
  river finds

The passage of arms

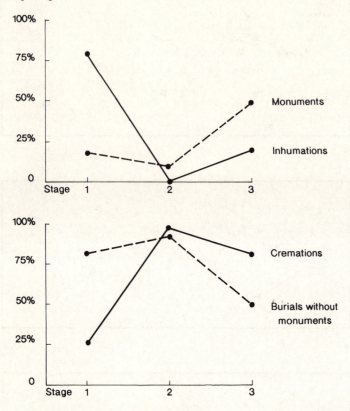

Fig. 23 Changes in the burial rite and the provision of a covering monument in the Later Bronze Age sequence in the Paris Basin. The diagram records the ratio of cremations to inhumations and the proportion of burials with or without a covering monument. In Stages 2 and 3 it seems as if monuments are found mainly with inhumations. Cremations, however, were less often accompanied by earthworks. (Data from Brun 1986)

that the dead person's property no longer circulated among the survivors, but the choice of watery locations for this activity suggests a still more powerful link with the existing history of deposition in these places.

As we mentioned in Chapter 1, river finds lack a real archaeological context, and in such cases it is impossible to consider associations between different artefact types. There is, however, one clue that may shed light on the processes at work. Some collections of metalwork are so extensive that they may have been accumulated over a lengthy period, or by a large number of people. A striking example is provided by the finds from Duddingston Loch near Edinburgh, which included nine swords, twenty-three spearheads and a bucket, as well as a quantity of animal bones (Callender 1922). It may be that these deposits are the successors of the funeral gifts formerly associated with barrows, but sometimes they were provided by a greater number of people. At all events such transactions might have played a part in the rites of passage.

So far these links are entirely circumstantial. Can further evidence be adduced in support of such connections? One possibility is that river metalwork results from a new way of disposing of the dead. Rather than bury individuals beneath a sizeable mound, bodies may have been deposited in watery locations, with fine metalwork of the types that would normally have been placed in the grave. It has always been assumed that bodies would have been cremated, making the recognition of water burials impossible. It now seems that this view was unduly pessimistic, at least in one part of Western Europe. Recent excavation at British sites dating to the Later Bronze Age has suggested that cremation was only one way in which the dead were treated. A series of high-status settlement sites have produced groups of unburnt human bones, suggesting a process of excarnation similar to that evidenced in the Neolithic period (Burgess 1988, 565–7; Thomas in press).

Other groups of unburnt bone, this time accompanied by metalwork, are known from an unusual class of deposit on the Continent dating from this period. These sites consist of caves or rock fissures that were filled with human remains, animal bones and finds of Late Bronze Age artefacts (Maier 1977; Warmenbol 1988a; Burgess 1988, 567). In one case these had been dropped through the opening of a rock fissure and could not have been recovered, and in another instance the cave itself was the source of a river. Although these indications cannot be given much weight, again they suggest that an alternative tradition of exposure or primary burial complemented the cremations or inhumations already known.

In the light of this information it seemed to be worth asking whether unburnt human remains could have been deposited together with metalwork, and, if so, whether any had been recorded by archaeologists. The published literature is rather unhelpful here. Some accounts of the discovery of metalwork do refer to finds of bones, but these were rarely recovered or identified. Even so, a few cases are of interest. For example, human bones were recovered from Duddingston Loch (Callender 1922), the swords found in British rivers were occasionally accompanied by skulls (e.g. Phillips 1941, 134) and skulls or other human remains come from three wooden structures in the wetlands of Holderness (Smith 1911).

In order to set these chance observations in context, Ken Gordon and the writer recently undertook a study of the finds from the River Thames, which provide a large and apparently representative sample of the kinds of metalwork deposited in rivers (Bradley and Gordon 1988). This material extends from the Neolithic period to the first millennium AD, but includes large groups of Bronze Age and Iron Age weaponry, which have been well studied in recent years. The original accounts of their discovery, usually during the nineteenth century, were searched for information concerning other material found at the time, and then the relevant museum collections were examined in case they contained human remains.

It soon became obvious that the weapons had been found together with a large number of human skulls, but those skulls had been forgotten once greater interest was taken in the artefacts. Many of the skulls still survived, and nearly 300 extant examples were traced; still more were described in the original accounts of these discoveries. It was clear that they had been deposited in an unfleshed condition; there were very few mandibles, and other body parts were absent from the museum collections, even though ordinary animal bones had been retained. The skulls showed a bias towards males aged between about 25 and 35, and had been recovered from the river during the same campaigns of dredging as the metalwork. The two distributions proved to be strikingly similar.

Dating such material is obviously a problem. Statistical analysis showed that the main group of skulls was very like examples of later prehistoric origin and thus could be of the same date as the metalwork, but this was not decisive. For this reason six skulls from the Thames were submitted for radiocarbon dating, and four of these fell within the period of the Later Bronze Age weaponry from the river. Since so few unburnt bones are known from the Later Bronze Age, this is a striking observation. Although absolute proof is lacking, it does seem likely that the weapons were deposited in the river together with human remains.

There are the first indications of similar evidence from the Low Countries, where so many human remains have been found in dredging that they are described as belonging to the 'River Valley People' (e.g. Erdbrink, Meiklejohn and Tacoma 1987 and references cited in that paper). Most of these are of Pleistocene age, but among them are some much younger finds, principally skulls. Five of these now have radiocarbon dates in the Bronze Age or Early Iron Age (Gowlett, Hedges, Law and Perry 1987, 132–3). Unfortunately, less is known about river metalwork in this region, although one major group is recorded from the Scheldt (Warmenbol 1986, 153) and another has been found in the Meuse (Roynams and Van der Sanden 1980, 191–203).

It is important not to press the evidence too hard. At present we are not aware of human skulls from many rivers with Bronze Age metalwork, and it remains to be seen whether these finds represent the exception or the norm. At all events it is clear that the distribution of weapons in the River Thames extends over a wider area than the finds of human skulls that have been recognised to date, and both there and in the Low Countries the radiocarbon dates run on into the first millennium AD. We can suggest that at least *one* major group of weaponry could have been deposited together with human remains, but we cannot say whether this was common practice. Significant progress depends on the excavation of *in situ* deposits, if any become available.

Burials and hoard finds

If it was Torbrügge's study of river metalwork that had a decisive influence on the way in which this material was approached, Hundt's account of hoards from northern Germany has had a similar impact on research (Hundt 1955). Both there and in southern Scandinavia, metalwork is more common in bogs than it is in rivers. Hundt's work has much the same point of departure as Torbrügge's paper, for again deposits of metalwork found in specialised locations show an essential continuity with the finds from earlier burials. This is well illustrated by evidence from Denmark which shows that in most areas complex artefacts moved from graves to hoards during Period IV (Kristiansen 1978, 162–3).

Again this change coincides with other developments. Cremation was adopted only gradually, but it is clear that such burials are accompanied by a much smaller range of items than the inhumation graves of earlier periods. Some of the types that had been placed in these graves were now deposited in watery locations. At the same time, large burial mounds were no longer built, although older earthworks were sometimes reused as the setting for later hoards and the contents of their graves could even be robbed (Rittershofer 1987). At this level, then, there are striking similarities with the sequence in Western Europe, and the same factors may have been important in both areas.

At another level there are important contrasts to consider. The dominant feature of the West European sequence is the translation of *weapon* deposits from burial mounds to rivers, but in southern Scandinavia such finds of weaponry were gradually eclipsed by finds of ornaments, and these predominate in the Later Bronze Age hoards. Comparison with finds from burials suggests that this change may also be one from male-associated artefacts to those associated with women (Kristiansen 1984a, 86 and 91). By contrast, the rate at which weapons were deposited in West European rivers may have increased over the same period.

A second contrast may reflect the locations in which these hoards were deposited. We have already seen how difficult it is to talk about the quantities of material that were being placed in rivers; it is harder still to establish any associations between different types of artefact. In Northern Europe, where so many finds come from bogs, there is often quite detailed evidence concerning the contexts of these hoards. It is possible to recognise individual sets of ornaments amongst this material, an argument strengthened by comparison with grave groups from neighbouring areas. It is clear that some hoards could contain one set of personal equipment, but frequently a single deposit includes *several* sets of ornaments (Levy 1982, ch. 6). This is a crucial distinction. It suggests that such collections might contain the property of more than one person, in which case the purposeful arrangement of the artefacts in these groups may also mean that they had been deposited on the same occasion. In this way hoarding may have permitted *more extravagant consumption* of metalwork than the provision of grave goods.

There is a further contrast with the evidence of river finds. The deposits of ornaments and weapons that characterise the North European sequence are complemented by a series of artefacts which appear to lack an everyday function. These are usually regarded as ceremonial items and include such extraordinary objects as musical instruments, figurines and 'cult wagons' (Broholm 1946). Some of these are elaborately decorated. In view of the contexts in which so much of this material is found, it is hardly surprising that water symbols are important on these objects. They include the boats mentioned in Chapter 2, as well as images of wading birds. Opposed to these is a second series of images linking the sun, the horse and wheeled chariots (Levy 1982, 104–7). To a large extent the same iconography is found in Scandinavian rock art, which actually depicts such objects in use in elaborate ceremonies (Malmer 1981). However they are to be interpreted, they first appear during the Earlier Bronze Age, but were deposited in much greater numbers during Period V. These finds have some parallels in Ireland (Eogan 1964, 313–14) – another area in which large amounts of metalwork were deposited in bogs – and may adopt motifs from a much wider area, but for the most part they contrast sharply with contemporary river finds in Western Europe.

In the latter area the circumstantial links between grave goods and river finds were strengthened by the discovery of large numbers of human skulls in the Thames. Such evidence is even more elusive in Northern Europe, where finds of animal bones do survive from a small number of hoards. Only at Radjbjerg, where a deposit containing two lures has been excavated, is there evidence for both human and animal remains. Again the human bone was unburnt and disarticulated (Broholm, Larsen and Skjerne 1949, 21–2).

These Northern European hoards do have features in common with the finds from burials, but they owe almost as much to a tradition of 'ritual' hoarding that was already well established when barrow building lapsed. In this respect they differ from the river finds of Western Europe. Unlike the latter material, they overlap with a series of deposits of ceremonial equipment. In Western Europe river finds took over a tradition of votive deposits in wet places and may have annexed it to a programme of conspicuous consumption. The opposite could have happened in Northern Europe, where the customary grave assemblage was increasingly assimilated into an established tradition of ceremonial offerings, vividly documented in Scandinavian rock art. This contrast is illustrated by the difference between deposits of personal weapons in Western Europe and the cosmological imagery characteristic of the finest metalwork in Northern Europe. If one tradition emphasised martial prowess among the living, the other referred more directly to the power of the supernatural and to an iconography drawn from exotic places. We shall return to that contrast later in this chapter.

On the other hand, all connection with past practice had not been severed. If human remains are virtually absent from the North European hoards, older burial mounds could be selected as locations for these deposits; the same can be true of Later Bronze Age cremations. Nearly all the hoards from these mounds date from Period IV, the phase in which such barrows first went out of use. Usually these hoards contain female ornaments. Only two 'ritual' hoards had been deposited on these such sites in Period III, and by Period V the hoards from older mounds seem to have an entirely utilitarian character (Levy 1982, 26–42). These patterns are unlikely to be coincidental. The chronology and associations of the finds both emphasise the links with funerary ritual, whilst the absence of human bones in the best-documented bog hoards strengthens the connection between those deposits and the finds of ceremonial objects.

How far can we extend these arguments to the hoards of Western Europe? Are any of these related to the commemoration of the dead? In fact there is very little basis for discussion, although the recognition of human skulls in the Thames certainly recalls other discoveries from the British Isles, but this time from dry land. These include both hoards and single finds. As they have recently been discussed by Roger Thomas (in press), they need not be considered at much length.

Thomas notes that occasional dry-land finds are associated with human bones. These finds share one important feature with the weaponry from rivers. In several cases the swords appear to have been deliberately broken or bent across the blade. These features are characteristic of the treatment afforded to material in Continental graves (e.g. Warmenbol 1988b), and emphasise the element of deliberate destruction that accompanied the provision of offerings. The same characteristics have been noted with finds that have not been discovered with bones, and suggest that such practices may have been more widespread than first appears. Thomas also notes that the original accounts of a number of finds refer to human 'bones' rather than skeletons, again emphasising the possibility that such remains had already received preliminary treatment. This is consistent with the evidence from the Thames.

In addition to these finds, there are tantalising suggestions that some British *ornament hoards* had been discovered with human bones. These have been considered by Robin Taylor, who suggests that once again they may be associated with funerary ritual (1982, 15–16). This is particularly interesting since some of the hoards may contain complete sets of personal ornaments. The crucial difference between these collections and the weapon finds, however, is that they occur on land, whereas weapons are more characteristic of watery locations. Here we should note that although most of the Scandinavian 'ritual hoards' do come from bogs, between 23 per cent and 41 per cent of those identified by Levy were discovered on dry land (Levy 1982, 26–42).

It is difficult to take these arguments further when so much of the crucial evidence is poorly recorded. However, even these few finds may be sufficient to urge caution in our interpretation of apparently mundane deposits of metalwork. Broken weapons may be a feature of graves and deposits containing scattered bones, but they are also a major feature of the Late Bronze Age founders' hoards, which supposedly consist of worn-out items awaiting recycling by the smith. In the same way, founders' hoards frequently contain half-melted objects which are thought of as scrap metal. In the light of this discussion, a certain ambiguity remains. This is also true when we consider that the small metal objects found with cremation burials can look just the same as the material in these deposits. Where metalwork is found in direct association with bones, every effort must be made to ensure that all the evidence is analysed.

Votive and utilitarian deposits

When it comes to studying utilitarian hoards, it would be easy to adopt an agnostic position. Our evidence is extremely ambiguous. If we accept that many of these hoards are connected with the organisation of metalworking, we find it difficult to explain why so much material was deposited and never recovered. If we treat every metal hoard as evidence of intentional deposition, however, it is just as hard to understand the contents of these collections.

Despite this problem, two observations are widely accepted. There is little doubt that during the Late Bronze Age increasing numbers of broken objects enter the archaeological record. At the same time, metal analysis reveals that a growing proportion of bronze metalwork was made from non-local raw materials and that large parts of Europe were linked, however indirectly, to the same source areas (Northover 1982). There were certain changes in these networks during this period – for example, there was a shifting balance between Atlantic and Central European metal sources – but no one would doubt that many of the objects found in the archaeological record were made from reused materials. As more attention is paid to metal analysis, and to the detailed study of how different items were made, it becomes difficult to reject traditional interpretations of these hoards entirely. On the other hand, it is all the more important to discuss them against a wider background.

Let us begin by considering the evidence from two hoards which are unusual because they were recovered by careful excavation. Their contexts and contents were recorded in great detail, and the individual objects have been analysed in the laboratory. The Villethiery hoard comes from the Yonne in north-central France (Mordant, Mordant and Prampart 1976), and the hoard

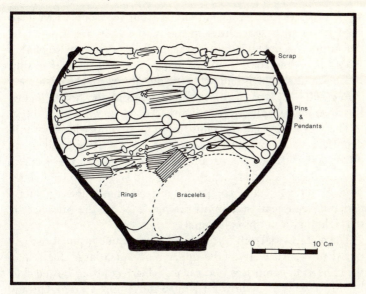

Fig. 24 A reconstruction of the Villethiery hoard, north-central France. (After Mordant, Mordant and Prampart 1976)

from Petters Sports Field, Egham, is from a settlement site in the Thames valley (Needham in O'Connell 1986, 22–60).

The Villethiery hoard dates from the 12th century BC and was apparently deposited in isolation. It comprised 900 metal objects which had been buried inside a pottery vessel (Fig. 24). The great majority of these artefacts were personal ornaments, mainly pins. The contents of the hoard had been carefully subdivided and some may have been packed in separate bags. Rings and bracelets were found in distinct groups on the bottom of the pot, and both had been covered by collections of bronze pendants and small bundles of pins. The remaining artefacts tended to be found in the upper part of this vessel, whilst the ornaments as a whole were covered by a deposit of more fragmentary items, interpreted as scrap metal.

It seems likely that the ornaments in this hoard were freshly made, and they were in mint condition. Meticulous examination of the technology and decoration of these objects suggested the work of several different individuals, but they appear to have been using such specialised methods that they are thought to constitute a single school. In the traditional terminology this would be a 'merchant's hoard', consisting as it does of freshly made artefacts which had yet to be distributed to the customer. The careful storage of the different types in the hoard makes this an eminently plausible solution.

The more fragmentary items found in the upper levels of this deposit have a quite different character. As well as small ornaments, they include ingots and pieces of broken axes, sickles, swords, daggers and spearheads. It would be usual to view these finds as scrap metal, brought together to make new artefacts, and this argument is certainly strengthened by the presence of the eight ingots in this collection.

The metalwork from Petters Sports Field came from more than one deposit. All were in the upper filling of a large ditch, and the collection comprises two caches which had been buried side by side in bags or shallow pits, and a third more scattered group from an equivalent stratigraphic position against the ditch terminal. The material probably dates from the end of the Bronze Age. It was found on the edge of a contemporary settlement, which has produced other evidence of metalworking. In particular, the mould for a bronze axe was recovered during earlier excavation on the site.

The material in the hoard falls into five broad categories, although some of the objects are extremely fragmentary. The main types comprise: tools (axes, knives, sickles and gouges); weapons (swords, spearheads, a ferrule and a chape); ornaments (a bracelet and a pin); sheet metalwork (cauldrons and a bucket); and metalworking residues (sheet bronze, bronze plate, casting jets, bronze waste and ingot fragments). Unlike the Villethiery hoard, newly made objects played little part, although there was one unfinished axe.

In the traditional interpretation this would be a 'founder's hoard', dominated as it is by broken objects and metalworking debris, but the fact that it was recovered by excavation means that this idea can be investigated in some detail. Analysis has concentrated on three aspects of this material: its metal composition; the treatment of its constituent elements; and its possible place in the manufacturing process. In each case the distinction between the two caches has proved to be all-important.

Two metal sources were represented among the finds. One consisted of unalloyed copper, to which lead would have been added, and the other of alloyed metal with a likely origin in northern France. Virtually all the metal with a high lead content was found in the same cache, suggesting that the two collections had been formed in order to make different types of artefact. The same impression is provided by the treatment of the objects in these groups. One group had been broken up to a greater extent than its counterpart, perhaps suggesting that the separate caches were to be melted down in crucibles of different sizes. This is likely to have occurred if they were intended for making different types of artefact.

Several kinds of fragmentary artefacts may have contributed raw material to this process, including tools, weapons, ornaments and sheet metal. In this respect the collection from Petters Sports Field recalls the earlier hoard from Villethiery, but in this case scrap metal predominates, rather than newly made objects. The British material has another distinguishing feature, since it contains metalwork from a number of different regional traditions. Whilst most of the types did have a local circulation, in four cases (a bugle-shaped fitting, a chape, one type of sickle and a distinctive form of socketed axe) the items deposited in the hoard were at the edge of their wider distribution. In this case an explanation was offered for the non-recovery of this material: since it might have been deposited at the end of the Bronze Age, the raw material in the hoard could have lost its value with the adoption of iron. If so, it might not have been worth taking the trouble to retrieve it.

In both these cases detailed analysis provides convincing support for the traditional way of looking at utilitarian hoards. Where less information is available, greater caution is required. Three features that link these hoards do seem to characterise a large number of deposits, and where at least two of these can be clearly documented it is hard to refute the orthodox interpretation. First, both hoards contain newly made items. These predominate at Villethiery, but there is an unsharpened axe from Petters Sports Field which is probably to be interpreted in the same way. This approach will only realise its full potential if the contents of hoards are investigated by careful wear analysis, as they have been in Scandinavia and southern England (Kristiansen 1978; Taylor 1988). Secondly, both of the hoards contain a range of metalworking residues, as well as the more ambiguous collections of broken objects that are usually described as scrap metal. Between them they include most types of evidence for metalworking – ingots, slag, casting jets and plate scrap – although neither contains a crucible or a mould. Whilst offerings might be made of raw material *per se,* it seems unlikely that small casting jets and fragments of slag would be accumulated for this purpose. Lastly it is clear that both hoards had been buried in locations where recovery would have been easy, had the occasion arisen. In fact the Petters hoard may have been placed in the top of a silting ditch, not because it was an easy place to bury it, but because the earthwork itself provided a convenient marker. It need hardly be added that this last observation is not enough to establish the interpretation of any particular hoard. Even so, these kinds of evidence are widespread, especially during the Late Bronze Age when we know that a large amount of metal was being recycled.

If we do accept the merits of the traditional interpretation, at least where hoard finds are documented in detail, we meet with a different problem. It may not be so difficult to distinguish between 'ritual' and 'non-ritual' hoards, but it is hard to understand how the two were related to one another. In order to investigate this question, we must return to some characteristics of the Petters and Villethiery hoards which have yet to enter the discussion.

One feature that these hoards have in common is the presence of both axes and sickles. This would be unproblematical, but for the fact that the two types so often dominate collections of Later Bronze Age metalwork. In many cases just one of these artefacts may account for the complete contents of a hoard (Pl. 11). Both the objects may have played a specialised role during the Early Bronze Age, but students of later periods tend to interpret them as everyday tools. The situation may be rather more complex than this bland outline suggests. There is no doubt that many of the axes *had* been used before they were deposited, just as there is no question that a far greater number of tools were being made during this period. Nevertheless, it is hard to see how an 'industrial revolution', as Burgess terms it, could be based so largely on the production of one kind of artefact (Burgess 1968, 17). The same is true of sickles. The Later Bronze Age does see a major reorganisation of food production, in which the harvesting of cereals was undoubtedly an important element, but again the number of these objects to enter the archaeological record seems to be quite disproportionate. Harding (1976) has tried to bring both types of evidence together and to define the agricultural tool kit used during this period, but this approach raises certain difficulties. There are many cases in which axes *are* associated with sickles, as they are in both of the hoards considered here, but axes are most common in Western Europe and sickles in Central and Eastern Europe. In each area large numbers can be found in hoards, but their main areas of circulation do not coincide. It is improbable that West European land use was based mainly on the axe and that in Central Europe farming depended on an abundant supply of sickles, and it seems more likely that these types possessed a dual role, serving both as everyday tools and as standard units of metal.

This would help to resolve several difficulties experienced in the study of utilitarian hoards. It would make the rarity of obvious ingots much easier to understand; although these are present in both the Petters Sports Field and Villethiery hoards, they are by no means common in other deposits. It might explain why so much of the material apparently reduced to scrap metal consisted of these two types of object, sometimes to the exclusion of other artefacts entirely. It would help to account for the number of 'merchants' hoards' containing apparently unfinished axes, and it would also account for a strange group of axes produced at the very end of the Bronze Age which were so poorly made that they could never have been used at all. These Breton socketed axes are found in very large numbers and frequently occur in hoards without any other kind of artefact. They were made in a restricted range of weights and have sometimes been claimed as a type of primitive currency – 'hache-monnaie' (Briard 1965). A comparable phenomenon is represented by the Hallstatt B winged axes imported into Scandinavia. Again, these are often

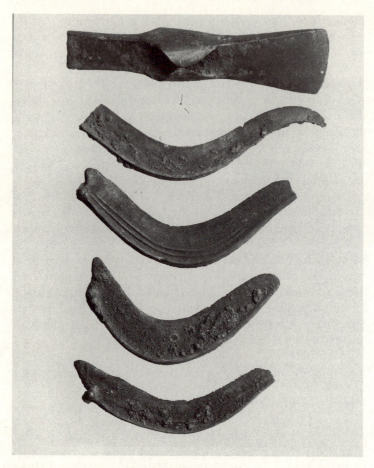

Plate 11 Hoard containing four sickles and a palstave from Lamenz,
Saxony. Photograph: British Museum.

unfinished or damaged, leading Thrane to suggest that they were
important as a source of metal (Thrane 1972).

Having drawn attention to the potential role of axes and sickles
as standard units of raw material, let us turn to the striking mixture of types that are present in both these hoards. During the
Early Bronze Age an elaborate protocol seems to have governed
the uses – and certainly the deposition – of different types of

artefact. Although the roles of particular types could change, similar conventions were in force in the Later Bronze Age. In Western Europe we saw how axes lost their status, as weapons were deposited in rivers rather than burial mounds. We also saw the contrasting contexts of ornament sets in Scandinavia and the British Isles, and the ways in which these were deposited in separate locations from the finds of weaponry. In the utilitarian hoards these divisions can break down completely. The Petters Sports Field hoard includes a bracelet, but it also contains swords, spearheads, a ferrule and a chape. These are specialised types, like the bucket and cauldrons represented in this group, but they were also associated with a variety of tools. Very much the same happened at Villethiery. Apart from an extraordinary number of fine ornaments, the hoard contains three types of weapon (dagger, sword and spear), as well as the axes and sickles considered earlier. Again it seems as if the formal divisions expressed in other types of deposit no longer retained their mystique.

This is a general characteristic of utilitarian hoards, and one which to some extent runs counter to the broader developments traced in this discussion. Where categories are mixed, however, the objects themselves are often destroyed. This is a particular feature of the Late Bronze Age, and it is for this reason that such tendencies are more strongly exemplified in the Petters Sports Field hoard than they are in the earlier deposit at Villethiery. Nowhere is this development more clearly illustrated than in the Carp's Tongue hoards in Britain. Here the fragmentation of elaborate metalwork reaches its zenith, and a whole class of fine weapons is best known from fragments included in collections of scrap metal (Coombs and Bradshaw 1979; Burgess and Colquhoun 1988).

Both these features can profitably be considered together with an observation made about several of the items in the Petters Sports Field hoard. Four of the types found there are outside their main distribution. This often applies to the unexpected combinations of artefacts found in 'mixed' hoards of this kind. At its simplest it seems as if items which had been deposited in a very structured manner are most likely to appear in scrap hoards *outside* their normal distribution. The same applies to collections of material containing objects that are not found together in wet deposits. In effect specialised deposits of a particular type of artefact may be ringed by more varied deposits in which these same items shed their exclusive character (Bradley 1985a and 1987).

This happens very widely and the range of variation can be illustrated by a few examples. First, it is worth considering the question of association. We have already seen how the most specialised deposits of this period maintained a fairly rigid separation between categories, and often between deposits of tools, weapons and ornaments In the Middle Bronze Age of southern England it even seems as if material in these three groups may have been made and distributed separately (Rowlands 1976). In this case the most specialised deposits are probably the weapons found in the Fenland, the Thames and other watery locations, and the ornament hoards, most of which are located nearer to the south coast. This would suggest two distinct patterns of deposition whose contents and distribution scarcely overlap (Bradley 1984, fig. 5.2). At the same time, most of the Middle Bronze Age tool hoards do not include other categories of material. When we consider those cases in which the contents of the three groups do overlap, we encounter a striking geographical pattern (Fig. 25). In the Thames Valley, where the most elaborate weapons were deposited in the river, the three classes of material were kept apart, but outside this area an increasing proportion of the hoards includes a mixture of these different types of material. The rigid categorisation of artefacts that is found in the Thames valley proves to have been less tenacious in more distant areas (Bradley 1985a).

The same tendency is apparent in Denmark, where the ornament hoards have such a distinctive character. Here it seems that we can recognise separate groups of male- and female-associated hoards, defined by finds of weapons and ornaments respectively (Levy 1982). It is likely that we can also recognise whole sets of women's ornaments. During Period V it seems as if the most complex of these hoards are to be found in Jutland. These appear to have been deposited with some formality, and they can contain as many as five sets of personal ornaments. With notable exceptions, those in other areas are somewhat simpler. In the light of our discussion of the British evidence, it is interest-

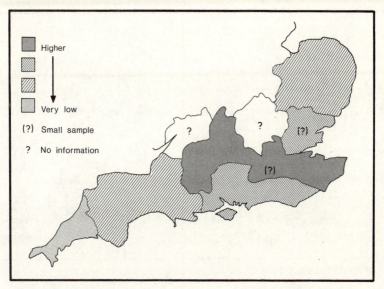

Fig. 25 The proportion of unmixed hoards in the Middle Bronze Age
of southern England, plotted by former counties. (After Bradley 1985a;
data from Rowlands 1976)

ing to consider those cases in which the specifically female-associated artefacts are found in the same deposits as male-associated
weapons (Fig. 26). Such 'mixed' groups avoid the most complex
ornament hoards of Jutland and are found some distance away,
on Funen and Zealand. In some cases it is tempting to relate
these deposits to the accumulation and processing of the metal
itself, as 63 per cent of the mixed hoards of Period IV and 55
per cent of those dated to Period V contain scrap or metalworking
debris. Half the hoard finds of socketed hammers also come from
groups of this kind (Bradley 1987, 355).

So far it has appeared that the characteristic crossing of categories seen at Petters Sports Field and Villethiery can happen
towards the edges of the areas in which particular artefact types
had been employed in a specialised manner. The same may also
apply to the treatment afforded to these objects in ostensibly
non-ritual hoards. Consider the case of the British Middle Bronze
Age rapiers published by Burgess and Gerloff (1981). This is

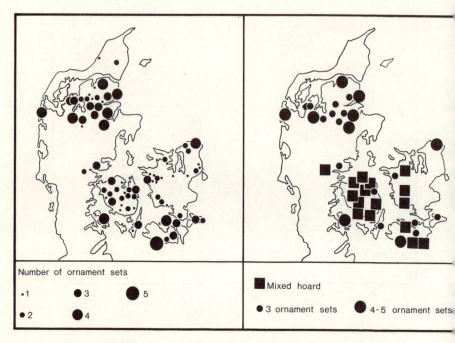

Fig. 26 The distribution of Period V ornament hoards in Denmark, showing the number of personal sets in each hoard (left) and the concentration of mixed hoards on Funen and Zealand (right). (After Bradley 1987; data from Levy 1982)

another group of finds which in normal circumstances were deposited in extremely specialised locations. The majority are known to come from rivers or bogs, particularly in the Thames and the Fenland, whilst less exactly provenanced examples often retain a distinctive patina from their deposition in water. A smaller number of finds, however, do come from hoards, where they can be associated, not with other weapons, but with tools and ornaments. It is notable that except in the Fenland, where the two patterns overlap, the distribution of these 'mixed' deposits rings the distribution of water finds, with most examples near to the coast (Bradley 1987, 355–7). This is consistent with the types of spatial patterning considered earlier, but in this case we can also take into account the distinctive condition of these

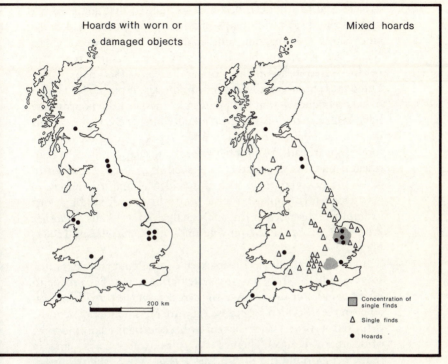

Fig. 27 The distribution of dirks and rapiers in hoards and single finds in England, Scotland and Wales, showing those hoard finds containing worn or damaged objects (left) and mixed hoards in which rapiers are found with tools and/or ornaments (right). (After Bradley 1987; data from Burgess and Gerloff 1981)

weapons. Very much the same pattern is revealed when we plot the distribution of those hoards which are specifically noted as containing worn or broken rapiers. Again, these are often found near to the coast and virtually enclose the distribution of more specialised deposits from watery locations (Fig. 27). It is particularly striking that this exercise highlights many of the hoards with mixed contents considered earlier (*ibid.*).

Very much the same pattern can be seen in the simple contrast between the distribution of particular types of river metalwork and their occurrence in dry-land hoards. In the British Late

Bronze Age this pattern becomes so marked that some 60 per cent of the distribution maps provided in O'Connor's detailed study show this phenomenon: single finds may be deposited in specialised locations, but artefacts of just the same types can be discovered in hoards in peripheral areas (1980, maps 1–82). Often these hoards are found near to the sea. A particular feature of this sequence is that the items in so many of the hoards may have been broken up for their metal content. Examples of this pattern include a variety of weapon types, among them basal-looped spearheads, Ballintober swords and chapes (Fig. 28). Continental metalwork is rarely published in a suitable manner to allow direct comparison with this evidence, and it is uncertain how frequently similar patterns are to be found, although one example is illustrated in Kubach's analysis of wet finds and other groups of Bronze and Iron Age finds in North Hessen (1983; Fig. 29).

A startling parallel to this pattern comes from an unexpected source. Only recently has any systematic attempt been made to investigate Later Bronze Age shipwrecks, which provide a valuable source of evidence because they are not intentional deposits (Muckelroy 1981). These have now been recognised off the coast of southern France (Hugues 1965; Bouscaras 1971) and in the waters around the British Isles (Dean 1984). Their contents share several striking characteristics. They contain a mixture of different categories of object, often in very large numbers, including tools, weapons and ornaments. Many of these are worn or fragmentary, and in some cases they seem to have been cut or broken for easier packing (Muckelroy 1980 and 1981) – this makes no sense at all unless these cargoes are regarded as raw material, rather than finished objects. A striking feature of these collections is that they contain a variety of artefact types which are outside their normal distribution, and in some cases the finds from a single shipwreck may draw on material from a number of widely separated areas. This is particularly true of the Middle Bronze Age hoard from Dover, which consisted of artefacts of French origin. Comparable material is rare or absent in southern England, but metal analysis shows that objects in purely insular styles could be made out of raw materials imported across the Channel (Northover 1982). This may provide some indication

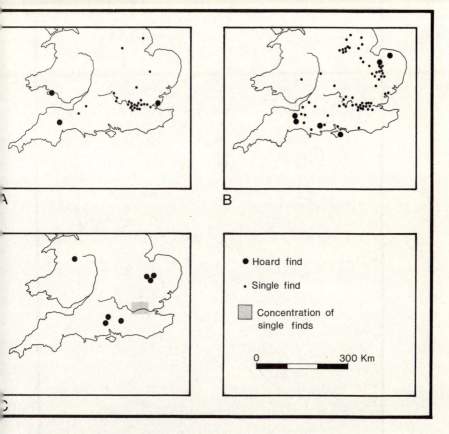

Fig. 28 The distributions of (A) Ballintober and related swords, (B) leaf-shaped basal-looped spearheads and (C) lozenge-section chapes in southern Britain, emphasising the distinction between hoard finds and single finds. (After O'Connor 1980)

of how efficiently the movement of such material was managed. As Muckleroy has pointed out (1981, 291), the contents of these shipwrecks have much in common with those of dry-land hoards.

In fact the general patterns exhibited by such material are so clearcut that it is easy to recognise exceptional cases. These are particularly important for any interpretation of non-ritual hoards. We have already noticed important differences between

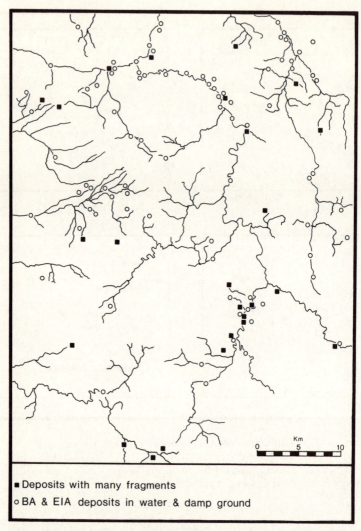

Fig. 29 The distributions of Bronze Age and Early Iron Age water finds and 'non-ritual' hoards in north Hessen, West Germany. (After Kubach 1983)

the finds from Villethiery and Petters Sports Field. There are differences of date between these collections, and the later of the two deposits contains a large component of scrap metal. This contrast is found much more widely and is consistent with the evidence of metal analysis, which suggests that the recycling of raw materials went on at an accelerated rate during the Late Bronze Age. This is important because eventually the so-called founders' hoards came to dominate the archaeological record so completely that these spatial patterns could be submerged. As we shall see, the paucity of river deposits from the same period also needs explaining, as does the non-recovery of so much of the metalwork. These questions will be addressed later in this chapter.

We have now drawn attention to a number of wider issues that have not received their due from specialists on Bronze Age metalwork. There are the curious problems posed by the over-representation of axes and sickles, and by their concentration in different parts of Europe. There is the difficulty created by the mixing of artefact types that had been kept rigidly separate in other deposits, and there are the special problems posed by the drastic treatment meted out to objects that under different circumstances would have been deposited with some formality. We have seen that to some extent these practices happened in separate parts of their distribution. At the same time, there are clear signs of chronological development, from a tightly struc-tured pattern in the Early Bronze Age to the virtual loss of order in the developed Late Bronze Age. How are all these features to be understood?

Interpretations

Introduction

At the end of Chapter 2 we were faced with a striking contrast in metal deposits between Central and Western Europe. Closer to the sources of this material large numbers of artefacts were being accumulated in hoards, and also in contemporary graves. There was evidence for the early development of ingots, which took the form of unfinished neck rings, and, as objects moved outside their local area of circulation, the rigid separation of different types sometimes broke down completely. In such cases they could be found together in hoards, which also provide evidence that artefacts were being used as a source of metal.

We contrasted those striking patterns with the very different evidence from areas further away from the metal sources. Here the hoards had a more distinctive structure, and contained smaller amounts of metalwork. They complemented the material found in graves but comprised a largely separate range of artefact types. There was no real evidence for the accumulation of scrap metal in these deposits.

To some extent this contrast could be explained by the proximity of major metal sources in Central Europe, and their absence in parts of Western Europe and throughout Scandinavia. This had influenced the process through which new raw materials were first adopted, and we identified a significant contrast between the treatment of metal artefacts in those areas in which they had been assimilated gradually into a Neolithic material culture, and others where they were introduced more abruptly, often through the Bell Beaker network.

A further contrast became apparent when we considered the evidence of contemporary occupation sites. In Central Europe the period that saw the largest metal hoards and some of the richest burials was also one in which a major class of fortified settlement came into being. This kind of settlement showed evidence of craft production and contained concentrations of exotic artefacts. Evidence of centralised food storage suggests that such sites dominated a wider hinterland.

By contrast, fortified sites of similar character were generally absent in Western and Northern Europe, where, with only limited exceptions, settlement sites are elusive, or of relatively ephemeral character. The major features of the second millennium BC were burial mounds like those in Central Europe, and in some areas there were elaborate ceremonial centres. The location of these sites was often determined by a long history of ritual activity, extending back into the Neolithic period, and newer monuments tended to cluster around much older constructions. To this extent at least, the dead seem to have eclipsed the living.

In Western Europe the Later Bronze Age marks a drastic break with such long-lasting traditions and has more in common with developments in Central Europe (Coles and Harding 1979, ch.

10; Rowlands 1984). Settlements are easy to identify, and some were extensive and remained in use over a long period. Hill settlements, and sometimes hillforts, were established in many areas and again provide evidence for the large-scale storage of staples, suggesting that they may have been integrated into the business of food production. Like the fortified sites in Central Europe, they seem to have played a part in the acquisition, and even the production, of fine artefacts. There is evidence of corresponding changes in the landscape, with an accelerated rate of clearance and indications of intensified agricultural production. In Britain and Ireland we find evidence for large-scale land division, with regular systems of fields and larger 'estates' (Bradley 1984, ch. 5; Darvill 1987, ch. 5).

These changes are undoubtedly reflected by innovations in the bronze industry. In general terms the rise of defended settlements ran in parallel with the development of an extended range of weaponry. More important, the changes in the productive landscape must have been effected with the aid of a new range of metal tools. During the Earlier Bronze Age a rather restricted set of metal implements was in use, and a variety of stone and bone artefacts continued to play an important role in everyday life. During the Later Bronze Age, however, a number of new types developed, some of them designed for very specific tasks. In Britain their adoption is reflected by a reduction in the range of stone tools being made (Ford, Bradley, Hawkes and Fisher 1984). A good illustration of these points comes from Harding's discussion of contemporary hoards in Central Europe, where the number of separate types increased between two and four times (1984, 142).

It was only during this phase that the past lost its hold over later generations. This is apparent in those areas where burial mounds were no longer built or maintained, and even when barrows were constructed these were much smaller than their predecessors. For the most part ceremonial monuments in Britain were deserted, or were preserved in islands of uncultivated land. The same is often true of large barrow cemeteries, but isolated mounds did not fare so well, and some were levelled by cultivation during the Later Bronze Age. In those cases in which ceremonial centres were destroyed or converted to more mundane uses, the

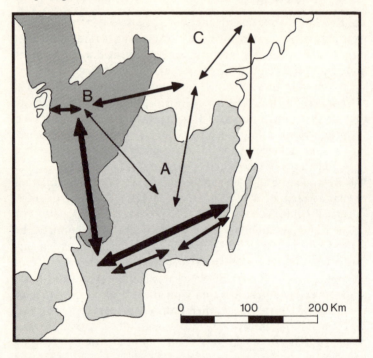

Fig. 30 The contrasting distributions of Later Bronze Age axes and swords in southern Scandinavia. The axe finds divide into three regional groups (A, B and C), whilst the relative strength of long-distance connections between different groups of swords are indicated by bars linking the main areas in which they are found. (Data from Larsson 1984)

older sites were affected first, before this process was extended to the later monuments (Bradley 1981a). Even so, very few were to remain inviolate throughout the first millennium BC.

The importance of being exotic

Access to the metal sources remained extremely important, but it is reflected in different ways. One of the characteristic features of the Later Bronze Age is the enormous distance travelled by some types of artefact. This is well illustrated by comparing the

132

distributions of axes and swords (Fig. 30). Whereas the axes cluster into a series of small regional groups, each with its own stylistic devices, the closest links between sword types may occur over considerable distances, with blank areas in between (e.g. Larsson 1984). This emphasises the importance of long-distance connections in the distribution of such metalwork, and there seems little doubt that the ability to acquire fine artefacts of exotic origin carried a considerable premium. This is also apparent from Sørensen's study of Late Bronze Age metalwork in Scandinavia (1987). Here it seems as if the distinction between local and foreign products was so important that it affected the manner in which these items entered the archaeological record. Still more significant, however, was the absolute *rarity* of individual types. Specifically in Scandinavia the importance of long-distance contacts is vividly illustrated by the evidence of Bronze Age rock art, in which depictions of weapons are most frequent in precisely those areas where the artefacts themselves are uncommon (Larsson 1986, 143). As we have seen, the art also carries references to an iconography of non-local origin.

We can see similar factors at work at the level of the individual site. At Bargeroosterveld in the Netherlands a small wooden shrine, dating from the Middle Bronze Age, was found during peat cutting in 1957 (van Zeist and Waterbolk 1961). This seems to have formed the focus for a series of metal hoards in the surrounding landscape, whose contents had been introduced from other parts of Europe. According to Butler, who analysed these finds, all but three of these objects had been imported from distant areas, extending from Central Europe to the Atlantic coast. In his words they are 'an astonishingly cosmopolitan lot' (1960, 108).

It is easier to understand the power of long-distance relations than it is to appreciate how important it was that *the metal itself* should be of non-local origin. This may seem a strange observation, but we have already suggested that similar considerations had mattered during earlier periods. It is quite remarkable that the distribution of 'wet' deposits is most obvious in those areas which lack suitable raw materials of their own. Thus the rivers which contain major groups of Bronze Age metalwork are effectively surrounded by the main ore sources, but do not extend

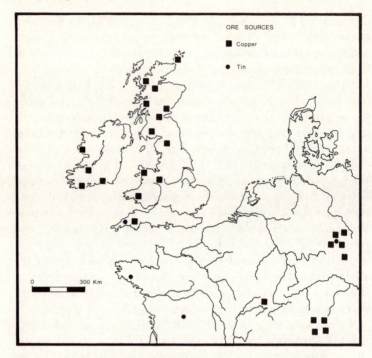

Fig. 31 The distribution of ore sources in Northern and Western Europe, compared with the major rivers containing metalwork. (Ore sources from Gimbutas 1965, Penhallurick 1986 and Tylecote 1987; the rivers are those considered by Torbrügge 1971.)

far into those regions (Fig. 31; Bradley 1989c). On a continental scale this is apparent from the long-established contrast between the distribution of Later Bronze Age grave finds and the discoveries of similar artefacts in bogs or rivers. Even on a more local scale, in Ireland and the British Isles, it is noticeable how the distribution of finds from watery locations is less pronounced in those areas in which metal could be obtained. So important were those considerations that they may help to account for the otherwise anomalous feature that in Britain artefacts made of European metal gradually eclipsed the products of local sources (Northover 1982). This may have been a deliberate choice on the part of a social élite, determined by cultural preference rather than economic circumstance. Normal laws of supply and demand did not apply.

There is another sense in which the sequence in Western Europe did not follow the pattern already established in Central Europe (Coles and Harding 1979, chs. 7 and 10; Rowlands 1984). In certain areas it involved a more active rejection of past practice. Many factors could have influenced this transformation. Climatic change and the wasting of marginal land may have sapped the economic fortunes of the existing system (Bradley 1981b). Changes in access to exotic goods may have undermined the position of the élite, as communities in different areas competed for access to such artefacts, leading to drastic changes in political geography (Rowlands 1980; Brun 1988). The situation is confused, although it is clear that changes happened rapidly, especially when compared with the stability of the earlier system.

Giving gifts

The changing contexts of metal deposits must be considered as part of these wider developments, but they differed markedly between Western and Northern Europe, and it will be necessary to treat these areas separately before we attempt to make any direct comparisons between them. In each case the most striking developments concern the changing contexts of the metal finds, and the abandonment of elaborate grave offerings in favour of new forms of consumption. Both areas provide hints of a transitional period that may prove to be very revealing. In Denmark, for example, a number of ornament hoards were deposited on the sites of older burial mounds (Levy 1982, 30–4), but nearly all of these hoards belong to the major period of change (Montelius IV). In Britain some of the last barrows to be built in the established Early Bronze Age tradition lack any burials, whilst others contain the customary grave offerings even when there is no sign of a body (Bradley 1984, 95). After that time, however, the contrast was complete.

The key to understanding the Later Bronze Age deposits in *Western Europe* probably lies with the interpretation of earlier grave goods. These can be regarded, not necessarily as the *property* of the deceased, but as a specific set of gifts provided by the survivors (Barrett 1989a). Sometimes they may have belonged to the dead person, but this cannot be demonstrated. Rich burials have a discontinuous history, and, as we suggested in Chapter 1, often appear most prominently in periods of conflict or crisis, when traditional norms might need reinforcing through the consumption of valuables. The provision of funeral offerings was firmly linked to the death of one individual, and that individual might be commemorated by an earthwork monument.

We have seen that in many ways the Later Bronze Age represented a break with the past. This applies to the continued use of specialised locations as much as it does to traditional practices like the provision of grave goods. The most important innovations were the adoption of flat cemeteries for part of the population and the construction of increasingly meagre burial mounds for others. To some extent the declining emphasis on monuments is associated with the destruction of the body by cremation, and possibly with a rite of excarnation in which the individual's remains might be dispersed.

If the provision of funerary offerings was detached from traditional locations and traditional burial rites, there would be scope for new developments. This is particularly true if the practice of making such gifts was assimilated into an equally long-lived tradition of votive offerings in watery locations – a tradition which hitherto had run in parallel to the provision of grave goods. In short, there was ample opportunity for the survivors to turn established practices to their own ends. And this they did.

The character of the new system is highlighted by the emphasis on weaponry. This is important for two reasons. First, it reminds us that river finds in Western Europe may be the sequel to *only some* of the funeral gifts of the Early Bronze Age. Female-associated artefacts are much less common in these locations. If women's graves had any successor during this period, it may have been the ornament hoards found on dry land (see Bradley 1984, 110–11). The dominance of weapon finds is also revealing, because it emphasises the potential for competitive display provided by these deposits. There is also evidence that warfare was of growing importance at this time, since some of the weapons found in rivers show signs of combat damage (cf. Savage 1979; Needham 1979, 113). Similarly, the Later Bronze Age saw the

increasing use of hill settlements, and even of defensive monuments (Coles and Harding 1979).

Such developments are certainly consistent with what is known
about other aspects of Later Bronze Age society (*ibid.*, ch. 10;
Rowlands 1984). Where the evidence has been studied in any
detail, there seems to be a concern with the definition of territory
and the enclosure of agricultural land. There may also be signs
that the food supply was regulated through centralised storage
in the earliest hillforts. It is hard to imagine a sharper contrast
with the Early Bronze Age system, in which access to the supernatural had been of equivalent importance and the landscape
of the living had been defined almost entirely by the monuments
surviving from the past. Given the new emphasis on food production, it is not surprising to find that feasting became an important
institution in the Later Bronze Age. This is evidenced by formal
deposits of animal bones, and possibly by specialised facilities
for the large-scale cooking of meat. Some of these sites have
produced finds of fine metalwork (Larsson 1986, 150–8; Barfield
and Hodder 1987; O'Drisceoil 1988).

We have already traced a long history of specialised deposits,
whose contents seem to reflect the decisive importance of exotica,
and of associations with faraway places. In Western Europe this
is most apparent from finds of foreign artefacts, but in Northern
Europe these connections are reinforced by an iconography which
is shared with another, more public medium – rock art. At times
close analysis of both kinds of information can suggest links
between widely separated areas. Such connections may provide
evidence of regular exchange partnerships between élites in different regions (Rowlands 1980). On the other hand, such links could
not be relied upon to uphold a system of stable ranking. The
prestige accrued through the acquisition of exotic goods was
always vulnerable to changes of fashion or to fluctuations in
the supply of artefacts from outside the local system. Again, the
formation of competing alliances might divert these items to other
groups.

There could be further problems within the local system, since
prestige is the common currency of non-market societies. This
is best created by 'inflicting debt' on rival parties (Earle 1989,
85). This programme could be put into practice through a cycle

of competitive feasting, which would ultimately reflect the success of the different actors in controlling food production. Otherwise it could rely on the mechanisms of gift exchange. As we saw in Chapter 1, this is an inefficient way of creating lasting obligations, since an advantage gained on one occasion can be lost at another. The debts created by one transaction can be discharged, as new obligations are created which give the advantage to the other party.

As Gregory (1980) has suggested, one way of resolving this problem is to make gifts to the gods. This is not done with the intention of soliciting a counter-gift, but precisely because offerings of this kind cannot be returned. This is particularly obvious where the transaction involves their physical destruction, or where they are deposited in locations from which they could not be recovered. Offerings of this kind provide the ideal arena for conspicuous consumption. They can be public and impressive. They allow direct competition between the rival parties, and offerings made in this way are taken out of circulation permanently. This means that it is more difficult for others to make up lost ground, since the supply that is available to them is automatically depleted by this process.

If some of the river finds are to be regarded as funeral gifts, it seems possible that they could have played a dual role. They may have been seen as offerings to the supernatural – or to the deceased individual – and to that extent they were taken out of circulation in perpetuity. At the same time, their deposition might provide the ideal opportunity for the mourners to stake a claim. Such lavish offerings might provide a way of fixing status and of claiming the prestige associated with the deceased. We have seen how this system took over from a long-established tradition of 'wet' deposits, and it is not necessary to suggest that all, or most of the weapon finds, were related to funerals or other rites of passage. In any event it seems possible that claims of this kind involved a request for support from the supernatural.

This may seem to be empty speculation, but there appear to be three sound reasons for favouring this approach. We have already mentioned the growing importance of fine weapons during this period, and the increasing role of hillforts in contemporary society. It is revealing that in some areas we find a complementary relationship between the use of defensible locations and the consumption of weapons. It is notable how the first defended sites in Britain have a different distribution from the main groups of river metalwork. The hilltop settlements are a feature mainly of western Britain, whilst most of the weapons are found in rivers discharging into the North Sea (Bradley 1984, fig. 5.3). Elsewhere the chronology of river finds and settlements of this type can show a rather similar relationship. Thus in Baden Württemberg hill settlements are mainly found in two periods: between Reinecke A2 and Reinecke C, and again between Hallstatt B1 and B3 (Beil 1980). Finds of swords, however, are most frequent between Reinecke A and Hallstatt A, and are less common in Hallstatt B, when these sites became important (Schauer 1971). It is perhaps revealing that the period with the fewest hill settlements in southern Germany (Jockenhövel 1974) was the time when a wide variety of sword styles was being made (Schauer 1971). If these patterns are more than a coincidence, they would suggest that the deposition of weapons played a role equivalent to the military posturing associated with fortified sites. It would be peculiarly apt to employ weapons for these flamboyant deposits, and their consumption in such large numbers might be regarded as a form of surrogate warfare. In Appadurai's striking phrase, such occasions could have served as 'tournaments of value' (1986, 21).

The major deposits of river weaponry have a very striking distribution. As Brun (1988) has recently observed, they are concentrated around the edges of a zone extending from the Rhine across much of France, within which Later Bronze Age artefacts show close connections with the Central European 'Urnfield' province. Further to the west, contemporary metalwork belongs to the Atlantic Bronze Age. The boundary between these two distributions remained fairly stable throughout the Later Bronze Age, and it is that boundary area that contains the major river finds (Fig. 32). Brun suggests that this was a period of political expansion and possibly warfare, and he compares the deposition of weaponry in these locations with the increasingly lavish potlatches that took place during the colonial period in North America. To a certain extent, these finds reinforce the boundary between two distinct cultural provinces, but they also appear

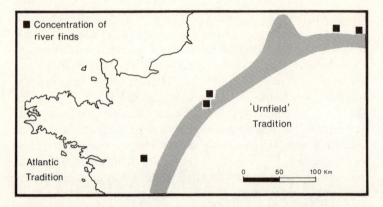

Fig. 32 The contrasting spheres of influences of the Urnfield and Atlantic traditions in France, compared with the locations of major deposits of river weaponry. (After Brun 1988)

to result from a kind of surrogate warfare (*ibid.*).

The last reason for applying Gregory's model to the river metalwork is very much simpler. In a few cases these finds are sufficiently well documented for us to work out the *rate* at which material was being deposited. This statement requires qualification, as the amount of metalwork available for study obviously depends on the intensity with which particular rivers have been dredged, and the steps taken to recover the material found on these occasions. This precludes direct comparison between the contents of *different* rivers, but it does allow the *rate of consumption* in separate periods to be compared. This involves working out the number of dateable finds in relation to the duration of each metalworking phase. This is likely to be a reasonably objective method, since it seems most unlikely that material of one phase was retrieved at the expense of other finds.

In England, Scotland and Wales the clearest contrast is between the quantity of Early Bronze Age daggers found in graves and their successors, the dirks and rapiers, which come from watery locations. Despite the various biases affecting their discovery, there are about 350 daggers and related types, and these were deposited over about 800 years (Gerloff 1975). There are roughly 400 dirks and rapiers from the same areas, but these were in

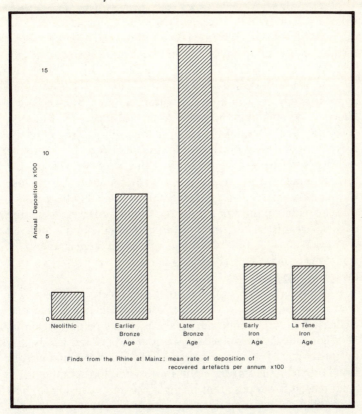

Finds from the Rhine at Mainz; mean rate of deposition of
recovered artefacts per annum x100

Fig. 33 The changing rate of consumption evidenced by prehistoric
river finds from Mainz, West Germany. (After Wegner 1976)

use over only half that period (Burgess and Gerloff 1981). In
short, the rate of deposition doubled. After that time there are
revealing statistics for finds of metalwork from the Thames,
which indicate a remarkably consistent rate of deposition, except
in Late Bronze Age 3 (Needham and Burgess 1980).

In other regions it is possible to see equally striking changes
in the rate at which river finds were deposited. In the Paris Basin,
for example, this increased almost fourfold between Bronze
Moyen and Bronze Final 2, before it fell sharply in Bronze Final
3; exactly the same trend is apparent among finds of weapons

from dry land in this area (Mohen 1977). Wegner's study of the river finds from Mainz reveals a rather similar pattern. Here the rate of deposition had been rising continuously since the Neolithic period and reached a peak in the Later Bronze Age (Fig. 33). At a more detailed level, finds of dated swords show an approximately even rate of deposition between Bronze D and Hallstatt B1, but this increased threefold during Hallstatt B3 (Wegner 1976). A similar pattern is found in an area in which grave finds and river finds overlap. In Upper Austria, where the two types of deposit were favoured in successive periods, the rate at which swords entered the archaeological record rose sharply between Hallstatt A and B3 (Ehrbach-Schönberg 1985). It seems unlikely that the increasing number of deposits in any of these areas is related simply to an increase in population, and the most plausible solution is that it reflects the more lavish provision of offerings. This is entirely consistent with the idea that these had a competitive aspect.

To sum up, it seems possible that in Western Europe a new system of metal deposits became established, not unlike that found in Central Europe during the previous period. Again its adoption may have involved competition for prestige goods, and the provision of generous offerings. To some extent funerary ritual provided the starting point for this development, but there is no reason to suppose that this was the only occasion for acts of conspicuous consumption. In Western Europe it is sometimes possible to relate the development of these transactions to evidence for the mobilisation of productive resources and the adoption of defensive architecture.

Regional differences

This pattern contrasts sharply with the sequence in Northern Europe, and it is to this that we turn our attention next.

We have suggested that in Scandinavia the identification between Later Bronze Age votive deposits and the dead was weaker, or that these finds were more closely integrated into an existing ritual tradition. The deposits of ceremonial equipment are a particularly distinctive feature of this area. There are three main ways in which the Scandinavian evidence differs from the developments which we have just considered, and all may be responsible for the singular course that events were to take.

First, it is important to recognise that metal was used rather differently in these two regions. It is not easy to make direct comparisons, as metalwork can be recycled, but there is some reason to suppose that more artefacts were in circulation across Western Europe than reached Scandinavia. Even though swords were used in the latter area during the Early Bronze Age and did not enter Britain until a later date, about 400 of them are recorded from the Nordic Culture area, compared with 1600 from Britain and Ireland (Bradley 1989d). At the same time, a varied tool kit was in use in the latter area, whilst stone and bone served a number of the same functions in Scandinavia (some of the relevant material was summarised in Chapter 2). When we consider that so much of the metalwork in Northern European deposits has a non-utilitarian character, it is worth asking whether bronze really played a central role in everyday life in the way that it did in other regions. A recent study by Levinson (1983) expresses similar doubts.

Secondly, the distinctive systems observed in Western Europe involved the intensification of food production. This is particularly apparent in the British Isles, but there is little to suggest that a comparable process was taking place in Northern Europe at this time. Although regular field systems are recorded in both regions, those in Britain can date from the Middle Bronze Age, whilst similar systems first appear in Northern Europe at the beginning of the Iron Age (Bradley 1978b). It is only then that there is much sign of agricultural reorganisation, and not until a developed stage in the pre-Roman Iron Age sequence was there much attempt to exercise control over the food supply (Parker Pearson 1984). Defended sites seem to be unrepresented in the Scandinavian Bronze Age, although they are found at a much later date, and it seems possible that society in this area lacked the economic infrastructure necessary to support a programme of conspicuous consumption on the scale observed in Western Europe. Viewed in this light, it is of interest that once the productive base was reorganised, early in the Iron Age, deposits of fine weapons soon appeared (*ibid.*).

Lastly, we have seen that the sequence in Scandinavia exhibits a much greater continuity than its counterpart in Western Europe. The break between the Earlier and Later Bronze Ages was rather less abrupt, and both periods are characterised by a series of distinctive deposits of ceremonial equipment. The importance of such material finds striking confirmation in the rock art of this period. This provides a further reason for believing that we may be studying two rather different societies. In Western Europe a close link may have existed between prestige and personal power, whilst in Scandinavia relations may still have been mediated to some extent through relations with the supernatural, and the trappings of warfare and aggression were less important.

The tradesman's entrance

So far this discussion has skirted the particular problems posed by utilitarian hoards, but it can do so no longer, as these are found on both sides of the North Sea.

The contents of these deposits are remarkable enough in themselves, but they also attract attention because they overlap with the contents of other, more specialised deposits. Indeed, they almost seem to be 'taking material away' from these collections. This applies to the mixture of unrelated types that can be found in these hoards, and to the drastic treatment afforded to particular artefacts.

We have already seen that the demand for metal was so considerable that careful attempts may have been made to measure the supply. This is surely a reason for the standardisation suggested by finds of axes and sickles, and in particular for the small non-functional axes made at the very end of this period. It may go further, and the scrapping of so many discrepant items in particular hoards could have been intended to achieve a set weight of metal. This will require careful investigation. At present the only evidence of a system of standard weights comes from the rare finds of goldwork (Spratling 1980).

The changing relationship between the non-ritual hoards and the more specialised deposits involves both spatial and chronological patterning, but neither is particularly easy to explain. We have seen how mixed hoards, or hoards with fragmentary material, tend to be found outside the areas in which the same types had played more specialised roles. There the tools, weapons and ornaments may have circulated separately, and individual artefact types entered the archaeological record with a curious formality. In contrast, these peripheral deposits, which in certain parts of Europe involve a significant emphasis on coastal areas, seem to stress the nature of these objects as metal and nothing more.

There seem to be two ways of viewing this evidence, although these may not be mutually exclusive. The first approach treats these collections as material brought together for the purpose of balanced dealing: artefacts are exchanged for their metal content, in standard units or as collections of fragmentary objects which have lost all identity. This view follows the work of Sahlins (1974, chs. 5 and 6), Godelier (1977) and Gregory (1982), all of whom postulate a general relationship between the nature of different transactions and the social distance between the parties undertaking them. It would be wrong to make a rigid distinction, but in their terms gifts pass between kin or close allies and may involve a subtle protocol, whilst *commodities* pass between strangers in more balanced transactions, where both parties may attempt to make a profit. This would be more likely to occur where objects had moved outside the areas in which they carried special meanings and their uses might be subject to sumptuary rules. For our purposes this might happen beyond the regions in which such objects played a specialised role. If particular styles of object were used to emphasise ethnic identity in opposition to other groups, the increasingly informal treatment of these artefacts might be found outside their normal distribution. There might also be a tendency to take the same attitude to types which had gone out of fashion and had lost their status in that way. This could explain the observation that many of the utilitarian hoards in Britain seem to date from the *ends* of particular industrial phases (Burgess and Coombs 1979).

In most cases such patterns will be difficult to recognise, since there will be such an element of subjectivity in defining boundary zones. In coastal areas, however, the problem may be less severe, since these could provide neutral places in which strangers might do business. This is a long-established tradition in European archaeology and is seen more clearly in the ports of trade of the Migration period (Hodges 1982). Its extension to Bronze Age studies is supported by the evidence of shipwrecks. Muckleroy's interpretation of this material has features in common with our hypothesis, since he suggests that the metalwork in these collections was traded as raw material precisely because it had moved outside the areas in which it had possessed a special significance (1981, 290–3).

There is another possibility to consider. We have already seen how difficult it would have been to secure an adequate supply of metals in those regions which were well away from the natural sources. Moreover the characteristic distributions of the finer objects sometimes suggest the existence of quite specific alliances between remote areas, through which these artefacts were obtained. There are also signs of the production of weapons and ornaments on some of the high-status sites excavated in Britain during recent years (Bradley 1984, ch. 5; Darvill 1987, ch. 5). There is not enough evidence to show that the supply of non-local metal was monopolised by any one group, although there are good reasons why they may have wanted to do this, especially if the ability to acquire the finest artefacts was a prerogative of high status. The location of rich settlements on rivers like the Thames (Needham and Burgess 1980), the Oise (Agache 1982, 268–70) or the Saône (Bonnamour 1976) may have made it easier to monitor the metal supply in areas remote from its sources.

If this were the case, the evidence of utilitarian hoards is very difficult to explain, for their accumulation would represent a *loss* to the system as a whole. Is it possible that these groups of material were formed by peripheral communities outside the main system of consumption, and in opposition to it? In such cases the types of object that were collected for their metal content would have no special meaning since they did not belong to the local system. They would be simply pieces of bronze, and, as such, a sought-after raw material. Those items could be reworked into more appropriate forms, in which case they might assume a new importance. On this interpretation, then, the spatial patterning that separates specialised from utilitarian deposits might arise because different interest groups were competing for access to *the same materials but using them in different ways.*

This might supply an explanation for the abrupt shifts in metal circulation areas identified by Northover (1982). Just as likely, these patterns arose from different combinations of these factors in different regions.

As we have seen, this marked duality is very much a feature of the Later Bronze Age, and the characteristic scrap hoards appear at a developed phase in the sequence, to some extent supplementing an established pattern of personal and 'merchants' hoards. They seem to be connected with the recycling of raw material indicated by metal analysis.

Recycling has been taken for granted by Bronze Age specialists. For them it is an indication of the smooth running of the metal industry, the ideal solution to the problems posed by a dependence on raw materials with a restricted natural distribution. It seems enough to explain the high level of metal production that was sustained across Western and Northern Europe. On the other hand, a rather different impression can be gathered from the role of recycling in periods whose economic background is better known. In the Viking Age, for example, Scandinavia became dependent on a supply of imported silver, in very much the same way as it had depended on the supply of prehistoric bronzes. Strikingly similar expedients were adopted to make the best use of this material (Graham-Campell 1982; Bradley 1988). Ornaments could double as ingots and were made from standard weights of metal. Silver objects which had circulated over a wide area of Northern and Western Europe could be collected in hoards, where they were broken up for use as hacksilver (Hårdh 1976). Again, the fragmentation of this material would allow it to be exchanged in prescribed weights. In the Viking Age, however, there is no sign of complacency. Silver artefacts were treated in such drastic ways because the supply of fresh material was unreliable. Indeed, major changes in the source of this metal are documented by inscriptions on the coins incorporated in the hoards. The first time that the silver supply was threatened, there was a period of widespread raiding overseas (Randsborg 1980, ch. 7), and later these pressures may have encouraged the wider use of base metal. This is evidenced both by the changing composition of ornaments (Dolley 1971) and by industrial residues from urban sites (Kevin Brown, pers. comm.). In the same way, the role of recycling in pre-industrial England has been investigated by Woodward (1985), whose study covers a wide variety of different materials, among them metals. Again this points in the opposite direction to the orthodoxy in Bronze Age studies. For Woodward such recycling is associated with conditions of poverty and chronic shortage. It may be imprudent to suppose that the Late Bronze Age was any different.

Questions of sequence were vital to the interpretation of the Viking hoards and their relation to a changing supply of silver. They may be equally important in understanding this period. How was the development of founders' hoards related to the chronology of other types of deposit? We have already considered the rate at which river metalwork was being deposited in three areas: the Thames Valley, the Paris Basin and the region around Mainz. We can also consider the chronology of the hoards deposited in Denmark. In each case there does appear to be a reciprocal relationship between utilitarian hoards and this material. By comparison with the Early Bronze Age, the artefacts from the Thames evidenced a high rate of consumption. This remained virtually the same in Late Bronze Age 1 and 2, but in Late Bronze Age 3 it fell by 60 per cent, before it resumed its former level. It is perhaps revealing that this fall in the number of river finds corresponds to a sudden peak in the deposition of dry-land deposits, some of them containing fragments of weaponry, together with other evidence of scrap metal (Needham and Burgess 1980).

Similarly, in the Paris Basin, Mohen's figures show that the rate at which weapons were deposited in rivers rose four times over between Bronze Moyen and Bronze Final 2, before it fell sharply in the following phase (Mohen 1977). Again, that decrease in river weaponry corresponds with a peak of apparently utilitarian deposits on dry land (Gaucher 1981). The sequence studied by Wegner (1976) has much in common with this outline. Dated swords were deposited at a roughly even rate between Bronze D and Hallstatt B1, but in Hallstatt B3 the rate of deposition increased three times over. There was a peak in the number of dry-land hoards deposited at this time, and thereafter the consumption of river metalwork fell away almost completely.

Lastly, there is the rather different evidence of the Danish

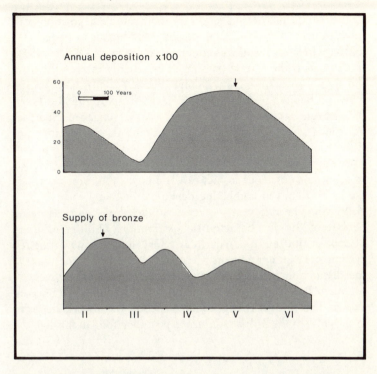

Fig. 34 The supply of bronze to Scandinavia, compared with the chronological distribution of 'ritual hoards'. (Bronze supply after Kristiansen 1984a, modified according to the length of the different archaeological periods; frequency of ritual hoards calculated from Levy 1982)

hoards. Here we have an additional source of information, as Kristiansen has employed wear analysis to shed light on the supply of metalwork coming into the local system. On this hypothesis a buoyant supply should be reflected by a short period of circulation and the deposition of unworn items; conversely, worn artefacts would indicate a period of shortage (Kristiansen 1978 and 1984a, 91–2). He argues that the main influx of metalwork came in Period II, and that after that time the supply decreased, although there were smaller peaks around the end of Period III and during Period V. On the other hand, Levy's study of the 'ritual' hoards suggests that their rate of deposition was lowest during Period III and considerably higher in Periods IV and V, when less metal was coming into the system (Levy 1982). It seems as if the rate of consumption actually increased whilst the supply of material was falling (Fig. 34). This may explain why the highest proportion of non-ritual hoards in the Later Bronze Age is found in Periods IV and V, suggesting that, as more metal was devoted to the supernatural, greater attempts were made to recycle what remained.

In each case deposits that have been interpreted as evidence of economic efficiency in fact reveal a crisis, the roots of which are to be found in competing demands for metalwork. This is clear from the different sequences studied here, and may also be reflected by the characteristic distributions of different kinds of deposit. Indeed, it is particularly revealing that when the recycling of weapon fragments was at its peak in the Thames Valley, the distinction between areas with river finds and those with founders' hoards disappeared completely (Needham and Burgess 1980). The drastic changes that overtook metalwork deposits at the close of the Bronze Age are to be understood in this light.

Crisis and denouement

How could these conflicts be resolved? We can usefully begin the discussion by considering the nature of some of the pressures experienced in different parts of Europe.

In Central Europe there are fewer indications of a crisis. Here metal could be obtained locally (Harding 1983), and there is less evidence for the extravagant consumption of artefacts known from rivers and votive hoards. This was a region in which more emphasis could have been placed on the changing *styles* of these artefacts than the materials of which they were made. With this went a commitment to a bronze tool kit, which was easy to maintain when metals were available in the same area. Here the main pressures on the bronze supply could have come through the need to provision more distant groups.

In Northern Europe the pressures on the metal supply can also be exaggerated. It is clear that a large amount of bronze went into the votive sphere, even at times when the supply of material from outside was subject to considerable fluctuation. It seems that an attempt was made to draw off some of these specialised items and to exploit them for their metal content, but we should not overemphasise this process, as there is evidence that bronze was used sparingly in everyday activities (Levinson 1983). For such purposes metal tools could be supplemented by artefacts made out of other materials.

It was in Western Europe that potential conflicts were more severe, for in this area a tradition of conspicuous consumption ran in parallel with a developed tool industry. We have seen how the metal supply was carefully monitored, and the distinctive distributions of scrap hoards and river finds even suggest that it was subject to competing claims. Similarly, the chronology of those different deposits reveals a reciprocal relationship between the two halves of our evidence. This is most apparent during the period of more unstable conditions suggested by the development of hillforts and hill settlements. Perhaps it is not so surprising that some groups of metal were concealed and never recovered.

The resolution of this problem perhaps followed a similar course to the sequence in Viking Scandinavia. The point was reached at which the only option was to make greater use of another material. Even then the adoption of early ironworking in different parts of Europe can only be understood in terms of a longer historical process.

In Central Europe, technological change posed no real problem. The new raw material had been known for some time before iron artefacts, particularly weapons, were generally deposited in graves. Their appearance may have been merely the culmination of a long-established tradition, and involved the substitution of one locally available material for another (cf. Champion 1980). It seems as if this was just another stage in the long quest for novelty that characterises the prestige objects of this period.

In Northern Europe, there is less evidence of sudden change, since so much of the bronze supply had apparently been devoted to the supernatural. Iron makes its first appearance only gradually and is not a regular feature of the archaeological record until several centuries after the large-scale movement of bronze artefacts had come to an end (Levinson 1983). During that interval

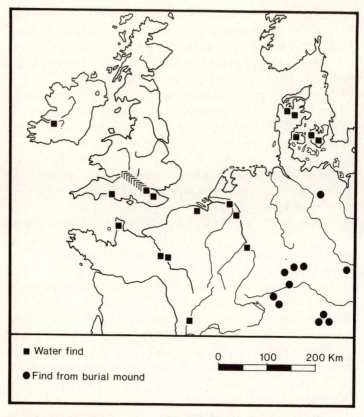

Fig. 35 The distribution of bronze Mindelheim and Thames swords in Northern and Western Europe, emphasising the contrast between water finds and those from burial mounds. (After Torbrügge 1971)

stone and bone tools continued in use. It was perhaps because the demand for bronze had been of such a specialised character that it was still being deposited in ritual hoards after comparable practices had largely lapsed in Western Europe (Larsson 1986, fig. 102). In fact some of the last deposits of bronze artefacts are composed of ornaments, apparently dedicated to the supernatural (*ibid.*, table 5.7). By that stage, however, there were fewer utilitarian hoards than ever before.

If the adoption of iron provided a potential solution to the problems experienced in Western Europe, it seems to have involved a major adjustment. This is because of the close identification between river metalwork and non-local materials, specifically bronze. There is no question that contacts between Western and Central Europe were so strong that the new material could have been adopted rapidly in the west; in any event there are indications that iron was already known but very little used. In fact the adoption of ironworking was somewhat retarded over the very area in which river metalwork was so important (Pleiner 1980 and 1981). Rather than adopt iron weapons when they first became available in Central Europe, communities in the west might continue to deposit bronze artefacts in rivers.

This is well illustrated by the changing context of sword finds during the all-important period of transition (Fig. 35). Gundlingen swords, for instance, were made of bronze and could have been produced in either Central or Western Europe (Cowen 1967; Schauer 1972). They are found in both these areas but conform to the geographical distinction between grave finds and river finds. Their contemporary, the Mindelheim sword, certainly was a Central European invention and was made in both bronze and iron. This had a more restricted distribution, but still the traditional contrast was maintained: iron swords were preferred in graves, whilst the bronze swords were deposited in rivers, largely in the west (Torbrügge 1971, Beilagen 16 and 17). In those regions in which bronze and iron swords circulated together, the situation is even more revealing. Gerdsen (1986) has studied the evidence from twenty-nine such areas, and in twenty-three of these iron swords dominated the burial evidence, whilst all the river finds considered in his monograph were made of bronze. These occurred in fifteen of the areas studied, but in no fewer then eleven of these, finds of iron swords were preferred for deposition in graves. Whilst some of this variation may be due to chronological factors, it also suggests that the choice of metal was significant. There are important differences in the rate at which iron was adopted in Western Europe, but enough is known to suggest that the more widely available material was accepted with a certain reluctance, and that it was less likely to be deposited in the traditional way.

All this amounts to saying that the Bronze Age/Iron Age

transition can only be understood against a longer background than is normally considered. The crucial change of technology was partly a result of the peculiar pressures to which the metal supply had been subjected. Those pressures had arisen from the demands of the *votive sphere,* and to that extent it is wrong to consider the change of technology as an 'economic' phenomenon. At the same time, that technological change was so protracted because the use of iron was incompatible with the traditional requirements of élites in Western Europe, for whom exotic artefacts and materials were essential if they were to maintain the kinds of consumption on which their positions depended.

In this chapter we have been concerned with evidence which is nominally 'Bronze Age'. This may seem an atavistic practice, an unnecessary act of obeisance to a model which has been under attack for years, but actually the difference between bronze and iron is crucial to our interpretation. Where this discussion does break with tradition is in suggesting that these two raw materials had different *meanings* for those who used them. If this is right, the change of technology may have had little to do with the mechanical properties of those metals.

Chapter 4

Coins of time and water

There the faint signs are left,
coins of time and water,
debris, celestial ash ...
  Pablo Neruda, *Extravagaria*

Introduction

It might seem that by the end of the Bronze Age events had run
their course; the supply of artefacts to the votive sphere was more
or less used up, and the various offerings had covered the full
range of possibilities. If so, there would be little virtue in extending
such a thematic account of this phenomenon into the Iron Age.

In fact the range of votive deposits had yet to be exhausted,
and it was not until the post-Roman period that developments
tended to repeat themselves. Quite new kinds of evidence first
appear during the Iron Age, and in some cases these are found
in different locations from those discussed in earlier chapters.
In order to avoid unnecessary repetition, this chapter concentrates on what was *new* during this period, and on the ways
in which traditional practices were altered. After a brief review
of some of the problems associated with this phase, it takes up
the sequence where the previous chapter left off and follows it
through to the Roman period.

All too often Iron Age archaeology is treated as a specialist
preserve, and this has held back discussion of its 'votive' deposits.
With certain exceptions (e.g. Collis 1984a), accounts begin with
the adoption of ironworking and then trace a sequence of changes
through to the eve of the Roman period (e.g. Filip 1977). The
Iron Age is studied as a time of rapid evolution, in which the
key issues become the precise level of complexity attained before
the Roman conquest – did prehistoric Europe see the emergence

155

of towns, a market economy and the institutions of the state? There is room for argument about all three of these questions, but behind each lies the clear assumption that the 'Iron Age' is a self-contained topic for study (Champion and Megaw 1985). The 'Bronze Age' supplies a background, where it is mentioned at all.

We shall take a rather different attitude to the later prehistoric sequence, since we have already argued that the adoption of iron-working did not result from any improvement of technology, but from the collapse of an already complex system which had linked communities across separate areas of Europe. It had its origin in the *breakdown* of an earlier socio-economic system. In these terms it begins as a period of devolution rather than evolution, a time of fragmentation rather than cohesion.

It is precisely because problems are considered on too short a time scale that Iron Age specialists have repeated many of the debates that have taken place in Bronze Age studies. Where Bronze Age specialists had their water finds, bog hoards and utilitarian finds, those working in Iron Age archaeology were operating within a cultural and chronological scheme which radiated outwards from two key groups of artefacts discovered in the nineteenth century: the grave goods from the cemetery at Hallstatt in Austria, and the water finds from La Tène in Switzerland. The material from the Hallstatt cemetery raises certain problems – Why were these graves so prolific? And do they represent the burials of an entire community? – but this is as nothing compared with the seemingly endless wrangling which has enveloped the material from La Tène. It is an argument which has dominated perceptions of Iron Age votive deposits, and for this reason we must start from that site. As with our discussion of the hoards from Petters Sports Field and Villethiery, we shall use that well-documented material to introduce the main themes in this chapter.

Fishing for swords

The Swiss lakes have produced some of the richest collections of archaeological material in Europe, including waterlogged settlements of both Neolithic and Bronze Age date (Harding 1980;

Coles and Lawson 1987, chs. 2–5). It was perhaps unfortunate that such evidence of domestic activity was already well known when the finds from La Tène came to light, since there was an automatic tendency to interpret them in similar terms. In fact there are three major groups of Iron Age material from similar locations in this region: Cornaux, Port and La Tène itself (Schwab 1972; De Navarro 1972; Wyss 1975). For the most part these will be treated together here. The main finds from La Tène came from the shoreline of Lake Neuchâtel and consisted of large amounts of timber and extraordinary quantities of fine metal-work. There were also discoveries of human and animal bone and other seemingly more mundane items, including craft tools and agricultural equipment (De Navarro 1972, 17). At first these were recovered in a quite chaotic fashion, by piecemeal dredging and by 'fishing' for the artefacts with tongs. Many of the objects were poorly recorded, and the finds themselves were so widely dispersed amongst public and private collections that fragments of the same sword are now in institutions in both East and West Berlin. When excavation did take place, it was of a very variable standard, and the best recorded parts of the La Tène site may not have been the most prolific (Vouga 1923). Even so, they were enough to suggest that some of the artefacts had been deposited in a former channel of the River Thiellein between two wooden bridges (Fig. 36). A similar bridge has now been excavated to modern standards at Cornaux, five km away, and has produced rather comparable evidence (Schwab 1972). There were apparently buildings on the water's edge at La Tène, but it is difficult to work out their original character or purpose.

It might seem that such discoveries were sufficiently like the finds discussed in the previous chapter for a votive interpretation to be accepted from the start, and this was certainly advocated from an early stage in the work. On the other hand, there was a tradition of 'lake villages' in this area which exerted a powerful influence over the interpretation of waterlogged sites. Even now there is a temptation to interpret these discoveries in everyday terms. Although the setting of the lakeside settlements is much better understood, there have been attempts to identify the Iron Age deposits as the sites of ports, with facilities for loading and unloading cargoes (Schwab 1972 and 1974). This might provide

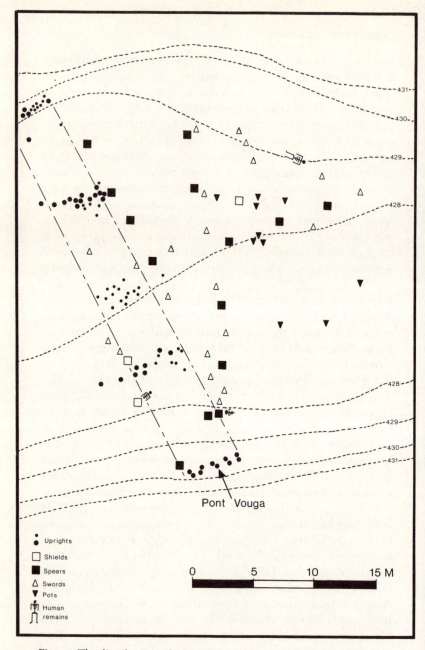

Pont Vouga

Uprights
Shields
Spears
Swords
Pots
Human
remains

0   5   10   15 M

Fig. 36 The distribution of selected deposits around the Pont Vouga
at La Tène, Switzerland. (After Vouga 1923)

158

one explanation for the concentration of fine objects, but it does nothing to indicate why they entered the archaeological record. This is thought to have happened because these sites were over-whelmed by a catastrophic flood, which caused the collapse of the bridge at Cornaux and resulted in a number of deaths; but even if flooding did happen at that site, there is no such evidence from La Tène (Berger and Joos 1977). Alternatively, it has been argued that La Tène was an armoury and that this explains the great concentration of weapons (Pittioni 1968). This seems most improbable and would certainly not account for the finds of human remains on the site (De Navarro 1972, 17–18). An earlier interpretation is that this material was left behind when the Helvetii embarked on the long migration documented by Caesar (Reinecke 1933, 150). It is not clear that La Tène was occupied by this group, and in any case the extended sequence of artefacts could only be explained in this way if the inhabitants had been running an antique shop. The evidence is so like the material discussed in earlier chapters that there seems every reason to interpret it along similar lines, and this view may be gaining support. We shall build on that conclusion by considering the distinctive features of other Iron Age deposits, in relation to the material from this complex.

The variety of deposits

One reason why the striking links between these collections and earlier water finds have escaped notice is because the Swiss material does not belong to the earliest part of the period. Indeed the name La Tène is applied to the second major phase of the European Iron Age. The apparent hiatus in the deposition of valuables may explain why at first these finds seemed to exist in isolation.

It is true that the decline in the long-distance movement of bronze is matched by a falling number of river deposits and the virtual disappearance of non-ritual hoards, but it must be asked at the outset why deposits of bronze were not replaced by similar finds of iron. The explanation is probably quite simple. The col-lapse of the Bronze Age system happened fairly rapidly, but the growth of the iron industry was rather slow. Settlement finds, and finds of industrial debris, seem to indicate that the large-scale production and distribution of metals was not resumed until the La Tène period (Collis 1984b, 87–92). The Bronze Age/Iron Age transition, then, need not mark a sudden change in metal technology, so much as a shortage of metal in general. In the votive sphere this may have been exacerbated by the reluctance of communities in Western Europe to deposit materials of local origin.

In fact the river deposits of the Early Iron Age reveal two striking trends: a more restricted distribution of finds of metalwork and a gradual decrease in their number. Even when the deposition of weaponry resumed on any scale, as it did in the La Tène period, fewer areas produce a significant number of finds, and these are not necessarily the regions that were most important in the Bronze Age. Votive offerings were less common in North-West Europe than they had been during the previous period, and the main groups are recorded from Britain and Ireland, southern Scandinavia and from the Swiss lakes. Rivers in northern France also include a significant number of weapon finds. It seems likely that this list underestimates their frequency in other regions, because most studies of Iron Age artefacts in Europe are based on discoveries from the numerous cemeteries of the period; for the most part comparable sites were absent during the Later Bronze Age. The same trends even apply where contemporary burials with grave goods are uncommon. Thus the number of swords found in Britain fell by about four fifths between Late Bronze Age 3 and 4 (Burgess and Colquhoun 1988), and when the sword was replaced by the dagger the number of finds fell by another fifty per cent. At the same time the distribution of water finds narrowed down to a limited stretch of the Middle Thames (Jope 1961).

In Ireland, where all too little is known about Early Iron Age settlements, the same process takes an even more extreme form (Champion 1989). Here there is a virtual gap in the archaeological record between the Late Bronze Age and the La Tène period, but in one sense the hiatus is unreal: it is almost certainly the result of the wider changes that affected offerings of metalwork. To some extent other types of material may have replaced fine objects in votive deposits. This is most obvious where finds still come from watery locations. The evidence from southern

Scandinavia is particularly revealing here, as it bears some resemblance to the Neolithic deposits found in the same area. Again, there are finds of pottery vessels containing meat or plant foods (Becker 1971), and discoveries of well-preserved bodies which provide evidence of human sacrifice, or perhaps of formal execution (Pl. 12). These 'bog bodies' had been carefully deposited in wet locations; they are discovered in isolation and are usually naked (Dieck 1965). One group has radiocarbon dates around the Bronze Age/Iron Age transition (Fischer 1979; Tauber 1979). If both these types of finds recall Neolithic deposits, other finds of this period have a very different character. A small number of metal ornaments continued to be deposited in watery locations, but a completely new development is represented by discoveries of wooden ploughs in similar environments (Glob 1945). The latter may not be so surprising when we consider the prominent part that had been played by scenes of ploughing in Scandinavian rock art (Malmer 1981, ch. 6).

To some extent deposits from the British Isles underwent rather similar changes. We have already seen how the deposition of weaponry in rivers gradually diminished during the Early Iron Age. At the same time, it seems as if specialised deposits of animal remains can be found on dry-land sites, both in this period and during the Middle Iron Age; the number falls off rapidly in the Late Iron Age when the deposition of fine artefacts was resumed on a significant scale (Wait 1985, ch. 5). Three main types of deposit are represented: complete or partial animal skeletons, which are normally without evidence of butchery; animal skulls; and groups of articulated limbs. These finds are regularly associated with corn storage pits (Pl. 13), and it seems possible that a symbolic link was intended between the sacrifice of food, or of whole animals, and the regeneration of the seed corn stored underground.

This is also suggested by finds of human remains dating from this period. We have already seen that a tradition of excarnation may have existed during the Later Bronze Age, at least on high-status sites. In the following period this became more common. By the Middle Iron Age, inhumation burials also appear with some frequency in the archaeological record. The human skeletal material seems to illustrate two striking trends. First, it seems

Plate 12 The bog body from Tollund, Jutland. Photograph:
Nationalmuseet, Copenhagen.

Plate 13 Human burial in an Iron Age pit at Danebury hillfort, Hampshire. Photograph courtesy of Barry Cunliffe.

as if isolated human bones, perhaps resulting from primary burial or exposure away from the settlement, were deposited within the living area during the Early Iron Age, with a significant proportion of the finds close to its perimeter (Wilson 1981; Wait 1985, ch. 4). In the next phase, however, a number of individuals were represented by inhumation burials and had been introduced whilst they retained their articulation. These are generally found within the main part of the living area, and often inside corn storage pits. Although it has been customary to think of these burials as 'casual' or in some way aberrant, they could be taken to suggest an increasingly powerful link between the deposition of bodies in storage pits (Pl. 13) and the concept of regeneration symbolised by the seed corn that had been kept there. There is a further connection between the ways in which some of the dead were treated and the formal deposits of animal remains that can be found in similar features within the settlements. This is not to suggest that the human remains have to be understood as 'offerings', but rather that a major emphasis was placed on types of deposit that stressed the links between the population and the fertility of its land, a topic discussed in very much these terms by Barrett (1989a). This is surely a parallel process to the placing of querns in these pits (e.g. Cunliffe 1984a, 443 and 1988), or the finds of food and agricultural equipment from the Scandinavian bog deposits.

Such practices may have a still wider distribution. For example, burials in Iron Age corn storage pits are now being found in northern France (Coudart, Dubouloz and Le Balloch 1981, 125). More important, a number of these tendencies contributed to the far more lavish deposits at La Tène, where their presence helps to distinguish this site from its counterparts in the Bronze Age.

The main links with La Tène are formed by finds of human remains, animal bones and possibly agricultural equipment. The human remains are particularly important here. They consist of isolated bones, principally skulls, as well as articulated skeletons (Vouga 1923, 135–42; De Navarro 1972, 17–18). They seem to have been strikingly like those recorded at Cornaux, where they are interpreted as victims of a catastrophic flood (Schwab 1972). On the other hand, the human remains from La Tène itself include one skeleton which seems to have had a rope around its neck, and a skull bearing knife marks. Some had possibly been deposited together with artefacts, and in one case a skeleton with a spearhead was found almost upright in the mud. The published plans of both La Tène and Cornaux also suggest that bodies could have been weighed down in the water by sizeable pieces of timber, as may have happened with bog bodies in Northern Europe (Dieck 1965; Vouga 1923; Schwab 1972). Such evidence makes it most unlikely that all these individuals had met with an accidental death. Again the skulls may have been deposited after the bodies had received preliminary treatment in a different location. Other cases are sufficiently similar to the bog corpses recorded in Scandinavia and elsewhere to raise the possibility of human sacrifice.

The animal remains from La Tène have been little studied, as most of the early excavators were concerned with recovering the finer artefacts. Even so, Vouga's monograph, which represents the fullest publication of the site, does include a detailed account of a large sample of animal bones found in excavation (1923, 131–4). We cannot say whether these were typical of the material on the site as a whole, but they are remarkable in being dominated by horse bones. This distinguishes them from contemporary settlement finds and again suggests that deposits of animal remains had played a specialised role on the site. Even though direct links are unproven, they recall the discoveries of weapons with horse skulls in European rivers (Brunaux 1988, 94–5) and the high number of horse bones in contemporary spring deposits in Scandinavia, where the faunal assemblage contrasts with that from nearby settlements (Stjernquist 1970).

Lastly, there is a range of artefacts from La Tène which are of a less striking character and could result from domestic activity on dry land. One possible source may be the ill-recorded timber buildings found there in the early excavation. On the other hand, it would be arbitrary to assume that all intentional offerings consisted of fine objects, and it is worth recording the occurrence in the excavated deposits of everyday items, including agricultural tools (Vouga 1923, 74–88). Their presence might be fortuitous, or it could suggest a further development away from the stereotyped assemblage found in the votive deposits of the Bronze Age. Similar items appear with increasing frequency among the river metalwork (Fig. 37; Fitzpatrick 1984), and, as we shall see, a more varied assemblage is also found at Iron Age shrines. Much the same range of material was placed on the bottoms of some storage pits in southern Britain (Cunliffe 1984a, 443 and 1988) or buried beneath Iron Age houses there and in the Netherlands

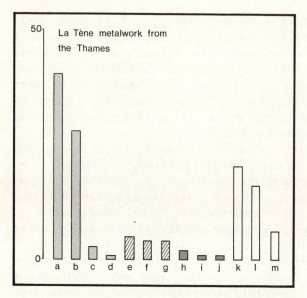

Fig. 37 Finds of La Tène metalwork from the River Thames – a: spears;
b: swords; c: shields; d: helmets; e: socketed axes; f: horse harness;
g: cart/chariot fittings; h: bronze cauldrons; i: tankards; j: spoons;
k: coins; l: brooches and m: currency bars. (After Fitzpatrick 1984)

(Cunliffe 1984a, 559; Therkorn 1987).

That last point may be tenuous, but it does deserve serious
consideration. If La Tène saw a wider range of deposits than
the finds of the Later Bronze Age, it only illustrates a more general
tendency in Iron Age archaeology. In addition to human and
animal remains and the deposition of agricultural equipment,
finds from similar locations include bronze cauldrons and bowls,
wood sculptures and occasional ceramic or metal vessels
imported from the Mediterranean.

The first of these is well documented in the British Isles and
falls into two chronological groups, one of which overlaps with
the transition from the Bronze Age, whilst the other belongs to
the Late Iron Age. It includes cauldrons as well as simpler bowls
made of sheet metal (Wait 1985, 31–5). Their dating is sometimes
uncertain, but they do appear to be associated with the serving
of food and drink, and in this respect they find close counterparts

in the styles of fine pottery recorded on dry land. They may be compared with the ceramic vessels found with offerings of food in Early Iron Age deposits in Scandinavia (Becker 1971). The same may also apply to the surprisingly numerous discoveries of Iron Age pottery from rivers in the Paris Basin (Freiddin 1982, 297 ff.).

The bronze vessels also recall a smaller and more controversial collection of river finds, those possibly imported from the Mediterranean world. Their discovery in rich Iron Age burials on the Continent is a well-known phenomenon, but this tends to occur in areas with fairly obvious geographical links to the south, and scattered finds in more distant areas are treated with greater reserve. These objects have a fairly restricted chronological distribution, with its main emphasis before 400 BC (Harbison and Laing 1974) – Late Iron Age imports are a separate matter and are usually found in settlements or burials. Like most fine artefacts, those found beyond the areas with rich burials lack any real archaeological context, and the majority have been dismissed as recent collectors' losses. This may be true in many cases, but it is striking that in Britain and northern France a significant number of these objects has been discovered in rivers. These hardly seem to be the obvious places for collectors to discard unwanted antiquities, and yet they do contain other objects of this period. It seems likely, then, that some of these pieces result from intentional deposits during the Iron Age. Again, they may have been associated with the serving of food and drink.

The sculptures raise even greater problems. Here their authenticity is accepted, but their dates are largely unknown (Detys 1983). This is a question that could usefully be resolved by dendrochronology. Nearly all this material consists of bold images made of wood, some with prominent genitals, which are thought to symbolise fertility. These discoveries are associated with watery locations, but this may be misleading since they would not have been preserved in other environments. Even so, the best-known groups of this material are the large collections from springs in Clermont-Ferrand and the source of the River Seine (Vatin 1972; Detys 1983; Romeuf 1986), and from Possendorf and Oberdorla, two bog deposits in Thuringia (Behm-Blancke 1958 and 1960). In the case of the two spring deposits the association with watery locations must have been intended, and both the German sites contained finds of human remains and metalwork. Two broadly comparable wooden figures were also associated with a wooden trackway at Oldenburg in the marshlands of Lower Saxony (Hayen 1971).

Finds of this kind have a very wide distribution, extending from Scandinavia and Ireland into central France, but very few have close dating evidence, simply because they so rarely occur in association with other artefacts. Even so, there are some suggestions that they first appear during the La Tène period. The Oldenburg trackway is dated to the third century BC (*ibid.*), whilst the wood sculptures from Oberdorla were found with a La Tène sword, as well as a quantity of animal bones (Behm-Blancke 1960). Equally important, the major group from the source of the Seine underlies a Roman temple (Detys 1983). Links with river finds are rare but extremely striking. The dredging of the Saône, which has been closely monitored by archaeologists, has produced a small amount of Hallstatt metalwork and a larger number of La Tène weapons, together with a male figure of just this type (Pl. 14; Bonnamour 1985). Occasionally this practice could have extended to pieces in other materials, and the famous male head from Bouray, dated to La Tène III, is made of bronze. It was found in the River Juive, not far from Paris (Megaw 1970, 142 and pl. 232).

At this point it is worth turning away from the detail of these deposits in order to highlight a few broader developments. The major difference between the water finds of the Later Bronze Age and those of the Iron Age is that they do not show such a close relationship to the contents of contemporary burials. This is true in two senses. The Iron Age is a period with an abundance of rich cemeteries; whilst Iron Age water deposits are fewer, they can certainly be found in the same regions as contemporary graves. This is particularly true of the Swiss evidence (Wyss 1975), but it also applies to the increasing number of river finds from northern and central France. At the same time, there are also literary references to the deposition of war booty in watery locations, where archaeological material is still lacking; the sacred lake at Toulouse is the most famous example of this phenomenon (Brunaux 1988, 42). In Scandinavia and the British

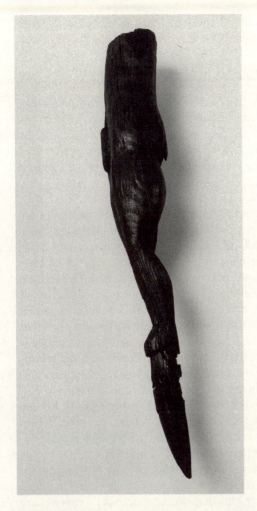

Plate 14 Part of a wooden figure from the river Saône at Seurre, Côte d'Or. Photograph: Musée Denon.

Isles, where the older contrast between grave goods and water finds continued, it now took a different form. Rich burials alternated with votive deposits in the Scandinavian sequence (Parker Pearson 1984), but burials with grave goods were uncommon in southern England until the later part of this period, when the number of river finds also increased (Whimster 1981; Wait 1985).

In that case, the burials tend to contain different artefact types from the river finds, whereas in Scandinavia the same kinds of material went into graves and votive deposits. In other areas, however, weaponry can be found in both these contexts during the same periods. Where the votive collections do differ from earlier finds is in the much wider range of material that they contain, and this seems to lessen their association with funeral rites.

Although the emphasis on male-associated artefacts certainly continued, there are signs that during the Iron Age this ran in tandem with a range of other deposits, more closely associated with fertility and the food supply. The interpretation of human sacrifices still poses a major problem, but the evidence of early Scandinavian traditions might suggest a link with the goddess of fertility, Nerthus, although this may not provide the whole explanation (Todd 1987, 166–7). The food offerings suggest a similar emphasis, but on a more modest scale, and the same may be implied by the deposits of animal and human bones in corn storage pits in Britain and France. The vessels containing food offerings found in Scandinavia may have their counterpart in the much finer bronze and ceramic vessels discovered in major rivers. More explicit links with human fertility seem to be suggested by some of the sculptures from watery locations, whilst the fertility of the crops may have been protected by the deposition of ploughs and other agricultural equipment.

Taken together, these different types of evidence suggest the emergence of distinctively new practices during the Iron Age. The long-established tradition of weapon deposits seems to have continued throughout this period, but their actual frequency was determined to some extent by the flow of metalwork through the system, with the result that fewer items were placed in water during the early years of the Iron Age than had been deposited in the Late Bronze Age. Similarly, the number of river finds increased, although never to their former extent, during the La Tène period, when there is evidence for metal production on an industrial scale in Europe and the British Isles (Collis 1984b,

87–92; Ehrenreich 1985). A further, more obvious influence on the supply of fine metalwork to the votive deposits was the provision of similar material in male graves at this time.

During the period of fragmentation that may have followed the collapse of the Bronze Age system, new alliances were formed, principally with the Mediterranean world, and a greater emphasis seems to have fallen on the reorganisation of food production at the local scale. Despite important differences between the archaeological sequences in separate regions of Europe, this was sufficiently pervasive for a new series of deposits to have developed that laid a special emphasis on the fertility of the land and the human population (Barrett 1989b). To some extent they took over from the more overtly military deposits of the previous period, but increasingly the two types came to overlap, as they did at La Tène itself. When the deposition of metalwork was resumed on a large scale, as happened by about 300 BC, it no longer had the close association with mortuary rituals that had dominated the Bronze Age evidence. To some extent it was now combined with a wider series of rituals that stressed the importance of food production. Finds from Gaul are exceptional in containing a significant quantity of human bones, but it was only in outlying areas like Britain and Scandinavia that deposits of artefacts can be regarded as surrogate burials. Otherwise they had assumed a much more flexible role.

The changing character of deposits

Let us return to the evidence from La Tène. So far we have stressed how it can illustrate the merging of two distinct strands in the history of votive deposits: the provision of weapons and other fine metalwork, and the offerings of food and materials associated with natural fertility. In other respects the development of this site, and its neighbours at Port and Cornaux, exemplifies a series of new developments, and each of these will be considered in its wider context. It provides evidence that offerings were becoming increasingly institutionalised during the later years of the Iron Age. They included a growing proportion of standard items, beginning with coins and ingots and perhaps ending with model artefacts. They took place at special locations, with a variety of structural features from shafts to timber shrines, and sometimes they were located on the borders between the territories of emerging polities.

The first of these points can hardly be controversial. We have already suggested that the expansion in the provision of votive offerings is due to broader changes in industrial production. This may have ended the shortage of metal that occurred late in the Bronze Age. The increased evidence for craft production is matched by growing evidence for the standardisation of its products. Metal was produced in consistent units – the iron ingots or 'currency bars' that have generated so much discussion (Allen 1967; Jacobi 1974). Salt was made in cakes of standard sizes, and these may have been distributed within their moulds (Bradley 1975). Storage pits inside hillforts may have been dug to accommodate standard quantities of grain (Cunliffe 1984a, 131), and sufficient weights have been found in excavation to suggest that these were also made in prescribed units (*ibid.*, 408–12). The same may apply to the gold ornaments produced during this period, which are sometimes found in hoards with coins (Allen and Nash 1980, 33; Furger-Gunti 1982).

The currency bars are directly relevant here, since their adoption marks a very interesting transition. In those areas with an abundant supply of iron and a high rate of production, such units could be made into ingots which had a shape all of their own, but where the iron industry was operating on a smaller scale, currency bars often took the form of unfinished sword blades (Allen 1967; Marien 1970, fig. 47; Jacobi 1974, Abb. 57). Although they could not have been used as weapons without reworking, the overlap between these groups is illustrated by a collection from Appleford in the Thames valley, where the edges of half these artefacts had been sharpened to look like sword blades, whilst the remaining half had been left blunt (Brown 1971).

This pattern would be of anecdotal interest were it not for the fact that currency bars now entered the votive deposits alongside finds of weaponry. This is an important feature of the well-documented material from La Tène, but it occurs much more widely. It is evidenced by major river deposits, including the Iron Age metalwork from the Thames (Fitzpatrick 1984) and the remarkable water find from Llyn Cerrig Bach on Anglesey (Fox 1946, 97), and is also found among the deposits from dry-land shrines in Britain and northern France (Horne and King 1980; Wait 1985, 186 and 385–93). The standardisation of offerings did not stop at these objects, however, and there are also finds of Iron Age coins from La Tène, although their exact contexts on the site remain in doubt. The unexpectedly high representation of gold coinage in this collection again highlights its unusual character, and Allen (1973) suggests that these were among the last votive deposits on the site before it was deserted. Although coins would be difficult to recover, they again appear among the Iron Age metalwork from the Thames (Fitzpatrick 1984), and Haselgrove has drawn attention to their discovery in other wet locations, including springs and beaches (1987, 119 and 135). They complement the much larger collections of such finds from excavated temples and shrines, where the proportion of forgeries is so high that Henig has postulated the existence of a special temple money (1984, 22–3). The later sites also include small personal ornaments and can contain a more restricted range of weapon types. It appears that at some stage the weapons were replaced by models.

Mention of these sites introduces a second development during this period. It is a natural temptation to compare La Tène with earlier water finds, dating from the Bronze Age, but the site itself does have one unusual feature. Apart from the buildings on the water's edge, whose exact nature remains in doubt, the site is characterised by two massive constructions identified as bridges; as we have seen, a third very similar example has been excavated recently at Cornaux (Schwab 1972). The layout of La Tène poses many problems, and now that a third bridge has been discovered in association with weapons and human remains, it may be time to envisage a less mundane interpretation. Perhaps these formidable timber constructions were intended specifically for the placing of offerings in deep water; on the roughly contemporary site at Hjortspring in Denmark this was done by sinking a collection of weapons and animal bones in a wooden boat (Rosenberg 1937). It may be incorrect to interpret these features at La Tène as *bridges* in the normal sense at all. There may be a precedent on Bronze Age sites like Fengate Power Station (Pl. 15), but a

Plate 15 Excavation in progress on the prehistoric timber structure at Fengate Power Station. The markers show the positions of the timber uprights. Photograph courtesy of Francis Pryor.

rather closer parallel seems to be provided by the timber causeway running into the River Witham at Fiskerton in Lincolnshire, which was associated with a group of Iron Age weapons, tools, pottery and animal bones (Field 1983). Again, one interpretation would be that these features were built specifically to aid performance of the rituals that took place on these sites. The same might apply to the less well-defined timber structures at Pommerouel in Belgium, which were associated with a similar range of material (De Boe and Hubert 1977; Hubert 1982).

In general terms all these finds may be assigned to the developed

La Tène period. This is important as it would make them broadly contemporary with developments that were taking place on dry land. Again we have seen how the major Bronze Age deposits occur in apparent isolation, except for those in burials. During the later years of the Iron Age, two major groups of non-utilitarian monuments came into being; we also know from Classical writers that natural locations such as springs and groves were used in rather the same ways.

The best-known monuments to emerge during this period are the sites described as *viereckschanzen*. These have a wide distribution in Western Europe. They consist of square or rectilinear earthwork enclosures, some of which contain deep shafts (Brunaux 1988, 65–7). The best known of these sites is at Holzhausen, where an upright post was found at the bottom of the shaft. Analysis of the surrounding soil revealed traces of flesh or blood (Schwarz 1975). Deep shafts of this kind do have a long ancestry, beginning in the Later Bronze Age (Piggott 1963), and can be found in isolation, but the idea of a formal enclosure seems to be a new development. These monuments first appear during the late La Tène period. They have been discovered in some numbers, but few have been excavated on any scale, and, as Brunaux points out, not all may have been used for ritual purposes (1988, 35).

The other group of sites consists of shrines, which may again be found inside an enclosing earthwork – Holzhausen in fact combines the two principles, as it contains a small shrine as well as the shaft mentioned earlier. The other shrines are found mainly in northern France and southern Britain, and where there is adequate structural evidence they appear either as circular timber buildings like those in contemporary settlements, or as rectilinear structures that anticipate the characteristic ground plan of the Romano-Celtic temples built in stone (Wait 1985, ch. 6; Horne 1986). These can contain concentrations of offerings, but another focus for such material is provided by the enclosure ditch (Brunaux 1988, ch. 2). On a small number of sites in Britain such buildings are found towards the centre of major hillforts, where they occur amidst structures for the storage of foodstuffs (Wait 1985, ch. 6). In Gaul they were also found at the entrances of Iron Age oppida (Brunaux 1988, 6–7).

If the *viereckschanzen* are primarily associated with sacrificial offerings – whether of humans or animals is uncertain – the shrines contain a far more varied range of deposits (Fig. 38). They include animal burials as well as very large numbers of bones, and in this respect they recall the evidence from ordinary settlements, and also some of the water deposits mentioned earlier; one of the richest of these, at Gournay in Picardy, was actually located beside a ten-hectare pool (Brunaux, Meniel and Poplin 1985). The finds from these sanctuaries can be complemented by discoveries of human remains. Usually they are disarticulated, and resemble those well known from earlier periods. Recent work in northern France has identified some Iron Age shrines which contain very large amounts of human skeletal material. One such site, at Ribemont-sur-Ancre on the Somme, contained a strange structure built out of human bones, accompanied by 112 weapons, most of them spearheads (Cadoux 1984). Skulls were completely absent, and in several cases it seems as if bodies had been carefully dismembered as part of a funerary ritual; there are few injuries to suggest that these deposits were the result of human sacrifice (Brunaux, Meniel and Poplin 1985, 147–64).

As at La Tène, the finds of human and animal bone are complemented by discoveries of weaponry. This material can be damaged or broken to such an extent that some pieces are barely recognisable. It was perhaps displayed in the open air for a long period before its deposition (Rapin and Brunaux 1988, 145–67). At French sites like Gournay these objects occur in such large numbers that the density of the weapons can only be compared with the deposits from La Tène. Smaller numbers of weapons are also found at the British sites. During the Late Iron Age it seems possible that a gradual change took place from more elaborate deposits of weaponry to the deposition of spearheads. The reasons for this will be considered in due course. In addition, it may be that weapons could be replaced by miniature copies, although the chronological evidence is not sufficiently clear, and this phenomenon could postdate the Roman Conquest (Green 1987).

All these deposits are augmented by collections of coins, but again there is some uncertainty as to how high a proportion

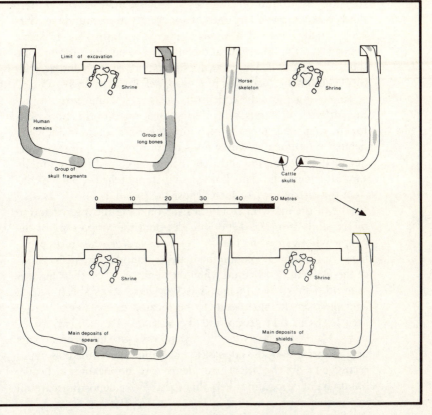

Fig. 38 The distributions of selected deposits in the Iron Age shrine at Gournay, northern France. (After Brunaux, Meniel and Poplin 1985; Rapin and Brunaux 1988; and Brunaux 1988)

of this material was deposited before the Roman period (see Haselgrove 1989). Coins probably came into use to facilitate the payment of essentially social obligations (Allen 1976), and we have already seen how some of those from ritual sites show an emphasis on specialised types, as if they are a form of temple money. Where any evidence exists, it seems likely that this material had been deposited in a series of small hoards, in and around the shrine (e.g. Magnard 1978, 307–9). As we have seen, currency bars are also found on these sites. Finally, material of all these kinds is accompanied by finds of apparently more mundane character. Small personal ornaments played a major role in votive deposits for the first time, and continued to be important during the Roman period. The same applies to finds of tools and agricultural equipment, including ploughshares (Brunaux 1988, 93–4).

Taken together, these deposits seem to include virtually all the varieties of intentional offering mentioned in this book, but for the first time since the Neolithic these are found inside well-defined monuments. Water finds continue to play a major part during the same period and seem to have contained a substantially similar assemblage. This link is only strengthened when we consider the distribution of such deposits.

One of the many uncertainties surrounding the interpretation of the finds from La Tène is in deciding the affiliations of the people who were using the site. As we have seen, this raises problems for those who explain the material found as the possessions of the Helvetii, left behind when they embarked on their famous migration in 58 BC. In fact it is very hard to establish such a firm link, as the sites seem to be located in the likely border area between that group and the Sequani (De Navarro 1972, 325). Moreover, as Allen (1973) points out, La Tène and its neighbours are on the edge of the distributions of the coin types recovered from the site. The evidence is by no means conclusive, but on balance it seems likely that these votive deposits are found in a border zone.

Such evidence is extremely tenuous, but it does not stand in isolation. Greater precision can be attained in an area with a plentiful inscribed coinage. This requirement is met by the Late Iron Age period in southern Britain, where the coins of a number of tribal federations are clearly distinguished from one another on stylistic considerations, and, more importantly, by inscriptions. The distributions of these coins have been analysed by statistical methods on the assumption that the spheres of influence of different populations would be marked by a concentration of their own coins and a corresponding scarcity of the coins of neighbouring groups (Kimes, Haselgrove and Hodder 1982).

This method has put the established procedure of inferring political territories on a sound statistical basis and has resulted

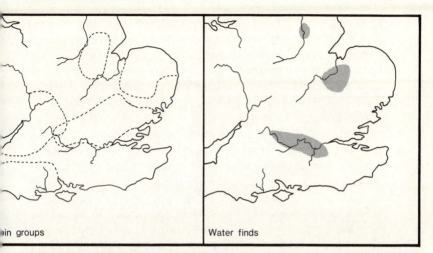

Fig. 39 Political units in Late Iron Age England, calculated from coin distributions (left), compared with the distribution of major groups of metalwork from watery locations (right). (Territorial divisions after Kimes, Haselgrove and Hodder 1982; metalwork finds after Wait 1985)

in the identification of five clearly defined territories in this area, separated by boundary zones which may be up to 30 km wide. These correspond well with basic topographical features in this area, and most of the borders are found along major rivers or in regions of contemporary wetland. In the light of our discussion of La Tène, it is of considerable interest that all the major areas with water finds of metalwork are in these border zones. They include the Thames, the Fen Edge, the Trent, the Witham and the Humber (Fig. 39). This is not to say that all the Iron Age metalwork found in those areas belongs to the same period as the coins themselves – some of the La Tène metalwork is certainly of earlier date – but it does suggest that such geographical divisions may have been of some antiquity.

It seems possible that similar considerations influence the locations of some of the Iron Age shrines, as well as a number of major collections of coinage. These often occur with rivers or springs, and also seem to be associated with tribal boundaries (Wait 1985, ch. 6; Haselgrove 1987, 133 and 137). This relationship is by no means exclusive, but it is supported by the recent identification of groups of coin deposits associated with beaches. In some cases several separate deposits seem to have been made over an appreciable period (*ibid.*, 119). Again the preference for liminal areas is important, and the same seems to be true in northern France, where the sanctuary sites are either found at the centre of political territories or seem to reinforce their boundaries (Brunaux 1988, 12).

In this respect the situation in the Middle and Lower Thames is most revealing. During the Later Bronze Age it had contained a major concentration of settlement sites, including a number which seem to have been of high status, and a concentration of ditched field systems. In the Late Iron Age there has always been a feeling that sites of equivalent importance ought to have been located here, perhaps in the area now occupied by London, but so far suitable candidates have failed to materialise (Kent 1978). The major sites are found instead at some distance, in Essex and Hertfordshire. Although linear earthworks, probably of late prehistoric date, are known to the north-west of London, attempts to find an oppidum to precede the Roman city have met with little success, and the only real concentration of artefacts recorded in the appropriate area consists of finds from the river, including a number of coins (Merrifield 1983, 9–12). An equivalent group of dry-land finds has yet to be identified.

Despite a massive campaign of excavation, relatively little later prehistoric material has come from the site of the Roman city, and what there is tends to have its main emphasis in the Bronze Age (Merriman 1987). The Late Iron Age material is unexceptional. On the other hand, the Roman city does overlie one remarkable group of water finds which could date from this period. These are a collection of human skulls from the River Walbrook, a former tributary of the Thames which was buried beneath the Roman city in the mid-second century AD. Although it had been supposed that the skulls belong to victims of the Boudiccan uprising, there are problems in taking this view. Most of the skulls are those of younger males and none shows any sign of injury. More important, they had entered the river after they had lost their flesh (Marsh and West 1981). They have so much in common with the skulls from the Thames itself that it is very tempting to suggest that this area witnessed a continuous tradition of such deposits from the previous period, and certainly two of the three skulls from the Walbrook have radiocarbon dates that span the Late Iron Age and early Roman periods; a third skull was probably Roman (Bradley and Gordon 1988). The Walbrook itself contains so many Roman artefacts that these are sometimes regarded as votive deposits (Merrifield 1962). In addition, it includes at least four pieces of Iron Age metalwork (Bradley and Gordon 1988, 507). It is tempting to suggest that deposits of human remains were a major feature of this area. If so, during the late prehistoric period this could have been a border zone reserved for river deposits. Only when this ritual system ended with the Roman Conquest could such a strategic location be taken over for more mundane purposes.

The idea that a border zone might receive deposits of human remains is by no means new. It has also been suggested by Jankuhn (1977) for one area of Jutland (Fig. 40). In this case their chronology is rather better known, and two main groups of finds have been dated by radiocarbon. We have seen that one belongs to the early years of the pre-Roman Iron Age; the other dates from its closing stages (Fischer 1979; Tauber 1979). If we can extrapolate from these examples, there may be a parallel with the evidence from London.

Discussion

So far we have isolated a number of important tendencies in the votive deposits of the Iron Age, nearly all of which can be illustrated by the well-known finds from La Tène. The variety of separate deposits increased sharply over this period, extending well beyond the long-running contrast between grave goods and water finds to embrace collections of material more closely associated with fertility and regeneration. The artefacts deposited could change, as more standardised items, including ingots and coins, came to take the place of the lavish prestige objects whose deposition had become the norm. Such finds were increasingly associated with special types of site, or with locations which included facilities provided for the purpose, from the shafts of the *viereck-schanzen* to the wooden 'bridges' at La Tène. And the deposition of so much material could be at its most extravagant around

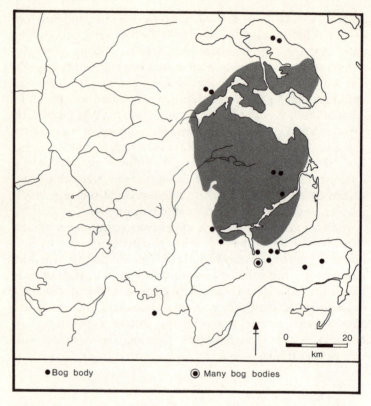

Fig. 40 The distribution of human remains from bog deposits in south-east Jutland, Denmark, compared with the extent of the main settled area. (After Jankuhn 1977)

the borders of emerging polities, as if competition between different territorial groups might even extend to their dealings with the supernatural.

It remains to establish what factors lay behind these develop-ments. At the beginning of this chapter, I criticised the tendency to write the archaeology of the Iron Age within an evolutionary framework. As we shall see, that temptation is not easy to avoid. But many of the questions that have dominated the literature do share a common emphasis: how far had native societies changed before that process was affected by the impact of the

Roman world? This applies as much to the use of coinage, as it does to the institutions of the state, and it is no surprise that even ritual practices must be considered in these terms. Whilst it is certainly possible to discern the outlines of a sequence in the evidence summarised so far, it is quite another matter to offer an explanation. The two poles in any discussion are easy to identify. On the one hand, there are certain developments which seem to have been under way before there is much possibility of strong outside influence; on the other hand, we can also scrutinise the evidence from the Roman provinces for indications that the intrusive system had incorporated native features which were present in some areas but did not occur in others. Here we can turn to what is known about Roman religion in its original source area.

To begin with purely native developments. First, there are those features which seem to form part of a much longer history of votive deposition, in some cases extending without a break from the Neolithic period. Pre-eminent among these was the deposition of valuables in watery locations – rivers, springs, lakes and bogs. The presence of weaponry among this material need occasion no surprise, as it simply continued a tradition established during the Bronze Age. Despite fluctuations in the metal supply, this practice had never ended completely (Fig. 41), and was of increasing importance once production had been resumed on any scale (e.g Zimmerman 1970, Abb. 5–7). When it did so, however, certain differences are apparent, and there may no longer be much connection between the water deposits of the Iron Age and the celebration of the dead. Indeed, there is evidence that such deposits had diversified and now contained a wider variety of artefact types.

To some extent that happened because these collections increasingly overlapped with a second series of intentional offerings, those associated with agricultural produce, and with human and animal fertility. These also had their roots in earlier practices, but they are most in evidence from the Bronze Age/Iron Age transition onwards. Even though Roman religion laid great stress on the sacrifice of animals and foodstuffs (Ogilvie 1969, ch. 3), the chronology of these finds rules out a direct connection here, and even the groups of human and animal bone from Late Iron

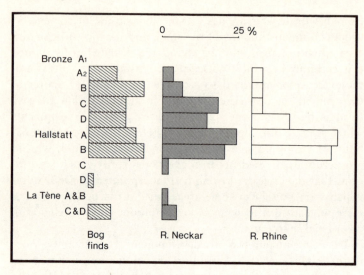

Fig. 41 The chronological distribution of water deposits in three areas of southern Germany. (After Zimmerman 1970)

Age shrines can be seen as the successors of these more informal practices. The same perhaps applies to the offerings of humbler artefacts, associated with different productive tasks, and in particular those connected with agriculture. Such finds have a long history, quite independent of contacts with southern Europe, whether these practices are seen in the water deposits of Switzerland and the British Isles, or the distinctive objects deposited on the base of corn storage pits. They may even suggest that votive deposits were being made by a wider section of the population.

It is more difficult to say whether the changes in the nature and location of votive sites resulted from outside influence, but it does not seem necessary to take this view. The construction of special facilities, whether enclosures, shafts, shrines or even 'bridges', owes little or nothing to exotic prototypes, and the process started too early to have been subject to pressures from outside. In any case the evidence of continuity is fairly strong. Thus timber structures like that at Fengate Power Station may originate in the Late Bronze Age (Francis Pryor, pers. comm.), just as the causeway at Fiskerton is found in an area which had already seen the deposition of river metalwork during the earlier period (Davey 1971). Similarly, the shrines at Danebury appear to be present throughout the hillfort occupation, which began in the Early Iron Age (Cunliffe 1984a, 81–7). The shafts of the *viereckschanzen* have their origin in a Later Bronze Age tradition, and even if some of the shrines had a distinctive rectangular ground plan, the circular buildings used for the same purpose are very like the houses found in contemporary settlements: so much so, in fact, that the two cannot be told apart with any certainty (e.g. Gregory 1981). Despite this element of local continuity, there was one most important change. It seems as if the rectangular shrines had their prototype among the small earthwork enclosures found in earlier Iron Age cemeteries. These were gradually embellished until they were no longer associated with burial sites, and once this happened, they provided a focus for the increasingly lavish consumption of valuables (Brunaux 1988, chs. 2 and 12). As so often in the past, a component of the funerary record was elaborated in another context.

The greater permanence of these structures can only be understood in the context of the social changes that were taking place at this time. As productive industries were revitalised, we find evidence for an unprecedented degree of political centralisation. This culminated in the development of enormous oppida and the emergence of polities with a strong enough power base to oppose the Roman advance (Collis 1984a, ch. 6). If these developments owed something to contacts with the Mediterranean world, the changes in ritual practices reflect those processes only distantly. The same social and economic changes may have lain behind the evidence of armed combat and the sharper definition of territorial boundaries during this period. It could be for this reason that both water deposits and sanctuaries were increasingly established in these areas. This greater stress on the definition of territories reflects far wider political changes at this time, but the idea of reinforcing those divisions by means of intentional offerings has a peculiarly local character.

Greater problems are created by the changing nature of the finds from these sites, in particular the more standardised offerings represented by coins, currency bars and possibly by model artefacts. The decreasing variety of weapons poses another problem, as spears became more important than elaborate or costly items. Here it is probably wise to look at the problem from the perspective of the Roman world. It is controversial whether certain *deposits* actually date from the Iron Age, no matter when particular artefacts had been produced. This applies to certain groups of native coinage (Haselgrove 1987, 126 and 1989), and almost certainly to the models of artefacts, which can include miniature weapons (Green 1987). In the case of coin finds, it does seem likely that some are genuinely pre-Roman deposits, but the chronology of the models remains uncertain. This is unfortunate since the finds from shrines in southern Britain, and especially from northern France, exhibit a wide range of contents (Horne and King 1980; Wait 1985, 385–93). To some extent these differences may arise because different kinds of offerings were required for different gods (Brunaux 1988, 23), but there may also be hints of a broader sequence. It is possible that the elaborate weapons were deposited during the earlier phases on these sites, along with currency bars, animal bones, human bones and personal ornaments. It seems likely that at a later stage they were complemented by finds of coinage, and that in some cases these came to play the dominant role (*ibid.*, 92). They could have supplanted the most elaborate weapons almost completely. As this happened, small spearheads became important, as if they symbolised more lavish offerings that were no longer considered appropriate (Bradley 1987). This may also be true of the later river metalwork, where spearheads play a prominent role (Fitzpatrick 1984).

This tidy scheme presents two problems. It describes a general tendency which certainly cannot be recognised on every site or in every area. Even where it does offer a plausible reading of the evidence, the chronology of such developments is imprecise, and it is hard to isolate the Roman Conquest in this sequence; this accounts for the controversial status of the pre-Roman coin hoards from these sites. A further complication is that the Roman annexation of North-West Europe was a gradual process, so that changes effected by the Roman presence in one area might colour developments among purely native groups in a neighbouring region (Haselgrove 1987, 134). Even with these qualifications, however, it seems possible that the standardisation of deposits evidenced at such sites extended into native societies whilst they still remained outside the Roman frontier.

It is profitable to look at the same questions from the Roman perspective. It is well known that Roman religion sought, wherever possible, to accommodate native practice into its institutional structure. The *interpretatio Romana* was a very flexible instrument, and this provides another reason why it is so difficult to distinguish formally Iron Age deposits from those of Roman date. The evidence from the post-Conquest period sheds light on a number of important issues. First, there were those elements in native practice that were found unacceptable. The best known of these was human sacrifice, which was the subject of Roman propaganda. These writings laid some emphasis on the role of the Druids, but as Todd has recently noted, we know very little about their real status or origins (1981, 255–6). It is uncertain when this priesthood developed or how long it remained important, and their political influence may have been exaggerated. It is hard to relate the literary references to the archaeological record and unwise to fall back on generalised interpretations based on 'Indo-European' social structure (*pace* Brunaux 1988, ch. 5). Suffice it to say that the Druids' activity was proscribed and that the prohibition was backed up by force. The second feature to be rejected by the Romans was the carrying of weapons by civilians, which was forbidden by the *Lex Julia de vi publica* (Mommsen, Krueger and Watson 1985, 816). This may account for the ending of weapon deposits, although it is an interesting sidelight on relations between the Roman and native populations that their place was taken by votive models of weapons, whose distribution is very similar to that of earlier water deposits (Green 1987).

In other ways the Romans assimilated the existing system. Many of the Iron Age shrines continued to be used, and the tradition of wood sculpture associated with springs carried on without a break (Detys 1983; Romeuf 1986). Most important, the characteristic rectangular shrines established during the Iron Age were rebuilt in stone according to very much the same ground plan. Their distribution emphasises the area over which native religion would have been affected most strongly as the Roman frontier advanced northwards, but it also highlights the tenacity of the pre-Roman way of doing things (Horne 1986; Roymans 1988). That is still more apparent outside the frontier in Scandinavia, where the deposition of weapons and other valuables in watery locations went on throughout the earlier first millennium AD, and sometimes involved prestige goods imported from the Roman world (Parker Pearson 1984). That distinctive system was to break down finally with the introduction of coinage.

Having stressed both similarities and differences, there is one fundamental way in which Roman religion had a different emphasis from native practice, and it is of the greatest importance to establish how far that influence was being felt in native societies before their annexation. This may provide a powerful index of social and economic change. Both native and Roman religion involved the sacrifice of animals and foodstuffs, and in the Roman world these were seen as a means of providing the gods with the *power* – effectively the physical strength – to change the fortunes of the living (Ogilvie 1969). Gifts, however, could be regarded in another manner. It was common for native warriors who were going into battle to take a vow that they would dedicate their spoils to the gods if they were victorious. This was a conditional promise, but it seems very likely that it accounts for the large deposits of weapons, animal bones and human remains found on sites in Gaul (Brunaux 1988, 103) and Scandinavia (Ilkjaer and Lønstrup 1982). Roman practice, however, extended across a whole range of human activity. This involved a more formal transaction in which the protagonist made a specific request of the gods. This was carefully recorded and is known as the *nuncupatio* (Henig 1984, 32–3). Its resemblance to a legal document is obvious. It stated that if the god performed a particular service for the suppliant, the latter would make a specific offering. If that did not happen, he or she was under no obligation, but if the request was fulfilled, the transaction had to be concluded by the offering that had been promised (*ibid.*). The second part of the transaction was known as the *solutio*. The whole arrangement bears a close resemblance to the Roman law of contract, and to all intents and purposes it involves a *payment* for services rendered.

Little could be more alien to the tradition of lavish offerings established in prehistoric Europe, a tradition which lent itself to conspicuous consumption and the quest for personal prestige. At first sight it epitomises all the differences between the native and Roman economic systems. But it does seem possible that some of the changes seen in pre-Roman deposits were already pointing in this direction. In particular, the appearance of less elaborate weaponry, currency bars and coins would all suggest that a significant change was under way and may have involved a similar relationship between the worshipper and the gods. The chronological evidence is insufficient to provide any guidance in this matter, but it is not impossible that some of these developments were happening under Roman influence. That influence was felt in so many areas, from building styles to political institutions, that it could have had its impact on native religion. And if it did so, it would have effected a more drastic transformation than any other in the prehistoric sequence.

Chapter 5

Irreducible objects

So step by step, book by book, though seeking each time only to write another book, I eased myself into knowledge. To write was to learn. Beginning a book, I always felt I was in possession of all the facts ...; at the end I was always surprised. The book before always turned out to have been written by a man with incomplete knowledge.

V. S. Naipaul, *Finding the Centre*

'Science! There are only scientists, my friend, and they're scientists only at certain moments. They are men ... groping ... with their bad nights or an excellent lucid afternoon. Do you know the first hypothesis of all science, the idea indispensable to every scientist? It's this: *the world is almost unknown*. This is a fact. Yet we often think the contrary: there are moments when everything seems clear, when all is fulfilled and there are no problems. At such times, there is no more science – or if you prefer, science is complete. But at other times, nothing is clear: there are only gaps, acts of faith, uncertainties; nothing to be seen but scraps and irreducible objects, on every hand.'

Paul Valéry, *Monsieur Teste*

Introduction

We have followed the prehistoric sequence for nearly four thousand years, but as this book draws to an end, other possible books come to mind. Our account has been extremely selective and has emphasised certain themes at the expense of others which might appear just as important. No doubt another version could consider the relationship between the production and deposition of fine objects, stressing technological factors where we have stressed social ones. An alternative account of the prehistoric material might emphasise different types of Neolithic artefact. It might analyse the circulation and consumption of goldwork in the Bronze Age, or the ornament hoards of the Iron Age.

Most accounts would converge, however, in placing a certain emphasis on the descriptions of sacrifice and votive offerings provided by Classical writers, but it is here that important differences of approach would probably be found. One way of treating this subject is to begin with those literary sources and to work backwards through the prehistoric material, subtracting the inessential from the more resilient core. This is very much the 'historical' approach advocated by Hawkes in 1954. Why has a different tactic been adopted here?

There are elements in this 'subtractive' approach which make it a dangerous course to follow. There seems little reason to suppose that Roman or Greek observers were in a good position to understand all the practices that they were describing, and in any event they were writing within well-defined philosophical traditions, even when their texts lacked an element of colonial propaganda (Piggott 1968, 28–32). Moreover, there is a danger that those who privilege these sources above the archaeological record will end up by writing conjectural history of the type so popular in the later nineteenth century, an essentially speculative narrative, enlivened by ancient or ethnographic local colour sundered from its original context. It was just this approach that was rejected by Hubert and Mauss (1964) when they embarked on their pioneering study of sacrifice. They chose to work from detailed religious texts. As archaeologists, we should also play our strongest card, and here the crucial element is sequence, not because it presupposes a notion of inexorable *progress* (*pace* Shanks and Tilley 1987b, ch. 3), but simply because it is the dimension which archaeology is best equipped to measure. It provides the critical element on which archaeological narrative depends.

When we study the sequence of intentional deposits, as we have done here, it soon becomes apparent that superficially similar collections of artefacts could be formed in quite different contexts and, apparently, for quite different reasons. Moreover, traditional practices, like the offerings of fine artefacts in watery locations, could be manipulated by interest groups within society. It will be only by studying those deposits in relation to their wider background that such changes can be appreciated; that is what is meant by 'contextual archaeology'. Thus at its simplest, it is impossible to transfer the accepted definition of a 'hoard' or a 'votive deposit' from one phase to another, for it is in the changing context of these finds that their roles will become more apparent. That is why period specialists, whose first-hand acquaintance with these finds is so much greater than my own, have failed to provide an acceptable interpretation of this material. As Pauli (1985) observed, it is *sequence* that provides all the vital clues.

A study which considers the changing character of one set of traditional practices over four millennia is necessarily concerned with what is called 'long-term history', but not just because it studies a lengthy sequence. That concept is helpful precisely because it describes the ways in which cultural practices were shaped and modified by living people, for whom they marked the edges of the social world. As Hodder says,

The historical approach ... argues that cultures are produced as organised and organising schemes of action that are meaningful to the individuals involved. These schemes are organised because of the human need to categorise and arrange, in order to perceive and act upon the world. The organisational schemes are arbitrary in the sense that their form and content are not determined by anything outside themselves. But they are not arbitrary in the sense that, once the continuous stream of human action begins, there are necessary historical links as one scheme is transformed into another. (1987, 2)

The same idea is expressed by Bloch in his study of ritual and history in Madagascar:

People act in terms of what they know and what they know is the product of their historically constructed culture. They may transform and change this culture but they do not do it from a zero starting base. (1986, 10)

In this sense it may be impossible, perhaps unnecessary, to explain the symbolic link that developed between votive offerings and watery locations, but once it had become established, we find almost unlimited permutations of that single relationship. Such associations could be remarkably tenacious, as earlier chapters have suggested.

Not all the examples of 'long-term history' used by Hodder and his co-authors illustrate this point effectively, as too many depend on documentary sources to provide archaeologists with a programme for research. Intentional deposits of valuables offer a rewarding subject for such a study, but this chapter is not intended as a recapitulation of the entire sequence described here. Rather, it reflects upon certain of its more striking characteristics and the wider lessons that can be taken from them. In particular, it points to a way in which more theoretical approaches can be reunited with the detailed studies of artefacts which at present exist in a vacuum.

In the long term

Chapter 1 summarised a series of debates in prehistoric archaeology concerned with the interpretation of intentional deposits of artefacts. Whilst the studies presented in Chapters 2, 3 and 4 adhere to traditional period divisions, the major issues can also be considered in relation to the sequence as a whole. Now it is time to return to some of the broader questions raised in our opening discussions.

Storage, concealment and loss

The sub-title of this book offers a choice of interpretations: do these complex deposits result from hoarding or votive activity? We shall consider the nature of sacrifice towards the end of this chapter, but at the outset we must address a rather more prosaic issue. How much of this material had been concealed with the intention of recovery?

As we saw in Chapter 1, most discussion of this question has been concerned with the evidence from the Later Bronze Age, and there has been an unfortunate tendency to project the same interpretations into the archaeology of other periods. Study of the sequence as a whole suggests that this has been misguided, for that period stands out from all the rest. It may have more metal objects available for detailed study, but this can be a disadvantage, for they have a far more complex structure than the finds of other phases. In fact this material is profoundly anomalous because the Later Bronze Age deposits have a *dual* structure. Some undoubtedly were intended as votive offerings, but others may result from the peculiar pressures exerted on the metal supply. The fact that so many deposits can be interpreted in utilitarian terms is evidence of an almost unique crisis in the flow of metals. The crisis may have meant that concerted attempts were made to divert some of the material into everyday activities and to make more use of what was still available. Most important, such circumstances could well account for its concealment. There is little way of telling whether similar material had been stored and recovered during other phases, but it may be no accident that so much metalwork was lost at a time when there are other signs of instability. The closest comparison appears to be with Viking silver hoards, and these provide evidence of rather similar political and economic pressures. This is not to say that all utilitarian hoards belong to the Later Bronze Age – for example, some of the 'emergency hoards' of the Late Iron Age may have been interpreted correctly (Haselgrove 1984, 86–7) – but it does seem that others are relatively uncommon, or are restricted to specific historical horizons. For this reason there is little basis for extending such an interpretation too widely: the common elements in the prehistoric sequence concern the non-utilitarian deposits.

When we turn to that material, we must be careful how we interpret such signs of continuity. Changes were normally effected *within* the cultural rules that seem to have determined the character of votive deposits. This did not exclude radical developments, but it did mean that until the period of Roman influence most of these were variations on readily identifiable themes. Drastic changes were more easily accomplished if those who promoted them appeared to be observing traditional norms.

We can see these processes at work on three levels: in the changing treatment of individual artefact type; in the changing context of intentional deposits; and in the subtle interlocking of votive offerings and sacrifices. Each of these elements needs to be treated separately.

The role of individual types

Despite the appearance of continuity provided by the contexts of these offerings, significant changes took place in the symbolic weight with which different types were imbued. Such contrasts are most easily recognised where they involve a chronological sequence, but they may also be identified by comparing the situation in different regions of Europe. In Chapter 2 we traced the way in which one such artefact, the stone axe, was endowed with a special significance and saw how this process was reflected in the finds from a series of specialised monuments, as well as those from watery locations. It was a process that only intensified as metals became available, so that in certain areas of Europe axes made of copper or bronze became important symbols during the later third and early second millennia BC. We saw how the axe was promoted from a work tool and how it gained added connotations as more emphasis was placed on objects originating in distant areas, until highly decorated bronze axes were probably divorced entirely from productive activities. At the same time, we also observed regional differences in the significance with which these objects were endowed, so that in areas with a long history of metallurgy, or with major sources of raw material, axes were often undecorated, whilst in those areas where metal-working was a recent introduction these objects shared their characteristic decoration with special types of funerary ceramics. At the same time, the contexts in which bronze axes were deposited might be dictated by much older traditions, extending back to the period when polished axes were being used. This illustrates the way in which new developments grew out of the cultural rules established in earlier periods. But what was represented as continuity could involve significant change.

One such change can be illustrated by tracing the role of axes into the later second millennium. At this stage, they seem to have lost much of their former importance, and in time they went back to being work tools, as weapons and ornaments became the main components of the votive deposits. Even so, the former importance of axes was recognised in the utilitarian sphere where such objects played a dual role, as everyday artefacts and as standard units of metal; to some extent the bronze sickle may have experienced the same change of identity. It seems likely that a similar process affected the votive deposits of the Late Iron Age. Here there is evidence that standard units of metal, imitating the forms of contemporary sword blades, could be placed in rivers or shrines, whilst the wide range of weaponry characteristic of these collections was gradually replaced by less extravagant deposits of spearheads.

There are two important points to stress in sequences of this kind. There is a real degree of continuity to be observed in the framing of these deposits. They are found in very similar locations in every period of prehistory, at least until the Late Iron Age. At the same time, the actual contents of these deposits may have been subject to constant revision, according to broader developments in the character of contemporary society. Thus the adoption of bronze provided an opportunity for more striking displays of exotica than the stone axes of the Neolithic period, but the increasingly unstable system of the Later Bronze Age encouraged displays of *weaponry* instead. Similarly, the more stereotyped character of the last Iron Age votive finds may reflect the changed economic circumstances of a periphery of the Roman world. Such changes were effected *from within* – by manipulating the conventions established during earlier periods.

The role of individual deposits

The same process determines the interplay between grave goods and water finds. At first it seems as if the compositions of both groups were bound by local rules. We have observed the subtle interplay between these categories of material as they vary from one region to another, or from period to period. In most areas the two traditions gradually coalesced, the votive deposits providing an opportunity for more lavish offerings than the burial mounds of the same period. This is not to say that all such finds were associated with funerary ritual, but it does seem that this change allowed more material to be deposited, and possibly by more people. Where such rituals may originally have been intended to emphasise the status and achievements of the deceased, we have suggested that votive deposits provided an ideal medium for flamboyant displays by the mourners.

It goes without saying that this is only one interpretation of that particular development, although it does seem to be supported by a variety of circumstantial evidence, from the presence of human skulls in the Thames to the increasing rate at which weapons were deposited in some of the main European rivers. For our purposes the important point is that again this change was effected by developing a tradition of votive offerings which was *already of great antiquity.* It involved the quantity and character of the artefacts being deposited, but again it could be represented as a development of an established system. It is because it was accomplished so smoothly that this transitional phase is difficult to characterise today.

In that case it seems as if a long-established tradition of making votive offerings had been subverted to create a medium for competitive consumption and had been assimilated to a separate tradition of funerary offerings. In other cases equally drastic changes might come about entirely from within. The clearest example of this development is seen in the Early Bronze Age of Central Europe, where the size of metal hoards increased dramatically during the period that saw the development of fortified settlements. In this instance the change did not involve the transfer of artefact types *from* the burial record. Rather, an already existing system of ritual hoarding could have been modified to provide a setting for acts of conspicuous consumption. The same may be true of the increase in river deposits of the Late Iron Age and, still more, of the finds from the sanctuaries that first developed during this period. Both seem to have been a development from much more parsimonious offerings, but they do not appear to have affected the character of contemporary burials. The location of some of these deposits around the borders of emerging polities suggests a still more profound modification of traditional practice.

Offerings and sacrifice

So far we have suggested that the provision of votive offerings and funeral gifts could have formed the basis for a programme of conspicuous consumption. If we are to understand these developments in greater detail, we will need to return to a distinction made in the opening chapter. There we saw how the separate ideas of offerings and sacrifices tended to be treated together in early anthropological literature. That distinction has not been particularly important in the later chapters, but now it has a part to play in our discussion.

Sacrifices are of living matter, whether plants or animals, whilst artefacts can only be offerings. This may seem to be a semantic

distinction, of little relevance to the argument, but in fact it is
very striking how these sacrifices have a chronological distribution all of their own. To some extent the same may be true of
offerings.

The term 'sacrifice' can be applied to a whole series of archaeological deposits dating from both ends of this sequence. In the
earlier stages of the *Neolithic* period, examples may include the
pots containing food found in Northern Europe, some of the
animal remains associated with chambered tombs and causewayed enclosures, and the dismembered bodies discovered in
watery locations in southern Scandinavia. In the *Iron Age*, there
are further finds of pottery containing plant and animal remains,
as well as deposits of meat joints and even of whole animals.
Still more striking are the finds of bog bodies so well documented
in Northern Europe. Although individual deposits could be interpreted in other terms, it is striking how many of these groups
are found at the same time. Still more striking is the fact that
all these types of evidence are found in both the Neolithic and
Iron Age periods, but are uncommon in between. Most of these
deposits appear to be geographically isolated, although some do
overlap with one another, or with finds of more complex artefacts. In the Neolithic period in southern Scandinavia, the
deposits containing human and animal bones avoid the distribution of amber hoards, although they do occur in the same areas
as ceramic vessels containing food. In the Iron Age, deposits of
human and animal remains are rarely accompanied by artefacts
– that is why Lindow Man has proved so difficult to date
(Gowlett, Hedges and Law 1989). When contemporary artefacts
were deposited, and particularly when they occur with these
remains, they tend to have a rather specialised character. Thus
axes play a conspicuous role in the Scandinavian Neolithic, and
wooden ploughs are found in Iron Age contexts. The grain storage
pits that contain animal deposits in Britain can also include finds
of quernstones or other everyday artefacts. Such tendencies must
not be exaggerated, but in most cases it seems as if these finds
were connected with beliefs concerning the fertility of the land.
This is not unexpected. The Early Neolithic period saw the first
experiments with domesticates, and the Early Iron Age witnessed
an unparalleled reorganisation of food production.

Having stressed the unexpected similarity between the first developments in both periods, we must consider how far these practices were altered in the later stages of the sequence. In both cases it seems as if votive offerings of artefacts assumed a rather different character. It is true that axes could be deposited with putatively 'sacrificial' deposits in Northern Europe, but these artefacts already had a dual identity as prestige objects and as work tools before the first copper axes were imported from Central Europe. It was only after that development had taken place that special monuments were built in which more lavish offerings were made. In Britain the equivalent stage in the sequence saw the first single burials, suggesting an equally drastic change.

In the Iron Age more complex deposits of artefacts came to *supplement* the traditional types of sacrifice found at sites like La Tène, but in this case there is no reason to suppose that such deposits ever went out of use. They are still found at Late Iron Age sanctuaries, and with the exception of the human sacrifices documented by Classical writers, they are evidenced throughout the Roman period. It was the votive offerings that to some extent changed their character, since weapons could no longer be used for this purpose.

In between these two extremes, during the *Bronze Age*, a strikingly different system had prevailed. Here the emphasis was on votive offerings, and the evidence of sacrifice is much more limited. Greater importance was attached to deposits of metalwork, first in burials and votive deposits, and later in watery locations. These changes were by no means uniform, and there are areas, such as Central Europe, where this scheme may not apply. Nevertheless, in those regions where bronze possessed an exotic character, votive offerings certainly came to predominate. This never happened in the Iron Age, where a wider range of material entered the archaeological record.

Perhaps a clue to the character of this system is provided by the importance of non-local metalwork in these collections, for when iron first became available it does not seem to have been thought of as an acceptable substitute. The finest items, which are so well documented in the votive deposits, must have been acquired by gift exchange. Is it possible that religious practices were also permeated by 'the spirit of the gift' (cf. Sahlins 1974, ch. 4)? The deposition of this material is surely a transformation of the very principles that had made it available in the first place. If gift exchange is a means of inflicting debt and accumulating prestige, votive deposits may have extended that process to relations with the supernatural. In that case it is no longer possible to create debtors, but, as we have seen, the crucial difference between 'gifts to men' and 'gifts to gods' is that votive offerings allow the continuous enhancement of prestige.

Again the sequence suggests that traditional practices were being subverted from within. A system of sacrificial offerings, entirely appropriate to societies in which fertility and food production were important, seems to have been drawn into a more antagonistic system of votive offerings, one that eventually assumed the character of surrogate warfare. During the Bronze Age this change was a development of competitive gift exchange, and sacrificial deposits lost much of their importance. In the Iron Age, however, the two traditions appear to have run in parallel and are often in evidence on the same sites. The continued preference for watery locations suggests that once again these changes were represented as developments of established custom. In practice, however, they broke with traditional norms and may have let to more far-reaching changes.

Summary

It is unnecessary to labour the point. In all three cases we have seen how changes in the system were accomplished by constant modification of the conventions that governed the provision of offerings. Only when Roman influence was felt in different areas were significant departures made from traditional practices.

On the other hand, it is customary to contrast such notions of continuity with those of change. In this case nothing could be more misguided, for it was precisely through an appearance of continuity that so much change could take place. Ritual activity is often said to involve a different conception of *time* from everyday affairs. It may involve archaic forms and procedures and can be conducted in archaic language. Its apparent antiquity is one feature which helps to protect it from challenge (Bloch 1977). At the same time, these are exactly the features that make it so susceptible to manipulation from within. There is no need for us to reify the 'ritual system' itself, for it is merely an abstraction with no motive force of its own. For just this reason it can provide an arena in which skilled participants use their knowledge of the accepted conventions to further their own ends. This is well shown in Bloch's study of the circumcision ritual practised by the Merina of Madagascar. Historical analysis shows that this ceremony hardly changed its character in two hundred years, but at the same time the scale on which it was carried out and the people who participated were affected by changing political circumstances:

From the formal point of view, the ritual seems to have altered surprisingly little in its symbolic aspects; the ritual acts, songs, the objects used. On the other hand, if we take a functionalist theoretical perspective, which stresses transformations in the ritual's role in the organisation of the social and economic system, the ritual seems to have changed fundamentally – passing from a descent-group ritual to a royal ritual and back again. Accompanying this change in the social function of the ritual have been changes that can be called logistic; these follow directly from the functional aspect and concern such matters as the number of people involved, the expense and the length of time given over to the ritual. (1986, 157)

These comments have a familiar ring, although they describe a ritual whose recorded history is two centuries rather than four millennia. Like the ritual described in Bloch's monograph, the deposition of votive offerings in watery locations is evidenced over a long period of time, but may have been utilised in very different ways from one period to the next, so that what started as an informal transaction between the living and the gods was transformed into one of the central political activities in prehistoric society. The success of such a stratagem is encapsulated by the sequence described in Chapters 3 and 4. The Later Bronze Age, the period when the provision of votive offerings was at its height, was actually a major period of political expansion, and it was when such offerings largely ceased, at the beginning of the Iron Age, that there is evidence of fragmentation and conflict. However arcane the means can seem to us today, Later Bronze Age societies had a staying power that their immediate successors lacked. Perhaps that is why the large-scale deposition of weaponry was eventually reinstated and why it was to have a still longer history outside the frontiers of the Roman Empire.

In the end

In the end, V. S. Naipaul says, to write is also to learn. None of the chapters of this book has taken the course that I had expected, and this concluding discussion is no exception. Like Valéry's Monsieur Teste, I make no claims to 'science', and one day's progress in this research has been followed by another day's dejection. As I commented at the start of this chapter, there are other books to be written on this subject. I can imagine some of their contents, but ultimately I prefer what I have written here. This has been an attempt to ease myself into knowledge, and I hope that it will have done the same for my readers, whether they agree with these interpretations or not. In either case it is enough to put these ideas forward for debate.

At best we have made some inroads into the petrified forest of artefact studies and may have found a path leading back to the real world. If that path leads archaeologists to study the most obtrusive of all their evidence, something will have been achieved. The study of finds from hoards and votive deposits is far too important to be left to the period specialist, when it could take its place near the centre of a revitalised social archaeology. Too often we seem to despair at the limitations of our evidence, but, for once, suitable material is available in abundance; those irreducible objects that will outlast the boldest attempts to explain them.

References

Abélanet, J. 1986. *Signes sans paroles: cent siècles d'art rupestre en Europe occidentale*. Poitiers: Hachette.

Abels, B-U. 1972. *Die Randeistenbeile in Baden-Württemberg, dem Elsass, der Franche Comté und der Schweiz*. Munich: C. H. Beck.

Acosta, P. 1968. *La Pintura Rupestre Esquématica en España*. Salamanca: Universidad de Salamanca, Faculdad de Filosofía y Letras.

Adkins, R. and R. Jackson 1978. *Neolithic Stone and Flint Axes from the River Thames*. London: British Museum (Occasional paper 1).

Agache, R. 1982. Information archéologiques: circonscription de Picardie. *Gallia Préhistoire* 25, 251–91.

Alexander, J. 1979. Islam in Africa – the archaeological recognition of religion. In B. Burnham and J. Kingsbury (eds.) *Space, Hierarchy and Society*, pp. 215–28. Oxford: British Archaeological Reports (BAR International Series 59).

Allen, D. 1967. Iron currency bars in Britain. *Proceedings of the Prehistoric Society* 33, 307–35.

1973. The coins found at La Tène. *Etudes Celtiques* 13, 447–521.

1976. Wealth, money and coinage in a Celtic society. In J. V. S. Megaw (ed.) *To Illustrate the Monuments* pp. 199–298. London: Thames and Hudson.

Allen, D. and D. Nash 1980. *The Coins of the Ancient Celts*. Edinburgh: Edinburgh University Press.

Anati, E. 1976. *Evolution and Style in Cammunan Rock Art*. Brescia: Centro Cammuna de Studi Preistorici.

Andersen, N. 1980. Sarup. Befastede neolitiske anag og deres baggrund. *Kuml* (1980), 63–103.

Aner, E. 1956. Grab und Hort. *Offa* 15, 31–42.

Appadurai, A. 1986. Introduction: commodities and the politics of value. In A. Appadurai (ed.) *The Social Life of Things*, pp. 3–63. Cambridge: Cambridge University Press.

Barfield, L. and M. Hodder 1987. Burnt mounds as saunas and the prehistory of bathing. *Antiquity* 61, 370–9.

Barrett, J. 1985. Hoards and related metalwork. In D. V. Clarke, T. Cowie and A. Foxon (eds.) *Symbols of Power at the Age of Stone-*

References

henge, pp. 95–106. Edinburgh: Her Majesty's Stationery Office.

1988. Fields of discourse: reconstituting a social archaeology. *Critique of Anthropology* 7.3, 5–16.

1989a. The living, the dead and the ancestors: Neolithic and Early Bronze Age mortuary practices. In J. Barrett and I. Kinnes (eds.) *The Archaeology of Context in the Neolithic and Bronze Age: Recent Trends*, pp. 30–41. Sheffield: Sheffield University, Department of Archaeology and Prehistory.

1989b. Food, gender and metal: questions of social reproduction. In M. L. S. Sørensen and R. Thomas (eds.) *The End of the Bronze Age in Europe*, pp. 304–20. Oxford: British Archaeological Reports (BAR International Series 483).

Barrett, J. and S. Needham 1989. Production, accumulation and exchange: problems in the interpretation of Bronze Age bronzework. In J. Barrett and I Kinnes (eds.) *The Archaeology of Context in the Neolithic and Bronze Age: Recent Trends*, pp. 127–40. Sheffield: Sheffield University, Department of Archaeology and Prehistory.

Baudou, E. 1960. *Die regionale und chronologische Einteilung der jüngeren Bronzezeit im Nordischen Kreis*. Stockholm: Almquist and Wiksell.

Becker, C. J. 1947. Mosefunde lerkar fra yngre Stenalder. *Aarbøger* (1947), 1–318.

1971. Mosepotter fra Danmarks jernalder: problemer omkring mosefundne lerkar og deres tolkning. *Aarbøger* (1971), 5–60.

1973. Problems of the megalithic 'mortuary houses' in Denmark. In G. Daniel and P. Kjaerum (eds.) *Megalithic Graves and Ritual*, pp. 75–9. Moesgard: Jutland Archaeological Society.

Behm-Blancke, G. 1958. Ein westgermanisches Moor- und Seeheiligtum in Nordwestthüringen. *Ausgrabungen und Funde* 3, 264–6.

1960. Latènezeit Opferfunde aus dem germanischen Moor- und Seeheiligtum von Oberdorla, Kr. Mülshausen. *Ausgrabungen und Funde* 5, 232–5.

Beil, J. 1980. Die Bronze- und urnenfelderzeitlichen Höhensiedlungen in Südwürttemberg. *Archäologisches Korrespondenzblatt* 10, 23–38.

Bender, B. 1978. Gatherer-hunter to farmer: a social perspective. *World Archaeology* 10, 203–22.

1985. Prehistoric developments in the American Midcontinent and in Brittany, north west France. In J. A. Brown and T. D. Price (eds.) *Prehistoric Hunter-Gatherers; the Development of Cultural Complexity*, pp. 21–57. London: Academic Press.

Bennike, P. and K. Ebbesen 1986. The bog finds from Sigersdal. Human sacrifice in the Neolithic. *Journal of Danish Archaeology* 5, 85–115.

Bennike, P., K. Ebbesen and L. Bender Jørgensen 1986. Early Neolithic skeletons from Bolkilde bog, Denmark. *Antiquity* 60, 199–209.

Berger, L. and M. Joos 1977. Zur Wasserführung der Zihl bei der Station

References

La Tène. In K. Stüfer and A. Zürcher (eds.) *Festschrift Walter Drack*, pp. 68–76. Zurich: T. Gut Verlag.

Berthoud, G. and F. Sabelli 1979. Our obsolete production mentality: the heresy of the communal formation. *Current Anthropology* 20, 745–60.

Bianco Peroni, V. 1979. Bronzene Gewässer- und Höhenfunde aus Italien. *Jahresbericht des Instituts für Vorgeschichte des Instituts der Universität Frankfurt am Main* (1978–9), 321–35.

Bishop, C., A. Woolley, I. Kinnes and R. Harrison 1977. Jadeite axes in Europe and the British Isles: an interim study. *Archaeologia Atlantica* 2, 1–8.

Blanchet, J-C. and B. Lambot 1977. Les dragages de l'Oise de 1973 à 1976 (première partie). *Cahiers Archéologiques de Picardie* 4, 61–88.

Blanchet, J-C, A. Cornejo, B. Lambot and S. Laurent 1978. Dragages de l'Oise de 1973 à 1976 (deuxième partie). *Cahiers Archéologiques de Picardie* 5, 89–104.

Bloch, M. 1977. The past and the present in the present. *Man* 12, 278–92.

1986. *From Blessing to Violence*. Cambridge: Cambridge University Press.

Bonnamour, L. 1976. Siedlungen der Spätbronzezeit (Bronze Final III) im Saône-Tal südlich von Chalon-sur-Saône. *Archäologisches Korrespondenzblatt* 6, 123–30.

1985. Les sites de la Saône aux âges du fer: problématique. In L. Bonnamour, A. Duval and J-P Guillaumet (eds.) *Les Ages du fer dans la vallée de la Saône*, pp. 25–31. Paris: Editions de C.N.R.S.

Bourdieu, P. 1977. *Outline of a Theory of Practice*. Cambridge: Cambridge University Press.

Bourdillon, M. and M. Fortes (eds.) 1980. *Sacrifice*. London: Academic Press.

Bouscaras, A. 1971. L'épave des bronzes de Rochelongues. *Archéologia* 39, 68–73.

Bradley, R. 1975. Salt and settlement in the Hampshire Sussex borderland. In K. De Brisay and K. Evans (eds.) *Salt – The Study of an Ancient Industry*, pp. 20–5. Colchester: Colchester Archaeological Group.

1978a. *The Prehistoric Settlement of Britain*. London: Routledge and Kegan Paul.

1978b. Prehistoric field systems in Britain and north-west Europe: a review of some recent work. *World Archaeology* 9, 265–80.

1981a. From ritual to romance: ceremonial enclosures and hillforts. In G. Guilbert (ed.) *Hill Fort Studies*, pp. 20–7. Leicester: Leicester University Press.

1981b. Economic growth and social change: two examples from Bronze Age Europe. In A. Sheridan and G. Bailey (eds.) *Economic Archaeology*, pp. 231–7. Oxford: British Archaeological Reports

(BAR International Series 96).

1982a. Position and possession: assemblage variation in the British Neolithic. *Oxford Journal of Archaeology* 1, 27–38.

1982b. The destruction of wealth in later prehistory. *Man* 17, 108–22.

1984. *The Social Foundations of Prehistoric Britain*, Harlow: Longman.

1985a. Exchange and social distance: the structure of bronze artefact distribution. *Man* 20, 692–704.

1985b. *Consumption, Change and the Archaeological Record*. Edinburgh: Edinburgh University, Department of Archaeology (Occasional Paper 13).

1987. Stages in the chronological distribution of hoards and votive deposits. *Proceedings of the Prehistoric Society* 53, 351–62.

1988. A comparative study of hoarding in the Late Bronze Age and Viking Economies. In G. Burenhult, A. Carlsson, A. Hyenstrand and T. Sjøvold (eds.) *Theoretical Approaches to Artefacts, Settlements and Society: Studies in Honour of Mats P. Malmer*, pp. 379–87. Oxford: British Archaeological Reports (BAR International Series 366).

1989a. Deaths and entrances: a contextual analysis of megalithic art. *Current Anthropology* 30, 68–75.

1989b. Darkness and light in the design of megalithic tombs. *Oxford Journal of Archaeology* 8, 251–9.

1989c. Hoarding, recycling and the consumption of prehistoric metalwork: technological change in Western Europe. *World Archaeology* 20, 249–60.

1989d. The role of Bronze Age metalwork in Scandinavia and the British Isles. In H-A Nordstrom (ed.) *Bronze Age Studies*, pp. 11–20. Stockholm: National Museum of Antiquities.

Bradley, R. and R. Chambers 1988. A new study of the cursus complex at Dorchester on Thames. *Oxford Journal of Archaeology* 7, 271–89.

Bradley, R. and K. Gordon 1988. Human skulls from the River Thames, their dating and significance. *Antiquity* 62, 503–9.

Bradley, R. and I. Hodder 1979. British prehistory: an integrated view. *Man* 14, 93–104.

Briard, J. 1965. *Les Dépôts bretons et l'âge du bronze atlantique*. Rennes: Travaux du Laboratoire d'Anthropologie de la Faculté des Sciences de Rennes.

Broholm, H. 1946. *Danmarks Bronzealder*, vol. 3. Copenhagen: Nordisk Forlag.

Broholm, H., W. Larson and G. Skjerne 1949. *The Lures of the Bronze Age*. Copenhagen: Nordisk Forlag.

Brown, D. 1971. A hoard of currency bars from Appleford, Berkshire. *Proceedings of the Prehistoric Society* 37 (i), 326–8.

Brun, P. 1986. *La Civilisation des champs d'urnes: étude critique dans le Bassin parisien*. Paris: Editions de la Maison des Sciences de l'Homme.

1988. L'entité Rhin – Suisse – France orientale: nature et évolution. In P. Brun and C. Mordant (eds.) *Le Groupe Rhin – Suisse – France orientale et la notion de civilisation des champs d'urnes*, pp. 599–620. Nemours: Mémoires du Musée de Préhistoire d'Ile-de-France.

Brunaux, J-L. 1988. *The Celtic Gauls – Gods, Rites and Sanctuaries*. London: Seaby.

Brunaux, J-L., P. Meniel and F. Poplin 1985. *Gourney I. Fouilles sur le sanctuaire et l'oppidum*. Revue Archéologique de Picardie, numéro spécial.

Burgess, C. 1968. The Later Bronze Age in the British Isles and north western France. *Archaeological Journal* 125, 1–45.

1978. The background of early metalworking in Ireland and Britain. In M. Ryan (ed.) *The Origins of Metallurgy in Atlantic Europe*, pp. 207–14. Dublin: Stationery Office.

1988. Britain at the time of the Rhine – Swiss group. In P. Brun and C. Mordant (eds.) *Le Groupe Rhin – Suisse – France orientale et la notion de civilisation des champs d'urnes*, pp. 559–73. Nemours: Mémoires du Musée de Préhistoires d'Ile-de-France.

Burgess, C. and I. Colquhoun 1988. *The Swords of Great Britain*. Munich: C. H. Beck.

Burgess, C. and D. Coombs 1979. Preface. In C. Burgess and D. Coombs (eds.) *Bronze Age Hoards*, pp. i-vii. Oxford: British Archaeological Reports (BAR British Series 76).

Burgess, C. and S. Gerloff 1981. *The Dirks and Rapiers of Great Britain and Ireland*. Munich: C. H. Beck.

Burl, A. 1976. *The Stone Circles of the British Isles*. New Haven: Yale University Press.

Burton, J. 1987. Exchange pathways at a stone axe factory in Papua New Guinea. In G. de G. Sieveking and M. Newcomer (eds.) *The Human Uses of Flint and Chert*, pp. 183–91. Cambridge: Cambridge University Press.

Butler, J. 1960. A Bronze Age concentration at Bergeroosterveld. With some notes on the axe trade across Northern Europe. *Palaeohistoria* 8, 101–27.

Cadoux, J-L 1984. L'ossuaire gaulois de Ribemont-sur-Ancre (Somme): premières observations, premières questions. *Gallia* 42, 53–78.

Callender, J. 1922. Three Bronze Age hoards recently added to the national collection, with notes on the hoard from Duddingston Loch. *Proceedings of the Society of Antiquaries of Scotland* 56, 351–65.

Callmer, J. 1980. Topographical notes on some Scanian Viking period and early medieval hoards. *Meddelanden från Lunds Universitets Historiska Museum* 3, 132–49.

Cannon, A. 1989. The historical dimension in mortuary expressions of status and sentiment. *Current Anthropology* 30, 437–58.

References

Champion, T. 1980. The early development of ironworking. *Nature* 284, 513–14.

    1989. From bronze to iron in Ireland. In M. L. S. Sørensen and R. Thomas (eds.) *The Bronze Age – Iron Age Transition in Europe* pp. 287–303. Oxford: British Archaeological Reports (BAR International Series 483).

Champion, T. and J. V. S. Megaw (eds.) 1985. *Settlement and Society: Aspects of West European Prehistory in the First Millennium* BC. Leicester: Leicester University Press.

Chappell, S. 1986. Alternative sources in regional exchange systems: a gravity model approach. *Proceedings of the Prehistoric Society* 52, 129–41.

    1987. *Stone Axe Morphology and Distribution in Neolithic Britain.* Oxford: British Archaeological Reports (BAR British Series 177).

Chenorkian, R. 1988. *Les Armes métalliques dans l'art protohistorique de l'Occident méditerranéen.* Paris: Editions du C.N.R.S.

Childe, V. G. 1950. *Prehistoric Migrations in Europe.* London: Kegan Paul, Trench and Trubner.

    1958. *The Prehistory of European Society.* Harmondsworth: Penguin.

Clark, G. and M. Neeley 1987. Social differentiation in European Mesolithic burial data. In P. Rowley-Conwy, M. Zvelebil and H. Blankholm (eds.) *Mesolithic North West Europe: Recent Trends* pp. 121–7. Sheffield: Sheffield University, Department of Archaeology and Prehistory.

Clarke, R. R. 1954. The Early Iron Age treasure from Snettisham, Norfolk. *Proceedings of the Prehistoric Society* 20, 27–86.

Cogné, J. and P-R. Giot 1952. Etude pétrographique des haches polies en Bretagne. *Bulletin de la Société Préhistorique Française* 49, 388–95.

Coles, B. and J. Coles 1986. *Sweet Track to Glastonbury – the Somerset Levels in Prehistory.* London: Thames and Hudson.

Coles, J. 1969. The Scottish Early Bronze Age metalwork. *Proceedings of the Society of Antiquaries of Scotland* 101, 1–110.

Coles, J. and A. Harding 1979. *The Bronze Age in Europe.* London: Methuen.

Coles, J. and A. Lawson (eds.) 1987. *European Wetlands in Prehistory.* Oxford: Oxford University Press.

Coles, J. and J. Taylor 1971. The Wessex Culture: a minimal view. *Antiquity* 45, 6–14.

Collis, J. 1984a. *The European Iron Age.* London: Batsford.

    1984b. *Oppida: Earliest Towns North of the Alps.* Sheffield: Sheffield University, Department of Archaeology and Prehistory.

Coombs, D. and J. Bradshaw 1979. A Carp's Tongue hoard from Stourmouth, Kent. In C. Burgess and D. Coombs (eds.) *Bronze Age Hoards,* pp. 181–9. Oxford: British Archaeological Reports (BAR British Series 67).

Coudart, A., J. Dubouloz and M. De Balloch 1981. Un habitat de la Tène Ancienne dans la valleé de l'Aisne à Menneville (Aisne). In

References

V. Kruta (ed.) *L'Age du fer en France Septentrionale*, pp. 121–30. Reims: Mémoires de la Société Archéologique Champenoise 2.

Cowen, J. 1967. The Hallstatt sword of bronze: on the Continent and in Britain. *Proceedings of the Prehistoric Society* 33, 377–54.

Cummins, W. 1979. Neolithic stone axes: distribution and trade in England and Wales. In T. Clough and W. Cummins (eds.) *Stone Axe Studies*, pp. 5–12. London: Council for British Archaeology (Research Report 23).

Cunliffe, B. 1984a. *Danebury: an Iron Age Hillfort in Hampshire*. London: Council for British Archaeology (Research Report 52).

1984b. Iron Age Wessex: continuity and change. In B. Cunliffe and D. Miles (eds.) *Aspects of the Iron Age in Central Southern Britain*, pp. 12–45. Oxford: Oxford University Committee for Archaeology.

1988. Celtic death rituals. *Archaeology* (April 1988), 39–43.

Darvill, T. 1987. *Prehistoric Britain*. London: Batsford.

Davey, P. 1971. The distribution of Later Bronze Age metalwork from Lincolnshire. *Proceedings of the Prehistoric Society* 37(i), 96–111.

Dean, M. 1984. Evidence for possible prehistoric and Roman wrecks in British waters. *International Journal of Nautical Archaeology* 13, 78–80.

De Boe, G. and F. Hubert 1977. Un installation portuaire d'époque romaine à Pommeroeul. *Archaeologia Belgica* 192, 1–57.

Déchelette, J. 1924. *Manuel d'archéologie préhistorique, celtique et gallo-romaine*, vol. 2. Paris: Picard.

Dehn, R. 1972. *Die Urnenfelderkultur in Nordwürttemberg*. Stuttgart: Müller and Graff.

De Lumley, H., M. Fontvielle and J. Abélanet 1976. Les gravures rupestres de l'âge du bronze dans la région du Monte-Bego. In J. Guilaine (ed.) *La Préhistoire française*, vol. 2, pp. 222–36. Paris: C.N.R.S.

De Mortillet, G. 1894. Cachettes de l'âge du bronze en France. *Bulletin de la Société d'Anthropologie de Paris*, 5, 298–340.

De Navarro, J. M. 1972. *The Finds from the Site of La Tène*, vol. 1. London: British Academy.

Detys, S. 1983. *Les Bois sculptés des sources de la Seine*. Paris: C.N.R.S.

Dieck, A. 1965. *Die europäischen Moorleichenfunde*. Neumünster: Karl Wachholtz.

Dolley, M. 1971. The nummular brooch from Sulgrave. In P. Clemoes and K. Hughes (eds.) *England Before the Conquest*, pp. 333–49. Cambridge: Cambridge University Press.

Driscoll, S. 1988. The relationship between history and archaeology: artefacts, documents and power. In S. Driscoll and M. Nieke (eds.) *Power and Politics in Early Medieval Britain and Ireland*, pp. 162–87. Edinburgh: Edinburgh University Press.

Dupré, G. and P. Rey 1978. Reflections on the relevance of a theory of the history of exchange. In D. Seddon (ed.) *Relations of Production*, pp. 171–208. London: Cass.

References

Earle, T. 1989. The evolution of chiefdoms. *Current Anthropology* 30, 84–8.

Edmonds, M. 1987. Rocks and risk: problems with lithic procurement strategies. In A. Brown and M. Edmonds (eds.) *Lithic Analysis and Later British Prehistory*, pp. 155–79. Oxford: British Archaeological Reports (BAR British Series 162).

Edwards, K. and K. Hirons 1984. Cereal pollen grains in pre-Elm Decline deposits: implications for the earliest agriculture in Britain and Ireland. *Journal of Archaeological Science* 11, 71–80.

Ehrbach-Schönberg, M-C. 1985. Bemerkungen zu urnenfelderzeitlichen Deponierungen in Oberösterreich. *Archäologisches Korrespondenzblatt* 15, 163–78.

Ehrenberg, M. 1977. *Bronze Age Spearheads from Berkshire, Buckinghamshire and Oxfordshire*. Oxford: British Archaeological Reports (BAR British Series 34).

Ehrenreich, R. 1985. *Trade, Technology and the Ironworking Community in the Iron Age of Southern Britain*. Oxford: British Archaeological Reports (BAR British Series 144).

Eogan, G. 1964. The Later Bronze Age in Ireland in the light of recent research. *Proceedings of the Prehistoric Society* 30, 268–351.

1983. *The Hoards of the Irish Later Bronze Age*. Dublin: University College, Dublin.

Erdbrink, D., C. Meiklejohn and J. Tacoma 1987. River Valley People: new additions to a series of fossil human remains from the Dutch–German border region in the Rhine Valley. *Proceedings of the Koninklijke Nederlandse Akademie van Wetenschappen* 90, 93–117.

Evans, J. 1881. *The Ancient Bronze Implements, Weapons and Ornaments of Great Britain and Ireland*. London: Longman, Green and Co.

Evans, J. 1955. *The Endless Web: John Dickinson and Co. Ltd. 1804–1954*. London: Cape.

Field, N. 1983. Fiskerton, Lincolnshire. *Proceedings of the Prehistoric Society* 49, 392.

Filip, J. 1977. *Celtic Civilisation and its Heritage*, second edition. Prague: Academica.

Fischer, C. 1979. Moseiligene fra Bjaeldskovdal. *Kuml* (1979), 7–44.

Fitzpatrick, A. 1984. The deposition of La Tène Iron Age metalwork in watery contexts in southern England. In B. Cunliffe and D. Miles (eds.) *Aspects of the Iron Age in Central Southern Britain*, pp. 178–90. Oxford: Oxford University Committee for Archaeology.

Fitzpatrick, A. and J. V. S. Megaw 1987. Further finds from the Le Câtillon hoard. *Proceedings of the Prehistoric Society* 53, 433–44.

Flanagan, L. 1978. Industrial resources, production and distribution in earlier Bronze Age Ireland. In M. Ryan (ed.) *The Origins of Metallurgy in Atlantic Europe*, pp. 145–63. Dublin: Stationery Office.

References

Ford, S., R. Bradley, J. Hawkes and P. Fisher 1984. Flintworking in the Metal Age. *Oxford Journal of Archaeology* 3, 157–73.

Fox, C. 1946. *A Find of the Early Iron Age from Llyn Cerrig Bach*. Cardiff: National Museum of Wales.

Freiddin, N. 1982. *The Early Iron Age in the Paris Basin*. Oxford: British Archaeological Reports (BAR International Series 131).

Friedman, J. 1979. Hegelian ecology: between Rousseau and the World Spirit. In P. Burnham and R. Ellen (eds.) *Social and Economic Systems*, pp. 253–70. London: Academic Press.

Furger-Gunti, A. 1982. Der 'Goldfund von Saint-Louis' bei Basel und ähnliche keltische Schatzfunde. *Zeitschrift für Schweizerische Archäologie und Kunstgeschichte* 39, 1–47.

Gaucher, G. 1981. *Sites et cultures de l'âge du bronze dans le Bassin parisien*. Paris: C.N.R.S.

Gelling, P. and H. E. Davidson 1969. *The Chariot of the Sun and Other Rites and Symbols of the Northern Bronze Age*. London: Dent.

Gerdsen, H. 1986. *Studien zu den Schwertgraben der älteren Hallstattzeit*. Mainz: Von Zabern.

Gerloff, S. 1975. *The Early Bronze Age Daggers in Great Britain*. Munich: C. H. Beck.

Gimbutas, M. 1965. *Bronze Age Cultures in Central and Eastern Europe*. The Hague: Mouton.

Giot, P-R., J. L'Helgouac'h and J-L Monnier 1979. *Préhistoire de la Bretagne*. Rennes: Ouest France.

Gladigow, B. 1984. Die Teilung des Opfers. Zur Interpretation von Opfern in vor-und frühgeschichtlichen Epochen. *Frühmittelalterliche Studien* 18, 19–43.

Glob, P. 1945. Ploughs of the Døstrup type found in Denmark. *Acta Archaeologica* 16, 93–111.

Godelier, M. 1977. 'Salt money' and the circulation of commodities among the Baruya of New Guinea. In M. Godelier *Perspectives in Marxist Anthropology*, pp. 127–51. Cambridge: Cambridge University Press.

Gowlett, J., R. Hedges and I. Law 1989. Radiocarbon accelerator (AMS) dating of Lindow Man. *Antiquity* 63, 71–9.

Gowlett, J., R. Hedges, I. Law and C. Perry 1987. Radiocarbon dates from the Oxford AMS system: Archaeometry datelist 5. *Archaeometry* 29, 125–55.

Graham-Campbell, J. 1982. Viking silver hoards: an introduction. In J. Farrell (ed.) *The Vikings*, pp. 32–41. Chichester: Phillimore.

Green, M. 1987. A votive shield model from Langley, Oxfordshire. *Oxford Journal of Archaeology* 6, 237–42.

Gregory, A. 1981. Thetford. *Current Archaeology* 81, 294–7.

Gregory, C. 1980. Gifts to men and gifts to gods: gift exchange and capital accumulation in contemporary Papua. *Man* 15, 628–52.

1982. *Gifts and Commodities*. London: Academic Press.

Groenman van Waateringe, W. and J. Van Regteren Altena 1961. Een

References

Vuustenen sikkel uit de voor-Romeinse ijzertijd te Den Haag. *Helinium* 1, 141–6.

Hagberg, U. K. 1988. The bronze shield from Fröslunda near Lake Vänern, West Sweden. In B. Hårdh, L. Larsson, D. Olausson and R. Petré (eds.) *Trade and Exchange in Prehistory: Studies in Honour of Berta Stjernquist*, pp. 119–26. Lund: Historiska Museum.

Harbison, P. 1969. *The Axes of the Early Bronze Age in Ireland*. Munich: C. H. Beck.

1978. Who were Ireland's first metallurgists? In M. Ryan (ed.) *The Origins of Metallurgy in Atlantic Europe*, pp. 97–105. Dublin: Stationery Office.

Harbison, P. and L. Laing 1974. *Some Iron Age Mediterranean Imports in England*. Oxford: British Archaeological Reports (BAR British Series 5).

Hårdh, B. 1976. *Wikingzeitliche Depotfunde aus Südschweden*. Bonn: Rudolf Habelt.

Harding, A. 1976. Bronze agricultural implements in Bronze Age Europe. In G. de G. Sieveking, I. Longworth and K. Wilson (eds.) *Problems in Economic and Social Archaeology*, pp. 513–22. London: Duckworth.

1980. *The Lake Dwellings of Switzerland: Retrospect and Prospect*. Edinburgh: Edinburgh University, Department of Archaeology (Occasional Paper 5).

1983. The Bronze Age in Central and Eastern Europe: advances and prospect. In F. Wendorf and A. Close (eds.) *Advances in World Archaeology* 2, 1–50.

1984. Aspects of social evolution in the Bronze Age. In J. Bintliff (ed.) *European Social Evolution*, pp. 39–45. Bradford University.

1987. *Henge Monuments and Related Sites of Great Britain*. Oxford: British Archaeological Reports (BAR British Series 175).

Haselgrove, C. 1984. Warfare and its aftermath as reflected in the precious metal coinage of Belgic Gaul. *Oxford Journal of Archaeology* 3, 81–105.

1987. *Iron Age Coinage in South-East Britain: the Archaeological Context*. Oxford: British Archaeological Reports (BAR British Series 174).

1989. Iron Age coin deposition at Harlow temple, Essex. *Oxford Journal of Archaeology* 8, 73–88.

Hawkes, C. 1954. Archaeological method and theory: some suggestions from the Old World. *American Anthropologist* 56, 155–68.

Hayen, H. 1971. Hölzerne Kultfiguren am Bohlenweg 42 im Wittemoor. *Die Kunde* 22, 88–123.

Healy, F. 1984. Farming and field monuments: the Neolithic in Norfolk. In C. Barringer (ed.) *Aspects of East Anglian Prehistory*, pp. 77–140. Norwich: Geo Books.

Helms, M. 1988. *Ulysses' Sail – An Ethnographic Odyssey of Power, Knowledge and Geographical Distance*. Princeton: Princeton

References

University Press.

Henig, M. 1984. *Religion in Roman Britain*. London: Batsford.

Herrmann, F-R. 1966. *Die Funde der Urnenfelderkultur in Mittel- und Südhessen*. Berlin: De Gruyter.

Hibbs, J. 1984. The Neolithic of Brittany and Normandy. In C. Scarre (ed.) *Ancient France*, pp. 271–323. Edinburgh: Edinburgh University Press.

Hodder, I. 1979. Social and economic stress and material culture patterning. *American Antiquity* 44, 446–54.

1987. The contribution of the long term. In I. Hodder (ed.) *Archaeology as Long-term History*, pp. 1–8. Cambridge: Cambridge University Press.

1988. Material culture texts and social change: a theoretical discussion and some archaeological examples. *Proceedings of the Prehistoric Society* 54, 67–75.

Hodder, I. and C. Orton 1976. *Spatial Analysis in Archaeology*. Cambridge: Cambridge University Press.

Hodges, H. 1957. Studies in the Late Bronze Age in Ireland, 3: the hoards of bronze implements. *Ulster Journal of Archaeology* 20, 51–63.

Hodges, R. 1982. *Dark Age Economics*. London: Duckworth.

Holgate, R. 1988. *The Neolithic Settlement of the Thames Basin*. Oxford: British Archaeological Reports (BAR British Series 194).

Hooper, B. and B. O'Connor 1976. A bronze spearhead and its shaft from the River Thames at Hammersmith. *Archaeological Journal* 133, 33–7.

Horne, P. 1986. Roman or Celtic temples? a case study. In M. Henig and A. King (eds.) *Pagan Gods and Shrines of the Roman Empire*, pp. 15–24. Oxford: Oxford University Committee for Archaeology.

Horne, P. and A. King 1980. Romano-Celtic temples in Continental Europe: a gazetteer of those with known plans. In W. Rodwell (ed.) *Temples, Churches and Religion: Recent Research in Roman Britain*, pp. 369–555. Oxford: British Archaeological Reports (BAR British Series 77).

Hornsey, R. 1987. Le Grand Menhir Brisé – success or failure? *Oxford Journal of Archaeology* 6, 185–217.

Houlder, C. 1976. Stone axes and henge monuments. In G. Boon and J. Lewis (eds.) *Welsh Antiquity*, pp. 55–62. Cardiff: National Museum of Wales.

Hubert, F. 1982. Site portuaire de Pommeroeul. Catalogue de matérial préhistorique et protohistorique. *Archaeologia Belgica* 248, 1–61.

Hubert, H. and M. Mauss 1964 (originally published in French in 1898). *Sacrifice: Its Nature and Functions*. Chicago: University of Chicago Press.

Hugues, C. 1965. La Découverte sous-marine de Rochelongues, Agde (Hérault). *Comptes Rendues d'Academie d'Inscriptions* (1965), 176–8.

References

(Hérault). *Comptes Rendues d'Academie d'Inscriptions* (1965), 176–8.

Hundt, H.-J. 1955. Versuch zur Deutung der Depotfunde der nordischen jüngeren Bronzezeit unter besonderer Berücksichtigung Mecklenburgs. *Jahrbuch des Römisch-Germanischen Zentralmuseums Mainz* 2, 95–140.

Ilkjaer, J. and J. Lønstrup 1982. Interpretation of the great votive deposits of Iron Age weapons. *Journal of Danish Archaeology* 1, 95–103.

1983. Der Moorfund im Tal der Illerup Å bei Skanderborg in Ostjutland (Dänemark). *Germania* 61, 95–116.

Jacobi, G. 1974. *Werzkeug und Gerät aus dem Oppidum von Manching.* Wiesbaden: Franz Steiner.

Jankuhn, H. 1977. Archäologische Beobachtungen zur Religion der festländischen Angeln. *Studien zur Sachsenforschung* 1, 215–34.

Jensen, J. 1972. Ein neues Hallstattschwert aus Dänemark: Beitrag zur Problematik der jungbronzezeitlichen Votivfunde. *Acta Archaeologica* 43, 115–64.

Jessup, R. 1939. Further excavations at Julliberries Grave, Chilham, Kent. *Antiquaries Journal* 19, 260–81.

Jockenhövel, A. 1974. Zu befestigten Siedlungen der Urnenfelderzeit aus Süddeutschland. *Fundberichte aus Hessen* 14, 19–62.

Jope, E. M. 1961. Daggers of the Early Iron Age in Britain. *Proceedings of the Prehistoric Society* 27, 307–43.

Kent, J. 1974. Interpreting coin finds. In J. Casey and R. Reece (eds.) *Coins and the Archaeologist*, pp. 184–200. Oxford: British Archaeological Reports (BAR British Series 4).

1978. The London area in the Late Iron Age: an interpretation of the earliest coins. In J. Bird, H. Chapman and J. Clark (eds.) *Collectanea Londiniensia*, pp. 53–8. London: London and Middlesex Archaeological Society (Special Paper 2).

Kibbert, K. 1980. *Die Äxte und Beile im mittleren Westdeutschland*, 1. Munich: C. H. Beck.

Kiernan, J. 1988. The other side of the coin: the conversion of money to religious purposes in Zulu Zionist churches. *Man* 23, 453–68.

Kimes, T., C. Haselgrove and I. Hodder 1982. A method for the identification of the location of regional cultural boundaries. *Journal of Anthropological Archaeology* 1, 113–21.

Kinnes, I. 1979. *Round Barrows and Ring-ditches in the British Neolithic.* London: British Museum (Occasional Paper 7).

Kopytoff, I. 1986. The cultural biography of things: commoditisation as process. In A. Appadurai (ed.) *The Social Life of Things*, pp. 64–91. Cambridge: Cambridge University Press.

Kristiansen, K. 1974. En kildekritisk analyse af depotfund fra Danmarks yngre bronzealder (periode IV–V). Et bidrag til den arkaeologisk kildekritik. *Aarbøger* (1974), 119–60.

1978. The consumption of wealth in Bronze Age Denmark. In K. Kristiansen and C. Paludan-Müller (eds.) *New Directions in Scandinavian Archaeology*, pp. 158–90. Copenhagen: National Museum

References

of Denmark.

1981. A social history of Danish archaeology, 1805–1975. In G. Daniel (ed.) *Towards a History of Archaeology*, pp. 20–44. London: Thames and Hudson.

1984a. Ideology and material culture: an archaeological perspective. In M. Spriggs (ed.) *Marxist Perspectives in Archaeology*, pp. 72–100. Cambridge: Cambridge University Press.

1984b. Krieger und Häuptlinge in der Bronzezeit Dänemarks. *Jahrbuch des Römisch-Germanischen Zentralmuseums Mainz* 31, 187–208.

1985. Bronze hoards from the Late Neolithic and Early Bronze Age. In K. Kristiansen (ed.) *Archaeological Formation Processes: The Representativity of Archaeological Remains from Danish Prehistory*, pp. 129–41. Copenhagen: Nationalmuseets Forlag.

(ed.) 1985. *Archaeological Formation Processes: The Representativity of Archaeological Remains from Danish Prehistory*. Copenhagen: Nationalmuseets Forlag.

1987. From stone to bronze: the evolution of social complexity in Northern Europe. In E. Brumfiel and T. Earle (eds.) *Specialisation, Exchange and Complex Societies*, pp. 30–51. Cambridge: Cambridge University Press.

Kubach, W. 1983. Bronzezeitliche Deponierungen im Nordhessischen sowie im Weser-und Leinebergland. *Jahrbuch des Römisch-Germanischen Zentralmuseums Mainz* 30, 113–59.

1985. Einzel- und Mehrstückdeponierungen und ihre Fundplätze. *Archäologisches Korrespondenzblatt* 15, 179–85.

Kyll, N. 1966. Heidnische Weihe- und Votivgaben aus der Römerzeit des Trierer Landes. *Trierer Zeitschrift* 29, 5–113.

Larsson, T. 1984. Multi-level exchange and cultural interaction in the late Scandinavian Bronze Age. In K. Kristiansen (ed.) *Settlement and Economy in Later Scandinavian Prehistory*, pp. 63–83. Oxford: British Archaeological Reports (BAR International Series 211).

1986. *The Bronze Age Metalwork in Southern Sweden*. Umeå: Umeå University, Department of Archaeology.

Lawson, A. 1980. The evidence for Later Bronze Age settlement and burial in Norfolk. In J. Barrett and R. Bradley (eds.) *Settlement and Society in the British Later Bronze Age*, pp. 271–94. Oxford: British Archaeological Reports (BAR British Series 83).

Le Roux, C.-T. 1979. Stone axes of Brittany and the Marches. In T. Clough and W. Cummins (eds.) *Stone Axe Studies*, pp. 49–56. London: Council for British Archaeology (Research Report 23).

1984. A propos des fouilles de Gavrinis (Morbihan): nouvelles données sur l'art mégalithique armoricain. *Bulletin de la Société Préhistorique Française* 81, 89–96.

Le Rouzic, Z. 1927. Dépôts rituels de haches en pierre polie découverts dans la région de Carnac. *Bulletin de la Société Préhistorique Française* 24, 156–60.

References

Le Rouzic, Z., M. Péquart and S.-J. Péquart 1923. *Carnac. Fouilles faites dans la région.* Paris: Berger-Lavrault.

Levinson, K. 1983. Jernets introduktion i Danmark. *Kuml* (1982–83), 153–68.

Levy, J. 1982. *Social and Religious Organisation in Bronze Age Denmark: An Analysis of Ritual Hoard Finds.* Oxford: British Archaeological Reports (BAR International Series 124).

Lewis-Williams, J. and T. Dowson 1988. Signs of all times: entoptic phenomena in Upper Palaeolithic art. *Current Anthropology* 209, 201–45.

L'Helgouac'h, J. 1965. *Les Sépultures mégalithiques en Armorique.* Rennes: Laboratoire d'Anthropologie Préhistorique de la Faculté des Sciences.

1983. Les idoles qu'on abat (ou les vicissitudes des grandes stèles de Locmariaquer). *Bulletin de la Société Polymathique du Morbihan* 110, 57–68.

Linders, T. and G. Nordquist (eds.) 1987. *Gifts to the Gods.* Uppsala: Boreas 15.

Lomborg, E. 1973. *Die Flintdolche Dänemarks.* Copenhagen: H. J. Lynge.

Madsen, T. 1982. Settlement systems of early agricultural societies in East Jutland, Denmark: a regional study of change. *Journal of Anthropological Archaeology* 1, 197–236.

1988. Causewayed enclosures in south Scandinavia. In C. Burgess, P. Topping, C. Mordant and M. Maddison (eds.) *Enclosures and Defences in the Neolithic of Western Europe,* pp. 301–36. Oxford: British Archaeological Reports (BAR International Series 403).

Magnard, M. 1978. Informations archéologiques: circonscription de Haute Normandie. *Gallia* 36, 295–313.

Maier, R. A. 1977. Urgeschichtliche Opferreste aus einer Felsspalte und einer Schachthöhle der Fränkischen Alb. *Germania* 55, 21–32.

Malmer, M. 1981. *A Chorological Study of North European Rock Art.* Stockholm: Almquist and Wiksell.

Marien, M. 1970. *Le Trou de l'ambre au bois de Wérimont, Eprave.* Musées Royaux d'Art et d'Historie. Brussels.

Marsh, G. and B. West 1981. Skullduggery in Roman London? *Transactions of the London and Middlesex Archaeological Society* 32, 86–102.

Mayer, E. F. 1977. *Die Äxte und Beile in Österreich.* Munich: C. H. Beck.

1979. Bronzezeitliche Passfunde im Alpenraum. *Jahresbericht des Instituts für Vorgeschichte der Universität Frankfurt am Main* (1978–79), 179–87.

Megaw, B. and E. Hardy 1938. British decorated axes and their diffusion during the earlier part of the Bronze Age. *Proceedings of the Prehistoric Society* 4, 272–307.

References

Megaw, J. V. S. 1970. *The Art of European Iron Age*. Bath: Adams and Dart.

Megaw, J. V. S. and D. D. A. Simpson 1979. *Introduction to British Prehistory*. Leicester: Leicester University Press.

Meillassoux, C. 1968. Ostentation, destruction, reproduction. *Economie et Société* 1, 93–105.

1981. *Maidens, Meal and Money: Capitalism and the Domestic Economy*. Cambridge: Cambridge University Press.

Mellars, P. 1987. *Excavations on Oronsay. Prehistoric Human Ecology on a Small Island*. Edinburgh: Edinburgh University Press.

Menke, M. 1979. Studien zu den frühbronzezeitlichen Metalldepots Bayern. *Jahresbericht der Bayerischen Bodendenkmalpflege* 18/20, 5–205.

Mercer, R. 1980. *Hambledon Hill – A Neolithic Landscape*. Edinburgh: Edinburgh University Press.

Merrifield, R. 1962. Coins from the bed of the Walbrook and their significance. *Antiquaries Journal* 42, 38–52.

1983. *London – City of the Romans*. London: Batsford.

Merriman, N. 1987. A prehistory for Central London? *London Archaeologist* 5, 318–26.

Miller, D. 1985. *Artefacts as Categories*. Cambridge: Cambridge University Press.

1987. *Material Culture and Mass Consumption*. Oxford: Blackwell.

Mohen, J.-P. 1977. *L'Age du bronze dans la région de Paris*. Paris: Editions des Musées Nationaux.

Mommsen, T., P. Krueger and A. Watson (eds.) 1985. *The Digest of Justinian*, vol. 4. Philadelphia: University of Pennsylvania Press.

Mordant, C., D. Mordant and J.-Y. Prampart 1976. *Le Depôt de bronze de Villethiery (Yonne)*. Paris: C.N.R.S.

Muckelroy, K. 1980. Two Bronze Age shipwrecks in British waters. *Antiquity* 44, 100–9.

1981. Middle Bronze Age trade between Britain and Europe: a maritime perspective. *Proceedings of the Prehistoric Society* 47, 275–97.

Needham, S. 1979. Two recent British shield finds and their Continental parallels. *Proceedings of the Prehistoric Society* 45, 111–34.

1980. An assemblage of Late Bronze Age metalworking debris from Dainton, Devon. *Proceedings of the Prehistoric Society* 46, 177–215.

1981. *The Bulford–Helsbury Manufacturing Tradition: The Production of Stogursey Socketed Axes during the Later Bronze Age in Southern Britain*. London: British Museum (Occasional Paper 13).

1988. Selective deposition in the British Early Bronze Age. *World Archaeology* 20, 229–48.

Needham, S. and C. Burgess 1980. The Later Bronze Age in the lower Thames valley: the metalwork evidence. In J. Barrett and R. Bradley (eds.) *Settlement and Society in the British Later Bronze Age*, pp.

References

437–69. Oxford: British Archaeological Reports (BAR British Series 83).

Needham, S., M. Leese, D. Hook and M. Hughes 1989. Developments in the Early Bronze Age metallurgy of southern Britain. *World Archaeology* 20, 383–402.

Nielsen, P. O. 1977. Die Flintbeile der Frühen Trichterbecherkultur in Dänemark. *Acta Archaeologica* 48, 61–138.

Nordbladh, J. and J. Rosvall 1981. *Hällristningar Kville Härad i Bohuslän*. Göteborg: Fornminnesföreningen i Göteborg.

Northover, P. 1982. The exploration of the long-distance movement of bronze in Bronze and Early Iron Age Europe. *Bulletin of the University of London Institute of Archaeology* 19, 45–72.

O'Connell, M. 1986. *Petters Sports Field, Egham: Excavation of a Late Bronze Age / Early Iron Age Site*. Guildford: Surrey Archaeological Society (Research Volume 10).

O'Connor, B. 1980. *Cross-Channel Relations in the Late Bronze Age*. Oxford: British Archaeological Reports (BAR International Series 91).

O'Drisceoil, D. 1988. Burnt mounds: cooking or bathing. *Antiquity* 62, 671–80.

Ogilvie, R. 1969. *Rome and her Gods in the Age of Augustus*. London: Chatto and Windus.

O'Kelly and C. Shell 1978. Stone objects and a bronze axe from Newgrange, Co. Meath. In M. Ryan (ed.) *The Origins of Metallurgy in Atlantic Europe*, pp. 127–44. Dublin: Stationery Office.

O'Shea, J. 1984. *Mortuary Variability: An Archaeological Investigation*. London: Academic Press.

Östergren, M. 1985. Metalldetektorn i praktiskt bruk. *Gotländskt Arkiv* 57, 11–28.

Ottaway, B. 1973. Early copper ornaments in northern Europe. *Proceedings of the Prehistoric Society* 39, 294–331.

Ottaway, B. and C. Strahm 1974. Swiss copper beads: currency, ornaments or prestige items? *World Archaeology* 6, 307–21.

Parker Pearson, M. 1982. Mortuary practices, society and ideology: an ethnoarchaeologocial study. In I. Hodder (ed.) *Symbolic and Structural Archaeology*, pp. 99–113. Cambridge: Cambridge University Press.

1984. Economic and ideological change: cyclical growth in the pre-state societies of Jutland. In D. Miller and C. Tilley (eds.) *Ideology, Power and Prehistory*, pp. 69–92. Cambridge: Cambridge University Press.

Pauli, L. 1985. Einige Anmerkungen zum Problem der Hortfunde. *Archäologisches Korrespondenzblatt* 15, 195–206.

Penhallurick, R. 1986. *Tin in Antiquity*. London: Institute of Metals.

Phillips, C. W. 1941. Some recent finds from the Trent near Nottingham. *Antiquaries Journal* 21, 133–43.

Piggott, S. 1963. The Bronze Age pit at Swanwick, Hampshire: a postscript. *Antiquaries Journal*, 43, 286–7.

1968. *The Druids*. London: Thames and Hudson.

Pittioni, R. 1968. Zur Interpretation der Station Le Tène. In E. Schmid, L. Berger and P. Bürgin (eds.) *Provincialia*, pp. 615–18. Basel: Schwabe.

Pleiner, R. 1980. Early iron metallurgy in Europe. In T. Wertime and J. Muhly (eds.) *The Coming of the Age of Iron*, pp. 375–415. New Haven: Yale University Press.

1981. Die Wege des Eisen nach Europa. In R. Pleiner (ed.) *Frühes Eisen in Europa*, pp. 115–28. Schaffshausen: Peter Meli.

Pryor, F. 1980a. Will it all come out in the Wash? Reflections at the end of eight years digging. In J. Barrett and R. Bradley (eds.) *Settlement and Society in the British Later Bronze Age*, pp. 483–500. Oxford: British Archaeological Reports (BAR British Series 83).

1980b. *A Catalogue of British and Irish Prehistoric Bronzes in the Royal Ontario Museum*. Toronto: Royal Ontario Museum.

1987. Etton 1986. Neolithic metamorphoses. *Antiquity* 61, 78–80.

Randsborg, K. 1974. Social stratification in Bronze Age Denmark: a study in the regulation of cultural systems. *Praehistorische Zeitschrift* 49, 38–61.

1978. Resource distribution and the function of copper in Early Neolithic Denmark. In M. Ryan (ed.) *The Origins of Metallury in Atlantic Europe*, pp. 303–18. Dublin: Stationery Office.

1980. *The Viking Age in Denmark*. London: Duckworth.

Rapin, A. and J.-L. Brunaux 1988. *Gournay II: boucliers et lances, dépôts et trophées*. Revue Archéologique de Picardie: numéro spécial.

Rech, M. 1979. *Studien zu Depotfunden der Trichterbecher- und Einzelgrabkultur des Nordens*. Neumünster: Karl Wacholz.

Reichel-Dolmatoff, G. 1978. Drug-induced optical sensations and their relationship to applied art among some Colombian Indians. In M. Greenhalgh and J. V. S. Megaw (eds.) *Art in Society*, pp. 289–304. London: Duckworth.

Reinecke, P. 1933. Die kaiserzeitlichen Germanenfunde aus dem Bayerischen Anteil an der Germania Magna. *Bericht der Römisch-Germanischen Kommission* 23, 144–206.

Renfrew, C. 1976. Megaliths, territories and populations. In S. De Laet (ed.) *Acculturation and Continuity in Atlantic Europe*, pp. 198–220. Bruges: De Tempel.

1977. Alternative models for exchange and spatial distribution. In T. Earle and J. Ericson (eds.) *Exchange Systems in Prehistory*, pp. 71–90. London: Academic Press.

1979. The tree ring calibration of radiocarbon: an archaeological evaluation. In C. Renfrew, *Problems in European Prehistory*, pp. 340–76. Edinburgh: Edinburgh University Press.

1986. Varna and the emergence of wealth in prehistoric Europe. In A. Appadurai (ed.) *The Social Life of Things*, pp. 141–68. Cambridge: Cambridge University Press.

References

Richards, C. and J. Thomas 1984. Ritual activity and structured deposition in Later Neolithic Wessex. In R. Bradley and J. Gardiner (eds.) *Neolithic Studies*, pp. 189–218. Oxford: British Archaeological Reports (BAR British Series 133).

Rittershofer, K.-F. 1987. Grabraub in der Bronzezeit. *Bericht der Römisch-Germanischen Kommission* 68, 5–23.

Romeuf, A.-M. 1986. Les ex-votos en bois de Chamalières (Puy-de-Dôme) et les sources de la Seine (Côte-d'Or). *Gallia* 44, 65–89.

Rosenberg, G. 1937. *Hjortspringfundet*. Copenhagen: Nordiska Fortidsminder 3.1.

Rosman, A. and P. Rubel 1971. *Feasting with Mine Enemy*. New York: Columbia University Press.

Rowlands, M. 1971. The archaeological interpretation of prehistoric metalworking. *World Archaeology* 3, 210–24.

   1976. *The Production and Distribution of Metalwork in the Middle Bronze Age in Southern England*. Oxford: British Archaeological Reports (BAR British Series 31).

   1980. Kinship, alliance and exchange in the European Bronze Age. In J. Barrett and R. Bradley (eds.) *Settlement and Society in the British Later Bronze Age*, pp. 15–55. Oxford: British Archaeological Reports (BAR British Series 83).

   1984. Conceptualising the European Bronze and Early Iron Ages. In J. Bintliff (ed.) *European Social Evolution*, pp. 147–56. Bradford: Bradford University.

Rowlands, M. and J. Gledhill 1977. The relation between archaeology and anthropology. In M. Spriggs (eds.) *Archaeology and Anthropology: Areas of Mutual Interest*, pp. 143–58. Oxford: British Archaeological Reports (BAR International Series 19).

Rowley-Conwy, P. 1984. The laziness of the short-distance hunter: the origins of agriculture in Western Denmark. *Journal of Anthropological Archaeology* 4, 300–24.

Roymans, N. 1988. Religion and society in Late Iron Age Northern Gaul. In R. Jones, T. Bloemers, S. Dyson and M. Biddle (eds.) *First Millennium Papers*, pp. 55–71. Oxford: British Archaeological Reports (BAR International Series 401).

Roynams, N. and W. Van der Sanden 1980. Celtic coins from the Netherlands and their archaeological context. *Berichten van de Rijksdienst voor het Oudheidkundig Bodemonderzoeck* 30, 173–254.

Rychner, V. 1987. *Auvernier 1968–1975: le mobilier métallique du Bronze Final*. Lausanne: Bibliothèque Vaudoise.

Sahlins, M. 1974. *Stone Age Economics*. London: Tavistock Publications.

Savage, R. 1979. Technical notes on the Watford sword fragments. In C. Burgess and D. Coombs (eds.) *Bronze Age Hoards*, pp. 221–8. Oxford: British Archaeological Reports (BAR British Series 67).

Schauer, P. 1971. *Die Schwerter in Süddeutschland, Österreich und der Schweiz*, vol. 1. Munich: C. H. Beck.

References

1972. Zur Herkunft der bronzenen Hallstatt Schwerter. *Archäologisches Korrespondenzblatt* 2, 261–70.

Schiffer, M. 1987. *Formation Processes of the Archaeological Record*. Albuquerque: University of New Mexico Press.

Schubart, H. 1972. *Die Funde der älteren Bronzezeit in Mecklenburg*. Neumünster: Karl Wacholz.

Schwab, H. 1972. Entdeckung einer keltischen Brücke an der Zihl und ihre Bedeutung für la Tène. *Archäologisches Korrespondenzblatt* 2, 289–94.

1974. Neue Ergebnisse zur Topographie von La Tène. *Germania* 52, 348–67.

Schwarz, K. 1975. Die Geschichte eines keltischen Temenos im nördlichen Alpenvorland. *Ausgrabungen in Deutschland* 1, 324–58.

Shanks, M. and C. Tilley 1987a. *Social Theory and Archaeology*. Cambridge: Polity Press.

1987b. *Re-Constructing Archaeology*. Cambridge: Cambridge University Press.

Shee Twohig, E. 1981. *The Megalithic Art of Western Europe*. Oxford: Clarendon Press.

Shennan, S. 1976. Bell Beakers and their context in Central Europe. In J. Lanting and J. D. Van der Waals (eds.) *Glockenbecher Symposion*, pp. 231–9. Haarlem: Fibula van Dishoek.

1986. Central Europe in the third millennium BC: an evolutionary trajectory for the beginning of the European Bronze Age. *Journal of Anthropological Archaeology* 5, 115–46.

Sherratt, A. 1976. Resources, technology and trade. In G. de G. Sieveking, I. Longworth and K. Wilson (eds.) *Problems in Economic and Social Archaeology*, pp. 557–81. London: Duckworth.

Simpson, D. D. A. and J. Thawley 1973. Single grave art in Britain. *Scottish Archaeological Forum* 4, 81–104.

Sklenàr, K. 1983. *Archaeology in Central Europe: The First 500 Years*. Leicester: Leicester University Press.

Smith, R. A. 1911. Lake-dwellings in Holderness, Yorkshire, discovered by Thos. Boynton Esq. FSA, 1880–1. *Archaeologia* 62, 593–610.

Sørensen, M. L. S. 1987. Material order and cultural classification: the role of bronze objects in the transformation from Bronze Age to Iron Age in Scandinavia. In I. Hodder (ed.) *The Archaeology of Contextual Meanings*, pp. 90–101. Cambridge: Cambridge University Press.

Spratling, M. 1980. Weighing of gold in prehistoric Europe. In W. Oddy (ed.) *Aspects of Early Metallurgy*, pp. 179–83. London: British Museum (Occasional Paper 17).

Stein, F. 1976. *Bronzezeitliche Hortfunde in Süddeutschland*. Bonn: Rudolf Habelt.

Stjernquist, B. 1970. Germanische Quellenopfer. In H. Jankuhn (ed.) *Vorgeschichtliche Heiligtümer und Opferplätze in Mittel- und Nordeuropa*, pp. 78–99. Göttingen: Vanderhoeck and Ruprecht.

References

Strathern, A. 1971. *The Rope of Moka*. Cambridge: Cambridge University Press.

Strömberg, M. 1971. *Die Megalithgräber von Hagestad*. Lund: Acta Archaeologica Lundensia 9.

Sweetman, D. 1985. A Late Neolithic/Early Bronze Age pit circle at Newgrange, Co. Meath. *Proceedings of the Royal Irish Academy, Section C* 85, 195–221.

Sylvest, B. and I. Sylvest 1960. Arupsgårdfundet. *Kuml* (1960), 9–25.

Tackenberg, K. 1974. *Die jungere Bronzezeit in Nordwestdeutschland, Teil* 2. Hildesheim: Landesmuseum zu Hannover.

Tauber, H. 1979. Kulstoff-14 datering af moselig. *Kuml* (1979), 73–8.

1982. Carbon-13 evidence for the diet of prehistoric humans in Denmark. *PACT* 7, 235–7.

Taylor, J. 1970. Lunulae reconsidered. *Proceedings of the Prehistoric Society* 36, 38–81.

Taylor, R. 1982. The hoard from West Buckland, Somerset. *Antiquaries Journal* 62, 13–17.

1988. Hoards – the interpretation and analysis of hoards of the Bronze Age in southern Britain. Ph.D. thesis, Reading University.

Therkorn, L. 1987. The interrelationships of materials and meanings: some suggestions on housing concerns within Iron Age Noord-Holland. In I. Hodder (ed.) *The Archaeology of Contextual Meanings*, pp. 102–10. Cambridge: Cambridge University Press.

Thomas, J. 1988. Neolithic explanations revisited: the Mesolithic–Neolithic transition in Britain and south Scandinavia. *Proceedings of the Prehistoric Society* 54, 59–66.

Thomas, R. 1989. The bronze-iron transition in southern England. In M. L. S. Sørensen, and R. Thomas (eds.) *The Bronze Age–Iron Age Transition in Europe*, pp. 263–86. Oxford: British Archaeological Reports (BAR International Series 483).

in press. Metalwork, rivers and the disposal of the dead in the British Later Bronze Age. *Antiquity* 64.

Thorpe, I. and C. Richards 1984. The decline of ritual authority and the introduction of Beakers into Britain. In R. Bradley and J. Gardiner (eds.) *Neolithic Studies*, pp. 67–84. Oxford: British Archaeological Reports (BAR British Series 133).

Thorsen, S. 1980. 'Klokkehøj' ved Bøjden. Et sydvestfynsk dyssekammer med velbevaret primaergrav. *Kuml* (1980), 105–46.

Thrane, H. 1972. Eyt nyt depotfund fra Sønderjylland og dansk fund af skaftlapøkser fra broncealder. *Aarbøger* (1972), 71–125.

Todd, M. 1981. *Roman Britain*. Brighton: Harvester Press.

1987. *The Northern Barbarians 100 BC–AD 300*. Oxford: Blackwell.

Torbrügge, W. 1971. Vor- und frügeschichtliche Flussfunde. *Bericht der Römisch-Germanischen Kommission* 51–52, 1–146.

Trigger, B. 1980. *Gordon Childe. Revolutions in Archaeology*. London: Thames and Hudson.

Tylecote, R. 1987. *The Early History of Metallurgy in Europe*. Harlow:

References

Longman.

Van der Waals, J. D. 1964. Neolithic disc wheels in the Netherlands. *Palaeohistoria* 10, 103–46.

Vatin, C. 1972. Wood sculptures from Gallo-Roman Auvergne. *Antiquity* 46, 39–42.

Verron, G. 1983. L'interprétation des dépôts de l'âge du bronze à lumière de prospections et de fouilles récentes. In J. Briard (ed.) *Enclos funeraires et structures d'habitat en Europe du nord-ouest*, pp. 263–80. Rennes: Laboratoire d'Anthropologie, Université de Rennes-Beaulieu.

Vestergaard, E. 1987. The perpetual reconstruction of the past. In I. Hodder (ed.) *Archaeology as Long-term History*, pp. 63–7. Cambridge: Cambridge University Press.

Von Brunn, W. A. 1959. *Die Hortfunde der frühen Bronzezeit aus Sachsen-Anhalt, Sachsen und Thüringen*. Berlin: Akademie Verlag.

Vouga, P. 1923. *La Tène: Monographie de la Station*. Leipzig: K. Hiersman.

Wainwright, G. 1979. *Mount Pleasant, Dorset: Excavations 1970–1971*. London: Society of Antiquaries (Research Report 37).

Wainwright, G. and I. Longworth 1971. *Durrington Walls: Excavations 1966–1968*. London: Society of Antiquaries (Research Report 29).

Wait, G. 1985. *Ritual and Religion in Iron Age Britain*. Oxford: British Archaeological Report (BAR British Series 149).

Wall, J. 1987. The role of daggers in Early Bronze Age Britain: the evidence of wear analysis. *Oxford Journal of Archaeology* 6, 115–18.

Warmenbol, E. 1986. British rapiers with trapezoidal butt found in Belgium. *Proceedings of the Prehistoric Society* 52, 153–8.

1988a. Le groupe Rhin – Suisse – France orientale et les grottes sépulchrales du bronze final en Haute-Belgique. In P. Brun and C. Mordant (eds.) *Le Groupe Rhin – Suisse – France orientale et la notion de civilisation des champs d'urnes*, pp. 153–63. Nemours: Mémoires du Musée Préhistorique d'Ile-de-France.

1988b. Broken bronzes and burnt bones. The transition from Bronze to Iron Age in the Low Countries. *Helinium* 28, 244–70.

Wegner, G. 1976. *Die vorgeschichtlichen Flussfunde aus dem Main und aus dem Rhein bei Mainz*. Kallmunz: Michael Lassleben.

Whimster, R. 1981. *Burial Practices in Iron Age Britain*. Oxford: British Archaeological Reports (BAR British Series 90).

Willroth, K.-H. 1984. Die Opferfunde der älteren Bronzezeit in Südskandinavien. *Frühmittelalterliche Studien* 18, 48–72.

Wilson, C. 1981. Burials within settlements in southern Britain during the pre-Roman Iron Age. *Bulletin of the London University Institute of Archaeology* 18, 127–69.

Woodman, P. 1978. *The Mesolithic in Ireland*. Oxford: British Archaeological Reports (BAR British Series 58).

Woodward, D. 1985. 'Swords into ploughshares': recycling in pre-industrial England. *Economic History Review* 38, 175–91.

References

Worsley, P. 1968. *The Trumpet Shall Sound: A Study of 'Cargo' Cults in Melanesia.* London: McGibbon and Kee.

Wyss, R. 1975. Sépultures, sanctuaires, sacrifices et leur relation avec l'habitat en Suisse à l'époque celtique. In P.-M. Duval and W. Kruta (eds.) *L'Habitat et la nécropole à l'âge du fer en Europe occidentale et centrale,* pp. 75–86. Paris: Libraire Honoré Champion.

Zeist, W. van and H. Waterbolk 1961. A Bronze Age sanctuary in the raised bog at Bargeroosterveld (Dr.). *Helinium* 1, 5–19.

Zimmerman, W. 1970. Urgeschichtliche Opferfunde aus Flüssen, Mooren, Quellen und Brunnen Südwestdeutschlands. *Neue Ausgrabungen und Forschungen in Niedersachsen* 6, 53–92.

Zvelebil, M. and P. Rowley-Conwy 1986. Foragers and farmers in Atlantic Europe. In M. Zvelebil (ed.) *Hunters in Transition,* pp. 67–93. Cambridge: Cambridge University Press.

Index

(Figure numbers are in italics)

adzes, 70
aerial survey, 31
agriculture, 44, 45, 47, 57, 65, 97, 184
  cereal pollen, 64, 65
  clearance, 65
  colonisation, 46
  equipment, 157, 164, 165, 166, 170, 178
  intensification, 131
  land, 57, 73, 131, 135, 137, 143
  produce, 183
  settlement, 45, 48
All Canning's Cross; ceramic style, 4 (22)
amber, 58, 64, 74
  beads, 64
  hoards, 58, 11 (59), Pl. 8 (60), 199
America, 36
animal bones, 11, 28, 58, 11 (59), 61, 63, 67, 74, 107, 108, 111, 143, 157, 161, 164, 165, 166, 168, 170, 173, 174, 176, 183, 186, 188, 198, 199
  burial, 176
  pig, 69
animals, 10
Appleford, 172
arrowheads, 70
Årupgård, 64
Atlantic tradition, 32 (140)
Austria, 88
  Upper, 142
'axe factories'/production centres, 46, 48, 65
axe-heads, 48, 49, 7 (50), 51
'axe-ploughs', 48, 49, 7 (50), 51
axes, 41, 43–5, 48, 51, 54, 55, 58, 94, 97, 99, 116, 117, 118–19, 120, 121, 129, 144, 199, 200
  British, 86

bronze, 196; decorated, 8, 196
  Continental, 66
  copper, 63–4, 75, 196, 200; shafthole, 86
  Cornish, 65, 13 (66)
  Cumbrian, 65
  decorated, 83
  depiction of in rock art, 48–9, 7 (50), 51, 53, 9 (54), 56, 74, 83, 84, 86, 90
  exchange of, 65
  flint, Pl. 7 (45), 66; British, 70, 75
  hafted, 84
  Irish, 8, 86
  jadeite, 66, 67
  metal, 35, 48, 64, 73, 83, 84, 85, 86, 87, 88, 89, 90, 99, 103; decorated, 86, Pl. 9 (87), 87
  Neolithic, 24, 27, 46, 51
  Papua New Guinea, 35
  polished, 44, 56, 57, 69, 73, 196
  Scandinavian, 67, 30 (132), 133
  socketed, 117, 119, 37 (166)
  stone, 35, 44, 47–8, 52, 58, 61, 65–7, 70, 71, 73, 74, 75, 80, 90, 91, 196, 197; hoards, 47, 63–4, 74; polished, 43, 44, 46, 8 (52), 56
  unhafted, 85, 86
  winged, 119–20

Baden Württenberg, 139
Bargeroosterveld, 133
barrow(s), 112, 131, 135
  burials, 101, 102, 103, 22 (104–5), 107
  cemeteries, 131
  long, 67
  round, 14 (72)
Bavaria, northern, 22 (104–5)

227

Index

Index

Index

Index

lakes, 5, 9, 183
Lamenz, Saxony, Pl. 11 (120)
La Tène,
  period, 159, 160, 170, 174–5
  site (Switzerland), 24, 156, 157–9,
    164–5, 37 (166), 166, 168,
    171–2, 173, 176, 178, 179, 181,
    200
  swords, 168
lead, 117
leatherworking, 12
Le Grand Menhir Brisé, 54–5, 10 (55)
Le Morte d'Arthur, 1–3, 4, 14, 40
Lindow Man, 199
literary sources, 1–4, 10–11, 15–16,
    23, 27, 28, 29, 32, 33–4, 37, 41,
    168, 182, 187, 192, 200
Llyn Cerrig Bach, Anglesey, 173
Llyn Fawr phase hoards, 4 (22)
Locheim, Rhine, 3
London,
  north-west, 180
  Roman, 180
'long-term history', 193
lunulae, 71
lures, 29, Pl. 6 (30), 98, 111

maceheads, 70
Madagascar, 193
Mainz, W. Germany, 33 (141), 142,
    148
male associations, 34, 122, 123, 170
  equipment, 24
  graves, 79, 94, 95, 171
marine resources, 57
material culture, 21, 31–6, 46, 70, 76,
    86, 130
Mediterranean, 83, 166, 171, 185
megalithic art, 46, 48–51, 6 (49), 7
    (50), 51, 52, 53, 56, 73, 86, 90
Melanesia, 35
menhirs, 48–9, 50, 51, 53, 56, 73, 74
'merchants' hoards', 116, 119, 147
Merina (of Madagascar), 202
metal, 80, 82, 85
  analysis, 23, 26, 82, 89, 114, 115,
    116, 118, 126, 129, 147, 149
  detectors, 31
  extraction, 97
  hoards, 10, 5 (32)
  industry, 15, 16–17

recycling of, 21, 26, 96, 118, 129,
    143, 147, 148, 150
  sheet, 116, 117, 166
  sources, 26, 88, 89, 19 (92–3), 95,
    98, 102, 114, 117, 129, 130, 133,
    31 (134), 146
  supply, 194–5
  working, 6, 16–17, 21, 23, 24–5,
    26, 27, 28, 29, 34, 42, 71, 73, 75,
    76, 77, 15 (78), 83–9, 91, 95–9,
    101, 103, 107–11, 113, residues,
    11, 12, 13, 89, 116, 118, 147
Meuse, River, 109
Migration period, 16, 146
mixed hoards, 9, 11 (59), 19 (92–3),
    121, 124, 26 (124), 125, 27
    (125), 144–5
model artefacts, 185, 187
Monte Bego, S. France, 83, 84, 85
monuments, 44, 46, 47, 48, 52, 64,
    65, 67, 68, 69, 82, 90, 98, 23
    (106), 130, 131, 136, 137, 151,
    172, 175, 178, 185, 196, 200
  defensive, 137
Morbihan, Gulf of, 46, 48, 51, 53, 66
moulds, 12, 25, 26
  clay, 23
  stone, 21
Mount Pleasant, Dorset, 73
multiple finds, 6
musical instruments, 111

neck rings, 88, 129
Nerthus, goddess of fertility, 170
Neuchâtel, Lake, 157
Newgrange, 73
'non-ritual' (utilitarian) deposits, 10,
    11–14, Table 1 (14), 15, 16, 23,
    29, 42, 66, 112, 114, 117, 118,
    119, 121, 123, 127, 29 (128),
    144, 145, 146, 148, 150, 152,
    156, 159, 194, 195
Nordic Culture Area, 143
North America, 139

Oberdorla, Thuringia, 167, 168
offerings, 11, 24, 28, 37, 39, 75, 95,
    103, 112, 113, 142, 164, 165, 170,
    171, 173, 175, 183, 184, 186,
    188–9, 192, 197, 198–201, 202

231

Index

Index

Index